From Object to Life

David Duncan

From Object to Life

Pari Publishing

Copyright © David Duncan 2010

First published in Italy in 2010 by Pari Publishing Sas.
All rights reserved. No part of this publication may be reproduced, transmitted or stored in a retrieval system, in any form or by any means, without permission in writing from Pari Publishing Sas, application for which must be made to the publisher.

A catalogue record for this book is available
from the British Library

ISBN 978-88-95604-08-4

Printed and bound in the United States

Book and cover design by Andrea Barbieri
Cover photos: Andrea Barbieri, Vassil Asjac

Pari Publishing

Via Tozzi 7, 58045 Pari (GR), Italy
www.paripublishing.com

Dedicated to my parents

Contents

11	Preface
15	One: Introduction
24	Two: Style
30	Three: The City under Repair
40	Four: Raw World
46	Five: Absorption World
48	Six: The Eternal Moment
51	Seven: The Eternally New World
55	Eight: Bubble World
57	Nine: Detachment
63	Ten: Object World
68	Eleven: Picture World
71	Twelve: Exposure World
74	Thirteen: Detail World
79	Fourteen: Wittgenstein the Philosopher
85	Fifteen: Simone Weil
89	Sixteen: Wittgenstein the Autistic
97	Seventeen: Association World
101	Eighteen: David Bohm
106	Nineteen: From Eternity's Point of View
110	Twenty: Reddish-Green
113	Twenty-One: The Well Adapted Concept World
117	Twenty-Two: If You Complete It, You Falsify It
119	Twenty-Three: The World Seen from Every Angle
126	Twenty-Four: Parallel Angles
127	Twenty-Five: Theology
128	Twenty-Six: Bewitchment by the Literal
130	Twenty-Seven: What is Joy?

132	Twenty-Eight: What's for Dessert?
136	Twenty-Nine: Not Object World
137	Thirty: Logic Fills the World
145	Thirty-One: Raw Math
147	Thirty-Two: Bubble Gum in the Storm
152	Thirty-Three: Lumps of Dough
155	Thirty-Four: Sighted Ethics
160	Thirty-Five: Mystical Views
162	Thirty-Six: Sufism
166	Thirty-Seven: One Night in the Sistine Chapel
168	Thirty-Eight: The Wheels have Come Off
172	Thirty-Nine: From Faulkner to Harry Potter
174	Forty: Abstraction
177	Forty-One: Free from Pictures
178	Forty-Two: Idolatry
181	Forty-Three: The Land of Black Grass
186	Forty-Four: Mountains and Desert
188	Forty-Five: Celebration
190	Forty-Six: Wittgenstein as Human
193	Forty-Seven: Gabriel Marcel
199	Forty-Eight: Creatures of Abstraction and Creatures of Life
202	Forty-Nine: Silence
204	Fifty: Talk
207	Fifty-One: '…'
209	Fifty-Two: Raw Faith
212	Fifty-Three: Raw Religion
216	Fifty-Four: Four Worlds
222	Fifty-Five: The Pilgrim
227	Fifty-Six: Gift World

231	Fifty-Seven: 'That Looks Close'
233	Fifty-Eight: Professional World
235	Fifty-Nine: Mask World
236	Sixty: Remarks
240	Sixty-One: Tony
245	About the Author
257	Notes
276	Bibliography
287	Acknowledgements

Preface

This book grew from the instinct and the passion to collect...

...books mostly – shelves upon shelves of them, usually arranged by author, but sometimes by color.

On the surface, the materials in the collection appeared to be wholly unrelated – writings by Einstein, Wittgenstein, David Bohm, Gabriel Marcel, Simone Weil, Native Americans and Sufis...and related works; biographies and expositions.

Einstein and Bohm were physicists, Wittgenstein and Marcel were philosophers, Weil and the Sufis were mystics, and Native Americans were...Native Americans.

It didn't matter that these works appeared to be unrelated; the instinct was sufficient.

For a few years I played with the idea of writing something around the most significant thoughts in this collection, but nothing came of it.

Only when I realized that I could write a book consisting entirely of *remarks* did the idea of a book make sense – only then did the idea possess integrity and the possibility of achieving something.

The style was primary.

There was something special about writing in remarks – almost a kind of magic.

For reasons I did not at first understand, discarding paragraphs and arguments for remarks felt like being freed from shackles.

The usual way of writing seemed inappropriate and lifeless; at times even unethical.

Writing philosophy in the traditional way – paragraphs to form conclusions – *that* was a mannerism – a cultural mistake...

One of the authors in my collection also wrote in remarks and felt their magic; the Austrian philosopher Wittgenstein.

That he and I shared the instinct to write in remarks was nothing more than a coincidence until an internet search on his name revealed a website on autism.

This was a complete surprise. No one in the world of philosophy had connected his name to autism, but apparently some autistics were convinced that he exhibited 'autistic traits.'

Knowing almost nothing of autism, I leapt into the literature. There were many books.

They said…

…that autistic children are often calmed by flickering lights – they instinctively wiggle their fingers before their eyes – yet curiously, I had spent two years experimenting with flickering lights, modeling their effects on vision. (There *are* irrelevant coincidences.)

…that verbal autistics often find explanations incomplete – asking for deeper answers – but I had devoted even more time to the study of the incompleteness of explanations.

…that some high-functioning autistics like to obsessively collect and arrange things, especially books, that they think in terms of colors, and that they often prefer short remarks to long, elaborate sentences.

Astonished, I returned to the books in my collection.

Reviewing the lives of Einstein, Bohm, Wittgenstein and Weil, I discovered that each possessed traits of very high-functioning autism.

No one had diagnosed them as autistic because in their day autism was defined only as a severe disability, and their traits were comparatively mild.

They were on the far end of the 'autistic spectrum.'

I was reminded of something else:

Over the years, I had written dozens of (unpublished) short stories and fables…

…like the story about a young girl whose language was silence…

…and the fable of a mirror maker who preferred to look at people in mirrors…

…and the fable of the bird who made too many plans.

Reading clinical descriptions of autism, I learned about its great silences, and how autistics avoid eye contact and make incredibly elaborate plans.

I was learning in words what I already knew.

I told the daughter of a friend about this long list of coincidences, and how every one of my stories subconsciously conveyed something about autism. She replied, 'Oh, Dave – that's so creepy, but in a good way.'

Yet there was more to these coincidences...

...and more to the use of remarks...far more...

Writing in the style of remarks felt alive. The larger mystery of this style remained hidden, but the key in some way was life, and that was enough to explain the remainder of my collection and suggest a parallel.

Autistics wish to emerge from their shells (so to speak), to escape from their half-living prisons into life, to find reality – to be truly human.

Other authors in my collection – Native Americans (who are not autistic) and the French philosopher Gabriel Marcel (who may have been) poured their hearts and purpose not into the modern goal of a world flooded with concepts, but into life, full and grand.

...and the mystical Sufis and Simone Weil (like Plato) wrote of escaping from the darkness of the cave into life...

They claimed that humanity lived in this darkness and didn't know it.

...as though from their perspectives, humanity was autistic in one trait – insensitivity to life.

The parallel was striking – these mystics saw mankind as we see profoundly autistic children – trapped, indifferent, blind to life.

An autistic child, innocent and oblivious, may try to move someone as if shoving a cardboard box out of the way. Parents will reprimand the child and try to convey the presence of a human being.

Yet a normal man or woman may commit some sin and be reprimanded by a Rumi or Buddha or Jesus for 'blindness to the living water' or for 'not having eyes to see or ears to hear.'

From the perspectives of saints and mystics, who use their hearts where others ask only for rules, who sense the sacred in everything and everyone, there seems to be only one possibility – it is humanity that is autistic.

It is humanity that needs to see more than objects and tools. It is humanity that needs to transcend its blindness to life.

Thus the title: *From Object to Life.*

The journey from object to life is harrowing and uniquely rich for those few with very high functioning autism.

But it is not so different for the rest of humanity, who languish inside invisible fortresses of their own, listening to the voices of the past but not understanding the words.

For centuries the arcane utterances of mystics and saints, removed in worlds and kingdoms of pure life, have only baffled us, for the instincts towards life within human kind have been tenuous and weak…

…and cultures which are drawn by the vision of an ordered world consisting of little more than policies and problems to solve – have served only to blind.

Perhaps now autism can help show the way.

One: Introduction

We fancied ourselves free from defects of sight,
Even as those affected by color-blindness.

Now at last our hidden disease has been revealed.[1] (Rumi, 13th century)

Imagine a profoundly autistic child. He does not understand.

He is climbing a woman as if she were a tree.

Immerse him in life, show him its many ways, for where you see life and significance, he sees only objects.

He lives in a world of objects – objects that move but never gesture, objects that make noises but never speak.

He is the center of his own world. He is blind to his blindness to life.

Give him rules, but show him your example; show him your heart.

With hard work and sacrifice he may come to understand.

And with time he may do more than blindly follow the rule not to climb people. He may come to see.

Imagine now some ancient figure of life – someone who meditates and prays and speaks of spirit and life.

In gentle words the figure speaks to those who have gathered…

You live in the small, closed prisons of the unliving, but do not know it…

…You act as if the world were just an object. You harm yourselves and others because you are blind. You swear by heaven as though it was a tool to be used…

…Which is more sacred, the religion that makes you the center of the world, or the religion that makes you least among all?

Some listen to these words, but it is hard to be told that you are blind.

Many who hear these words pass by. They protest, 'I feel fine; I don't know what you're talking about. I see life and reality as well as anyone.'

...as though they had been invited to participate in something grand but had chosen not to.

Yet others remain. They sense something large and significant, like the rush of the wind.

They follow examples. They are disciples; mimics of life, sincere and devoted.

Perhaps immersion in water will help – contact with reality, immediate, close and enveloping. This is one path towards life, a modern therapy for autistic children.

Today we know more of autism – we know that it is not confined to the child lost in his own confinement, trapped in some invisible cell that rocks back and forth.

We know that autism extends in mild ways and in bits and pieces to people of all kinds, all interests, all abilities – to the likes of Lewis Carroll, W.B. Yeats and Vincent Van Gogh.[2]

Today we refer to this vast constellation of disability, struggle and sparkling talent as the 'autistic spectrum.'

This book consists of a simple extension of the autistic spectrum – it sees all of humanity as autistic...

...and not in the usual clinical sense; not in the sense of a profound disability, but in the sense of being blind to life.

...and this is no disparagement, not a shadow cast over humanity, not a criticism...

...but a ray of hope that momentarily catches one unaware, for it appears in a place we did not expect...

...and follows a path we did not imagine.

Recognizing that humanity's journey is like that of an autistic child is not the recognition of a disability – it is the sight of unbounded possibility.

And we have all seen the sparks of this possibility – the selfless gestures, the caring remarks, the loving sacrifices – unconsciously, naturally, in all of humanity.

...sparks eager to become fire.

Ancient figures of life – Jesus, Rumi, Buddha, Lao-Tzu, mystics and saints – they experienced this possibility in full. They became this fire and called it Awakening, Enlightenment, Reality, the Kingdom and Good News.

They passed through some barrier and looked back, seeing others as trapped, as blind, as not awake, as self-destructive and insensitive to life.

They saw their followers as one sees autistic children – exhibiting strange mannerisms, strange instincts, apart from life and reality, asking the wrong questions, stuck in harmful and repetitive behaviors, afraid to look at themselves in mirrors.

They gazed at humanity as a caring mother gazes at her autistic child, with affection, poignancy, frustration, joy, and fervent hope.

In countless degrees and the subtlest ways we may be partially blind to *anything* we perceive – color, size, shape, reality...and life.

Shape blindness (often called 'form blindness') is not well known, but some people cannot distinguish squares from pentagons, or one fingerprint from another.

In its richness, blindness to life is like color blindness.

...and this comparison is apt, for 'blindness to life,' like 'blindness to color,' is not some fuzzy, mystical phrase, but a commonplace.

Color blindness is easily studied and well known.

Blindness to life is neither.

It is not just an autistic girl asking if she is alive.

Blindness to life has been hard to see because it has been in front of us all along.

As we shall detail in this book, autistics are known to be literal, to see people as objects, to be blind to significance, to find reality more in concepts than in life, to lack empathy and to blindly follow rules.

Yet saints and mystics past noted these traits in everyone.

Autistics are now called *mind blind*, to indicate their insensitivities to the feelings and intentions of others.

Yet it would be more accurate, because of the absence of a sense of the tangible reality of the exterior world and their interior selves, and all the examples we have given, to call them *life blind*.

There is also blindness to *pure life*.

To saints and mystics there is a glorious world of significance and life – a pure life – into which everyone is born, but to which almost everyone is innocently insensitive.

With respect to pure life…

To feel that everyone one does not know is a stranger, is a blindness to life.

To see everything and everyone first and foremost not as sacred, is a blindness to life.

To be unable to receive or give love in full measure is a blindness to life.

To worship fairness is noble, but to worship fairness for oneself is a blindness to life, for one excludes one's largest identity, purity of heart.

…and so there is a continuum – the *great autistic spectrum* – blindness to ordinary life among conventionally diagnosed autistics, blindness to the multiplicity and significance of life among many, and blindness to pure life among almost everyone.

Blindness to pure life is neither sensed nor imagined by most people, but this blindness *is* sensed and imagined by some extraordinary autistics.

The lives of three very-high functioning autistics described in this book, Wittgenstein, Weil and Bohm, and the partly autistic philosopher Gabriel Marcel, were dominated by this extraordinary sensitivity.

These autistics lived the blindness spoken of by mystics and saints, and felt it in their blood and bones. They were spiritually autistic; hypersensitive to their insensitivity to pure life, and they lived with this dilemma and wrestled with it each and every day.

They followed a dozen autistic instincts towards pure life, some wondrous, some powerful, some gravely dangerous. They knew nothing about autism.

This book is a book of autistic instinct – a book of autistic therapy and illumination.

It is a simple idea – the human path is the autistic path.

In retrospect, it is almost obvious – not because humanity is so clearly blind to life…

…but because so many ancient followers and disciples begged for directions, asking autistic questions like, 'Who is my neighbor?' – craving the structure and certainty of social rules – not life.

And sometimes, when these followers persisted, they were given rules. Though more often they were directed to ask better questions or to open their hearts or to accept a better life.

Autism is a world of disconnection – a bubble world, where problems are all too often presented to one's fears and one's analytical mind for solution, not to the heart – that is too painful.

…and so the autistic's temporary solutions to the difficulties of social life – rules – are not solutions at all, but stop gaps – not life, but games of life.

Autistic children require rules of behavior because they lack the instincts of behavior.

Yet the same holds true for humanity: the fact that a subject like ethics exists at all (a complex of moral concepts and rules of behavior) – points to the blindness of humanity to life.

Remarkably, moral rules and laws – the religious and legal foundations of civilization – are only stepping stones to something innate, something higher.

And to this day, the artifice of law is regarded as a deep and intricate subject, not as evidence of a broadly distributed disability.

In its beginnings the human-autistic path to pure life is easy to see, for it is shared by the paths of the victim and to some extent, the modern world…

…for the mind of the victim (of injustice, or crime, or violence or…) is also disconnected – withdrawn and hypersensitive, demanding, with ears closed and eyes seeing only the forces of contention…

…as much of modern culture is disconnected – abstract – distant – bureaucratic and impersonal – a game of civilization, not civilization.

Thankfully, autistics have a marvelous window in their prison cell, shared in subtler ways by all of humanity.

Autistics call it absorption in reality – resonance with reality – being reality.

…like the mildly autistic physicists David Bohm and Albert Einstein, who grappled with their scientific problems by feeling them inside, only later translating them into symbols.

…or like the profoundly spiritual autistic philosopher and mystic Simone Weil, who noted the deepest form of absorption:

Whoever endures a moment of the void either receives the supernatural bread or falls.[3]

To be absorbed in the world – to merge with color and be one with fluttering leaves…this taste of the free and the sacred is a great window – a great light through the autistic prison.

…and there are other wonderful and specifically autistic forms of perception – seeing in detail, seeing from all angles and seeing with detachment – that are highly regarded, even trumpeted by mystics and saints.

The path to pure life is very hard for most people, and even the idea of pure life is rather fanciful and removed except for a few, but something else can be gained from these remarks.

What is important is an awareness of the dimension that stretches from object to life.

One is constantly reminded of political dimensions (left and right), of pragmatic dimensions (rich and poor), emotional dimensions (happy and sad), and moral dimensions (good and bad). But here we portray the dimension of object and life. One might call it *the autistic dimension*.

In different ways, Wittgenstein, Weil, Marcel and Bohm, many mystics and Native peoples were aware of this dimension, and like instinctive compass needles their lives aligned along its axis.

It is perhaps best to illuminate this dimension with some examples.

A few years ago a Navaho grandmother refused to install a sink with faucets and running water in her kitchen. She preferred to use the well outside, and to thank the water each time she used the well. (I am not by this example proposing a Luddite philosophy – that is a generalization.)

But one should at least be aware of the grandmother's sentiments. For all I know someone with the best intentions may have come to her home and proposed that she '*utilize* her resources,' not understanding that she preferred to express her gratitude.

She wanted her life to remain, at least in part, a gift.

This leads to a second example. Some high functioning autistics (like George Orwell) have been especially sensitive to the absence of life in words.

The word *utilize* is one small horror of object world – like the squeal of chalk on a black board. It drains life from those who hear it and those who *utilize* it.

I contrast 'life' not with death, but with what one might call distance, hollowness, obliviousness, or inauthenticity.

Yet (and this is a third example) 'inauthenticity' is itself an inauthentic term – lifeless and abstract...like jargon.

As far as possible, hyper-domesticated words – abstractions lauded nowadays in schools for their 'generality' and 'utility' – words that end in 'icity,' 'ist,' 'ity' or 'ism,' and hollow words like 'utilize' are, for the purposes of life, avoided.

'Life' may be contrasted with 'object' not in the sense of a physical object, like a piece of dry wood, but in the significance that a piece of dry wood can never feel.

The dimension of object and life is alien to any culture immersed in the notion that making a living is solely a mechanical function, unrelated to making a life.

High functioning autistics are often regarded as impractical dreamers by those who are so buried in their daily responsibilities (functions) that they have forgotten how to make a life.

...and of course many autistics desperately need to make a living *and* a life.

We find life in many things – in family and society, in nature, in stories and traditions, in song and dance, in growth and achievement, in work, in play, in gifts and identity, in freedom and love; even in death (like catching and eating a fish).

Hypersensitive to the absence of a sense of life within themselves, Wittgenstein, Weil, Bohm and Marcel were hypersensitive to its absence in the world.

Often their greatest sensitivities were to misunderstandings of concepts related to life.

For instance, today one thinks of freedom as a kind of power or independence, not as it might be thought of – as a larger identity.

Or one values fairness only to produce alienation by mechanizing it into law, or values justice only to impoverish it by reducing it to a matter of contention.

In addition to being trapped in the lifeless rules of legal or competitive thought, one may easily be trapped in the modern world's object metaphor...

...asking (as a scientist today must) what sorts of *things* joy and pain are, for they must be 'things' of some sort, since every*thing* is a thing.

Autism is blessed with sensitivities that others cannot imagine.

Some self-confident autistics compare themselves to lighthouses, standing alone at the edge of the world, casting a beam into the darkness, sensing what the rest of the world cannot.

(Einstein once romanticized about working as a lighthouse keeper.)[4]

They display an attitude. They see themselves as guides for a disabled humanity.

They refer to their special insights and innate moral sense as 'beneficial mutations.'

They are sanguine about enlightening the 'normal' world, and in a wry way they always manage to place 'normal' in quotes.

Others are far humbler – seeing only their own flaws.

At his best Wittgenstein wrote: *I ought to be no more than a mirror, in which my reader can see his own thinking with all its deformities, so that, helped in this way, he can put it right.*[5]

Autistics are mirrors of incompleteness and perfection. They live in extremes. They dwell in multiplicity.

They reflect the deepest shadows and the purest rays of light.

Two: Style

Most readers enjoy the continuity of a single long strand of thought. For example, one lives the story of a novel by vicariously absorbing its sequential life.

In a conventional book of non-fiction, one similarly hopes to understand a 'line of reasoning.'

…a thread of facts, a threaded argument, or a fictional life threaded in words…

Read a book, get a spool of thread.

…as though *thread life* was required by the sequential nature of the verbal mind.

The style of this book is far richer, if the reader will allow it, and doesn't try to read the remarks as if they are always supposed to be smoothly sequential.

It is more difficult. The autistic mind is discontinuous. Like the loose threads of a tapestry that strive to connect, the thoughts of the autistic mind reach out in every direction.

…for there are many threads that require contact – connection. The verbal, sequential mind is secondary.

This book is a collection of remarks. The remarks are, for convenience, presented in one order. But one may easily reorder them.

One may journey among related remarks from different chapters to form entirely new stories – new emphases – new chapters – new books.

One may attend only to those remarks which seem most significant.

Or one may collect and assemble every use of the word 'gift' or 'grasp' or 'concept' or 'freedom.'

One may, in the long run, fabricate a network of thoughts – a kind of tapestry world. This is the way *Aspergians* think – those with a kind of high functioning autism, Asperger's syndrome (or at least it is the way I and some other Aspergians think).

Read a book – get a tapestry of thoughts – and a *tapestry life*.

Imagine a town in which each inhabitant writes his and her own version of the 'town story.' Each story conveys a distinct perspective, each creates a partial world.

Only by reading every story can one understand the town in full, reliving every perspective and life.

The Aspergian mind, like this book, like a town of variously coupled lives, is a cluster of minds. It finds truth and life not in any one story or any one sequence, but in multiplicity.

(Multiplicity is kin to autistic detachment – aloofness – standing back – seeing *all* the players so as to understand the play – seeing *all* the pieces in the puzzle.)

There is also the hard work of this style – the hard work of creating a coherent world with a life that is true to its rich and deep multiplicity.

Ideally this book would be a mobile – thousands of remarks, suspended, momentary and free – not just a sequence – not just a book…a mandala in 3D, designed to evoke life – then vanish in the caprice of a breeze, to allow new life.

And it would be for the reader to patiently, arduously search out and piece together different remarks – different thoughts – forming great and intricate patterns, rather like a scientist being unceremoniously handed a world and told, 'Here, you figure it out.'

The book started this way – a compilation of unrelated remarks, forcing the reader to pause in the way that an autistic pauses – at each thought – having to wonder whether one remark really followed another or was something completely new…and from the tangle of remarks having to construct a new and meaningful reality.

…but this was far too difficult to manage and understand (even by the author) and slightly less random remarks left friends and family baffled – so the reader is now presented with the less onerous task of reading a sequence of remarks.

The present form is good enough. It provides one very simple and instinctive autistic means towards life – remarks.

The style of this book is a form that slowly scrapes away at prison walls.

Remarks are closer to life in the attention they give to each thought. They are closer in contemplation.

Possibly they are meditative – not information so much as a succession of breaths.

Perhaps they are baby steps, cautious and small, lacking confidence in the whole, seemingly faithless to those accustomed to large schemes and easy conclusions, yet full of integrity and respect, faithful to every detail, to every feather and every sparrow.

The style is not argument (though some arguments do appear).

For thousands of years philosophers, scientists and theologians have tried to understand and structure the world by *arguing* for new pictures of reality.

But not all knowledge is *opinion* based on *argument*.

Not all we know consists of representations, ideas, concepts, theories and abstractions.

Some knowledge is immediate and unspoken, so natural to us it is almost invisible.

We perceive colors, shapes and sounds – we do not argue for them – they form the unspoken ground of our life. We also take for granted the ability to perceive life and reality in ourselves and others.

Life and reality – both are perceived, and both allow forms of blindness.

An autistic child once asked, 'Am I real? Am I alive?'

In this context (and perhaps in every context) these are not scientific questions. Nor are they part of some philosophical debate.

To paraphrase Wittgenstein, we are not *of the opinion* that people are alive and real. We *see* them as alive and real. Theories are not involved.

If you are the parent of an autistic child, you do not *argue* the child into seeing life.

Instead, (in the absence of some medical fix) you seek for a way to stimulate in the child the sense of life, hoping that they will somehow sniff it out, grow and mature.

But our world today, the modern world, *is* the world of concepts and theories. The predominant culture, the modern culture, is 'concept-first.' It tries to solve all of its problems with new concepts, new theories and new words.

To learn about some hypothetical reality like enlightenment or the Kingdom of God one says, 'Tell me about it. Convince me with an argument.'

...like trying to learn the sensation red by having the term defined...

...or like some autistic child who questions if she fully feels the reality of her own hand, so she searches in an encyclopedia under 'reality.'

She looks for a theory. She looks for an explanation. She looks in the wrong place.

How do you find life and reality? The answer is older than history: they are looking for you.

This sounds so strange to modern ears – to people accustomed to getting what they want by going after it and getting it (an approach that is of course fine for many desires – like picking an apple off a tree).

But primal peoples find it obvious that life can be obtained only by opening a door – by being silent or respectful, or grateful, or devout, or extraordinarily attentive, or vulnerable, or brave, or not wanting anything except to give.

They sing songs of gratitude every day. We do not. And for some of them, gratitude *is* their religion, with no shared doctrines, only shared stories, shared songs and dances and food, for their community is a family, not a theology.

...and I think it comes to be obvious to many autistics that life can be obtained only by allowing it...for, like primal peoples, autistics are born into worlds beyond their understanding and control – neural forests of shadows and gifts...

...where they are forced to accept their vulnerabilities – and understand that life is acquired not by being grasped, but by being allowed...

…like allowing a gift to oneself to be significant – allowing the vulnerability – for trying to grasp the gift – *trying* to possess it, would kill it, and trying to grasp the gesture by discerning a hidden motive would kill the giving, making life into an object.

Autistics are born to fear contact with life. They must fight for the courage to be vulnerable.

Object world is safer; it is distant – there is no contact.

There are many quotes in this book – not to avoid the effort of analysis, but to do justice to the autistic inclination to gather many small pieces that eventually show a coherent whole – like placing crayons in a row.

The quotes in this book carry a special significance. They were collected over thirty years, waiting on shelves until patterns emerged.

In this book, the goal is to respect life – to allow it, not to grasp it.

Conclusions are avoided. Paragraphs are avoided. Arguments are avoided.

The idea that mankind is autistic is suggested. It is made plausible, not argued for. It is the sort of notion one must feel deeply inside; a realization that transforms.

Our goal is not to domesticate language, not to control it and use it *only* as a tool. We are *applying* instincts whose validity we accepted long ago.

Four autistics, one borderline autistic and one non-autistic Native American play leading roles in this book. I could not have begun to write without the guidance of their insights.

Each one walked a different path towards life. Each path illustrates the possibility of achieving a larger life and identity.

Though they never met each other, their lives intertwine in a rich tapestry – a flying carpet of intricate, deep intelligence and character.

Ludwig Wittgenstein – the philosopher whose obsession was to escape the autistic 'bottle,' and who taught the modern world the great lesson that reality, as manifest in the simplest expressions of our language, is more than things.

Simone Weil – the activist and writer who touched the sacred, and whose every remark and action guided her to return.

David Bohm – the Aspergian physicist who devoted his life to a reality far deeper than the object world of science.

Donna Williams – the (contemporary) autistic whose personal insights into the human subconscious surpass a thousand theories.

Gabriel Marcel – the playwright and philosopher who endlessly circled the issues of life – fidelity, faith, mystery…and wrote that his plays and philosophical writings formed a whole.

…in similar fashion, though not in imitation, several short chapters in this book are stories about the journey from object to life – each a different path – each a different angle.

Dan – a Lakota elder – whose insights so clearly portray a culture far from objects and close to life.

I am, of course, indebted to the great figures of religion who swam in the ocean of pure life, and reached depths to which toe-dippers can only dream.

Three: The City under Repair

Autistics are human beings. They come in both genders, all races and all ages.

People without autism are called *non-autistics* or *neuro-typicals*.

Autistic traits range from mild to severe across an extraordinarily wide spectrum.

At one end of the spectrum is *classic* or *profound autism*…the child sitting alone, oblivious to others yet hypersensitive – throwing fits of frustration, unable or unwilling to communicate.

At the other end of the spectrum is high-functioning autism – and near it, *Asperger's syndrome*, after Hans Asperger, an Austrian pediatrician.

In his insightful book on Asperger's syndrome, Lawrence Osborne noted that possessing even a few Aspergian traits is now *fashionable*.[1]

Why should Asperger's be fashionable?

Status – Aspergian talent.

It is thought that many renowned mathematicians, physicists, engineers and computer scientists may have had some form of Asperger's – people like Einstein and Alan Turing.

(Einstein's traits were especially mild, but his obsessive wholesale scientific mentality, otherworldly isolation, sloppy dress, longing for harmony, love of determinism, delight in long explanatory trains, artistic playfulness, absorption in the music of Mozart, abhorrence of authority and lifelong alienation from the group loyalties of human society, all expressed the flavor of very high functioning autism.)

Biographical evidence amassed by the psychiatrist Michael Fitzgerald suggests that Aspergian abilities reach well outside the sciences…

Among the list of those diagnosed as having exhibited at least some Aspergian traits – Hans Christian Andersen, Herman Melville, William Butler Yeats, Lewis Carroll, Arthur Conan Doyle, George Orwell, Spinoza, Kant, Simone Weil, Mozart,

Beethoven, Erik Satie, Béla Bartók, Glenn Gould, Vincent Van Gogh and Andy Warhol.[2]

The great majority of Aspergians are not nearly so talented. They are overjoyed to simply make it through high school or college... or the day.

Most adult Aspergians have trouble holding onto jobs – they do better with their own interests, in their own way, at their own rate, with their own social interactions.

Some advocates for autistics reject the 'autistic spectrum' because the idea that any multi-dimensional human can be defined by a single location along a line (even the colorful line of a spectrum) can be just plain wrong.

For instance, even today some autistic adults are incorrectly labeled as low-functioning or retarded because they can't speak, but it turns out that they can communicate intelligently by typing.

Also, profoundly autistic children often seem to connect to the world in a deeply direct and spiritual way, with an access and insight that puts non-autistic spirituality to shame.

If you are interested in spooky stories about such things, see William Stillman's book, *Autism and the God Connection*.[3]

The idea that autism is only a disability is wrong. Dr. Asperger defined Asperger's syndrome in part as involving special talents like a deep, abiding interest in some obscure exclusive topic (like a particular airplane or dinosaur) – talents that unfortunately run afoul of the generic ideals of traditional non-autistic institutions like public school.

Besides the great Aspergian scientists and writers who create because their brains must create, besides the Nobel laureates who win their prizes because of the autistic ability to focus, there are autistic savants whose astonishing talents in art, music, and memorization confound the label of disability.

Asperger's and autism are complex. There are many traits and many exceptions.

The traits are so varied, it is often more accurate to speak of Fred's mind and Julie's way and Joe's tendencies...rather than Asperger's syndrome.

Aspergians sometimes remark that the psychologist's game of finding a category for them seems to be a kind of joke (and psychologists are often painfully aware of their oversimplifications, but are not in the business of creating the fine grained science of the future that requires a thousand additional categories).

The human brain is far more complex than its ability to understand its own nature.

Autistics are often said to be clumsy, but some become talented athletes.

Some Aspergians are fiercely dogmatic about science, religion or politics, yet others are utterly dispassionate about such things.

Some autistics have difficulties with depression or sexual identity, others don't.

Some autistics are very social, and most Aspergians have no special talent for math.

An Aspergian child may spend the day being kind to his friends and then lash out in a fit of temper and frustration.

Autistics of all stripes are often said to be mind blind – to lack empathy.

While it is true that autistics often have no concept of intent and are often unknowingly rude, as a general matter autistics are unusually gentle and sympathetic – sensitive to the world.

In recent years there seems to be a genuine and rather mysterious increase in the incidence of cases of autism.[4]

In Silicon Valley people routinely speak of an autism epidemic, and attribute it in part to the presence of two parents who are skilled in engineering and computer science.

Estimates of the proportion of people with autism today vary from 1 in 150 to 1 in 500. (The uncertainty arises from different standards of diagnosis and different studies.)

As to the causes of autism, the science is immature: theories are too many and too few.

Genetics clearly plays a role: if one identical twin is autistic, it is far more likely that the other will be autistic. Males with high-functioning autism greatly outnumber females. In one study, older fathers were found more likely to have autistic children.

Some have suggested that Asperger's is a male-oriented syndrome because males and Aspergians tend more to live in mental worlds of abstraction – rules and games, as opposed to reality.

The discovery of brain cells that respond in situations that evoke empathy has led to speculation that autism (in part) may be caused by a deficiency of these cells.

Yet this is only the beginning. Discoveries will no doubt be made of molecules in the brain related to feeling faith, feeling repentant, feeling that others are living beings, not objects, and feeling that others are valued and trusted beings, not strangers.

These potential discoveries suggest a medical path not only to life, but to what we have called pure life and others have called enlightenment, the Tao and the Kingdom – a seemingly cheap path, unless it works some magic on our attitude towards the significance of molecules.

The profoundly autistic mind, regardless of its talents, is damaged; it is a city under repair.

Profound autism consists of difficulties with *sensations, feelings, concepts,* and *behaviors,* all perhaps because of troublesome neural *connections.*

Sensations do not work – one may be hypersensitive or insensitive – or both – the sight of fluorescent lights or the sound of a shoe scraping over a doctor's floor may be painful and intrusive, yet the howl of someone crying may pass by, unnoticed.

Feelings are raw – unfiltered and confused. The feeling of 'exposure anxiety' may override everything and keep one from communicating at all. One may retreat in being defined – as when one is made vulnerable by being given a gift.

Concepts are not formed: like the children who see a nose, eyes and a mouth but not a face.

Behaviors are unusual: repetitive movements, rocking, flapping one's hands, panicking at noises and the arrival of human beings.

There is much instinctive behavior devoted to sensory *stimulation* (called *stimming*) like biting one's arm (to form neural connections or perhaps to blunt a greater interior pain).

And there is much behavior devoted to *relaxation* and *absorption*, like watching a steady, slow flickering light or twirling in a circle to decompress…and behavior devoted to *escaping* the world altogether by 'shutting down.'

Sometimes connections are tenuous – with the world and with oneself.

In profound autism, the world can be uncertain – dreamlike – like mist. The autistic boy Elijah asked his mother:

'*Am I two-dimensional?*'…

'*Am I three-dimensional?*'…

'*Are cartoons dead?*'…

'*Do cartoons get hurt?*'…

'*Is Pinocchio a <u>real</u> boy?*'…

'*Does Pinocchio get hurt?*'…

'*Am I a real boy?*'[5]

Consider friendship.

We connect to our friends by sensations, feelings, concepts and behavior. We *see* a friend, we *feel* friendship, we *think* about our friend, and we *behave* as a friend. Friendship is at least this – connection by these means.

But in autism, every form of connection is problematic.

In profound autism the damage may be severe, but with help that is equally profound in understanding and persistence, great repairs can be made…

…and contact with oneself can be gained, and the world *can* come into focus and begin to exist.

The other end of the autistic spectrum is another world. (The term 'autistic spectrum' is common parlance and useful, despite its flaws.)

In Asperger's syndrome the healing is easier than in profound autism, for the damage is less severe and the internal methods of healing are more sophisticated.

...and because Aspergians are verbal (sometimes too verbal) they have a channel to the world that allows internal repairs to proceed efficiently, rather than by trial and error.

Aspergian traits include:

...a tendency to enter states of deep contemplation (like a nun or a monk).

...'zoning out' by finding solitude and escape in some game or entertainment.

...joy in abstract system building – creating new forms of science or art (like Van Gogh or Einstein).

...being hypersensitive – to high frequencies, to pencil scratches... to almost anything.

...seeking control over an external world of seeming anarchy... creating a mini-tyrant...or an ardent, severe political activist (like Simone Weil), insisting that the world conform...

...speaking sometimes in a monotone – as if reciting from memory, like a machine.

...being pedantic and uncompromising...the 'little professor' who (like Wittgenstein) stops the discussion or stamps out of the room.

...obsessing on one narrow interest. The Aspergian exclaims, 'This subject is my soul!' (Like the teenager who exclaims, 'This music is my soul!')

...Identity, meaning and life are wrapped up in a wonderful, small, shiny package that others deem irrelevant...as though neural connections to a subject superceded connections to everything else.

...valuing logic over emotion (like Sherlock Holmes or Mr. Spock).

...lacking the ability and the interest to *listen* (to a political speech, or a sermon, to talk radio, to close friends while playing cards...) *to bond* and reinforce one's sense of community.

Listening to bond is not *listening to learn facts*. The former is closer to life, and to the horror of small talk.

...more power to small talk.

Better still is *listening to live* – attending to a remark to participate in some living quality of the remark, like immediacy...

...or some low and forgivable quality, like lashing out or pettiness...

...or some dim and forgivable quality, as in a one-dimensional remark...

...or some great and noble quality, like honesty or purity of heart.

More Aspergian traits:

...lacking social instincts, like not understanding a wink or table manners.

...being anti-social or society sensitive – finding numerous faults in 'the system.'

...being fascinated with detail and parts.

...loving impish, innocent, bizarre, literal and sarcastic humor. (In a recent radio interview, a famous American comedian began, 'Hi, it's nice to meet your voice.')

...thinking visually – forming pictures and caricatures to understand.

...or thinking in some other single mode – touch perhaps, or sound.

...having trouble with change and compensating by making elaborate plans.

...loving simplicity (in a sensory and conceptual world that overwhelms).

...loving truth – the whole truth – and clarity (deceit is too complex and social).

...loving animals (who are predictable and kind and who never deceive).

...having a desire for completeness and perfection, both moral and intellectual.

...wanting to generalize – perhaps to connect the disconnected portions of the brain, like writing in remark-details and not paragraphs, allowing *every* small detail an unbiased chance to connect, without destroying the detail.

...being dispassionate. This includes the love of long, dispassionate causal chains...

...thinking literally – seeing everything in physical terms – living in a world of objects and abstractions – seeing the world of engineering, mathematics or logic *as* the world.

...in some Aspergians, wanting a reason for everything – never content, never pattern-full, endlessly asking the five year old's question, 'Why?'

...being anxious – or in all too many Aspergians, feeling distraught or tormented.

Sometimes sensitive Aspergians express the intense pain of reality, as though in touching the face of God they were continually being scratched by a three-day growth.

As we shall see throughout this book, notable Aspergians have warned of the dangers of Aspergian traits present in all of humanity.

David Bohm pointed out the pitfalls of literalism, George Orwell wrote of the horrors of the mechanical mentality and the tyranny of control, and some of Hans Christian Andersen's fables expressed the deadliness of obsession. Herman Melville's *Moby Dick* was a grand adventure in obsession.

Wittgenstein fought tooth and nail the literalism embraced by philosophers and modern science, and a number of religious figures throughout history have warned about treating oneself and others – even those who are worshipped – only as *things* to be used – tools.

(In the Tao Te Ching, virtue itself (Te) is not a *thing* – not an abstraction, and the Tao – the nameless – is certainly not a thing – unapproachable by concepts.)

The film *A.I.*, an offshoot of a story by Brian Aldiss, conceived by Stanley Kubrick and developed by Steven Spielberg, presented a very dangerous Aspergian journey from object to life. The hero was a small robotic boy.

(The character was based on Pinocchio, the wooden boy who so desperately wanted to transcend his own nature: to be truly real.)

Pinocchio and the robot boy, like naïve and determined autistic children, barely survived the surreal, confusing circus known as 'the world,' but the robot boy finally found the 'place where dreams are born.'

Perhaps the best and least forgiving (most condescending) Aspergian film is Kubrick's *2001: A Space Odyssey*, which revels in the contrast between the sublime, isolated autistic existence of an astronaut on his way to Jupiter, immersed in ethereal harmony, infinite space and mechanism – versus the superficial, tacky, literally distant, violent world of human/ape society.

Even communication of the astronaut with his parents is autistic – delayed and unreal.

Mechanism, an object – a computer – one with whom he *can* communicate, tries to kill the astronaut, for ultimately it is soulless, originating from tools used to kill.

With desperate courage and perseverance the astronaut survives and discovers transcendence…his journey from object to life, and mankind's.

In surveying hundreds of web remarks, stories, articles and poems by autistics and Aspergians, the prevailing theme is struggle – with oneself and with the world.

The personal writings on autistic web sites display an appreciation for honesty and eccentricity, and the desire for respect as a distinct neural culture.

Yet a distinction is not a label. A distinction reveals a truth, a label hides it.

Autistics often voice resentments at being labeled – feeling that they are living in a box, then being boxed by doctors, teachers and the state, labeled for the purposes of treatment, education and financial support.

This is ironic. Autistics have trouble understanding facial expressions while living among those who far too often see a label and not a face.

Dogs see faces.

Yet seeing in labels is easily forgiven if one also sees humanity (including oneself) as a neural animal – a naming animal that survives in part by means of labels that simplify a complex world...

...an animal naturally blind to its own subconscious mentality – a mentality that can be invisible, dehumanizing and benevolent all at once.

...like a bureaucracy...or a culture.

Many Aspergians love science fiction, and some eagerly imagine future worlds with intellects so vast and hearts so full that labels no longer exist.

Complexity is finally allowed to exist, finally respected more than the oversimplifications of language and the tribe.

...and here, 'tribe' is used in its lowest sense – loyalty to a group and its narrow truths where that loyalty is blind and misguided.

(Aspergians often ignore the highest sense, where loyalty and devotion to others is sacred – for that I apologize.)

Some autistics are lucky: I have heard parents of autistic children praise state help for their children, and Aspergian children praise their (rare) flexible schools.

Autistics are immersed in concept worlds of their own creation.

They are not given their worlds, not given automatic concepts, as neuro-typicals are.

Their minds are not pre-fabricated. From raw materials they are self-made.

Yet autistics and non-autistics *are* cut from the same cloth. Both are beset with eyes that see objects, tools and labels where instead they should see life.

Sometimes autistics feel this distinction more forcefully, more painfully, and can better navigate the dangerous journey from object to life.

But the journey is together. As the old Native American said, 'We are admitted to an equal sky.'

Four: Raw World

The autistic world is many worlds – many *discrete* worlds. It is not a seamless whole like the non-autistic world…

…and each discrete world is, in its own way, *raw* – that is, unprocessed and alone.

A figurative comment like 'That thought is beneath you,' must be highly processed, for it connects two *completely different* worlds: the physical world of 'low' and the social world of character.

Sometimes the autistic world is a world of gestures or touch or art or music, but not worded language…

…and so the phrase itself is a disconnected fragment, not grasped, not understood…

…but the disconnection is only in words.

Sometimes the social world of character is overwhelming. It is too much *to be* good or bad…or low…or anything.

…and so the world of character is a disconnected fragment because it is not allowed.

Sometimes words refer only to objects because a world of named objects is easy.

In *literal world* language is *always* about objects. The comment, 'That thought is beneath you,' prompts the autistic child to look down.

In the profound autistic's completely raw *object world*, a human can have as little significance as a moving bag with eyes. A human can be a moving object, without life.

The ability to see significance is advanced. Seeing life and value in a face is advanced.

Similarly, seeing a motivation in someone's arrival is far more than seeing an object in motion.

Seeing significance may be regarded as 'extra processing,' but ironically, that is seeing it only as a kind of physical process – a collection of brain chemicals in motion.

Interpretation is more easily regarded as a kind of added processing or filtering. Seeing a stable, interpreted world is necessary for survival...and for communication, like seeing ink on paper as remarks, not as black squiggles.

Interpretation is seeing a representation – *seeing* something *as* something else – seeing a squiggle as an s.

Seeing-as is advanced.

Autistic worlds are not structured in this way – the absence of refinement and order – of subconscious interpretation – of automatic concept building – can be very mild or moderate or quite extreme.

Seeing the world completely uninterpreted can be a horror – as when a severely autistic child is frightened by the movement of his own foot – not knowing that *that* patch of color is his.

Yet in mild cases, seeing without interpretation can be a blessing – lacking a single strong way to conceptualize, and so drifting among different ways of seeing – seeing a forest *as* trees, *as* branches, *as* leaves and wood, *as* reflections of light – a multiplicity of forests.

This is seeing significance, multiplicity and life where others see only trees. It is a raw form of wealth, a raw treasury, free from the tyranny of concepts.

There is also the raw world of pure sensory absorption, where the autistic ignores thoughts and becomes one with the color blue, or the harmony of a popular song, or a campfire, or a small gray stone.

Perhaps the best raw world is innocence without guile.

There are many raw worlds – worlds of seeing in detail, seeing in parallel, seeing from every angle, seeing everything as new – or old – thinking by association...we'll describe these worlds and others in later chapters.

There is much to be said for unfiltered existence: raw perception, raw thought and raw life.

...autism reveals it, autism is the best and the worst of raw-world; it is the garden of roses and thorns.

Concept building (especially filtering by naming: 'That's a tree… now you're done…now you understand') creates stable objects and worlds. But this utterly natural process which sometimes gives life to vague feelings, also steals significance and life.

From the perspective of raw-world, concepts all too often blind – words blind.

From the perspective of raw-world, to hear the category words of others is to have an unbelievably rich and significant world made poor.

To utter such words is to miss the mark with every sound.

It is devilishly hard to realize that most of us live in a concept mediated world – a profoundly oversimplified, filtered world where much detail and life is lost.

We find it hard to believe that we are in many ways blind to reality, because we are 'hardwired' to see reality through conceptual glasses.

Yet the evidence is there: psychologists have conducted experiments showing that normal adults are bound to their concept-structures (frames, schemas and paradigms) where by contrast profound autistics are free from these inhibitions, perceiving the world directly – perceiving it raw.[1,2,3]

Autistic minds develop very slowly.

They are not 'pre-programmed' or 'hardwired,' as computer scientists might say.

It can take a lifetime to form concepts – a lifetime of painstaking effort to construct a personal world.

Non-autistics grow up quickly, and their concepts grow as well, making sense of the world by quietly and efficiently taking control…

…and in a strange way, making them immature – for like the children of the wealthy, they do not have to work…

…there is no need to find the truth – their concepts whisper that they *are* the truth…

…there is no need to construct a world – their concepts *are* the world.

For the sake of efficiency and survival, concept-structures form early in the minds of normal children, silently blinding them.

The infant mind is like a field that is traversed in all directions, and then a road is built and one walks only on the road, and soon the road vanishes from sight, but still one follows it, unaware that there is a road beneath one's feet, unaware that one is following a path, unaware even of the field.

When most children are six months old they can discriminate between different monkey faces, but not after nine months.[4]

They can distinguish phonetic differences in foreign languages when they are roughly five months old, but six months later differences only in their native tongue.[5]

Normal adults cannot listen to words and hear only raw uninterpreted sounds. They must hear speech – words with meaning.

Normal adults cannot see a face 'hollow' – with the nose sticking *in* the face – they *must* see an ordinary face. A hollow face sculpture is not seen as it is, except with a great amount of texture added to the nose and the benefit of a very close stereo view.

In a sense, normal adults see a spoon when it is half submerged in a cup of coffee. They would be shocked to reach for a spoon and pick up only a visible handle.

They complete the part and construct a whole. Autistics don't.

Whether autistics can see hollow faces I don't know.

But they can hear raw speech. Sometimes that is all they can hear, but sometimes they can switch from hearing speech raw to hearing it as meaningful.

Some autistics can *see* the world *as it is* – raw – without concepts. We know that they can. They draw it this way. They are autistic savants.

Autistic savants have tremendous talents but also suffer from tremendous disabilities – they may be able to recite Mozart from memory but be unable to communicate in words.

Consider the extraordinary skill of savant 'raw-sight,' where a three year old autistic girl draws a horse from memory in stunning, accurate perspective…[6]

...yet a normal, not especially talented child (or adult) draws a horse as a *collection of components* in a *side view*: a closed curve for a body, four stick legs, a neck, a head, a curved line for a mouth and dots for eyes.

The normal person draws a static abstraction; a concept, not an animal.

Yet the savant's drawing is unmediated, and the horse is moving... and alive.

How strange that most people say that they see people as alive, but draw them as stick figures.

Some people spend their lives hunting for more concepts.

Most people can be taught to draw with greater realism by being blinded to their unconsciously imposed concepts – their hidden idols.

For example, when a normal (untalented) adult draws a dog, she pencils in lots of lines to represent hairs. But the hairs are just a concept.

She must be trained to ignore her concepts and to far more accurately draw the actual shadows and textures of a dog's fur.

She can be shown only a small part of a dog – a keyhole view – without being told that she is looking at a dog – like looking at an isolated remark.

Or she can be shown the image of a dog upside-down or distorted beyond recognition to help her to ignore her preconceptions and draw what is actually there.[7]

...like the purposeful and humorous craziness of a handful of Sufi mystics, or the preposterous behaviors of some enigmatic Zen masters.

Raw world also has the wonderful advantage that one can possess a quality without believing in it.

A dog is loyal – it does not believe in loyalty. It does not have this concept. It does not need it.

If a dog could talk, it would say, 'I don't believe in loyalty,' despite being more loyal than any human.

The silent, raw principles of dogs are strong and resolute. Dogs abide.

Young children (autistic and non-autistic) who know a bit of language will retreat to baby talk when they are stressed. They fall back on reliable habits – primitive forms of connection to the world.

Adults do many things when stressed. Sometimes they are brave or noble. Sometimes they focus. Sometimes they shut down or relax. And these behaviors are easy to see.

But sometimes they fall back into object world…and that is hardly noticed.

…like the war-weary soldier who records his daily experiences by listing a sequence of facts – no emotions – no adjectives – just the life of an object in object world.

…or the man to whom an injustice is done, who cries out, 'I have my rights!'

…seeing himself only as an *isolated object* in pain, possessing some *abstract thing* called rights, relying on the *written rules* and *forces* of object world to amend the behaviors of adversaries who have been stress-demoted into object-people.

Lao-Tzu and Rumi saw us as cherishing a world of objects.

They saw us as worshipers of forms – the secondary and the apparent.

They said our *cultures* and *concepts* blind us to the primary and the real.

We imagine freedom to be the *right* to do what we please. And in the realm of power freedom *is* this sacred *thing*.

But there is a larger world, a larger realm, where freedom is more than power…better than power…

…something more mature, something of a large heart and identity – a form of life and participation that is neither written down nor guarded by force.

Five: Absorption World

There are phrases in Aspergian poetry that gesture towards an expressionless world of silence, light and shadow.

They reach deeper than language – language in an impediment, language annuls.

An obsessive interest in color, light and music is a kind of enchantment and awe.

One is absorbed in the world. One is without concepts. The self disappears in pure experience.

…like the autistic boy Elijah, who thought in colors and counted stones, and danced with dragonflies, and lined his crayons up in a row.[1]

Or like the (contemporary) autistic mystic, William Julien, who wrote:

Lay your Treasures in a row.

Your marked path will guide you to your heart.[2]

Or like Donna Williams, who wrote that her childhood body was a tool of resonance – not an individual – not a self.

Her body felt patterns. It thought in form and movement. Empathy was not of the conscious mind but of the body. A chair was a shape that moved…and away from her resonance with the felt world was the ego.[3]

Music and nature for her were more than enjoyed, they were celebrated:

My music spoke of the things I loved, of the wind and the rain, of freedom and hope, of happiness in simplicity, and of triumph over confusion.[4]

Shadows, especially the drifting shadows of leaves, shadows that calmly mottle a surface and give it life – are one of the joyful, deep experiences within the autistic spectrum.

And there are rare stories of autistic savants, like Nadia, entering her own special world of visual beauty. Between the ages of four and seven, she created drawings compared in beauty to cave paintings from 30,000 years ago.[5]

One is reminded of autistic children who wrap themselves in moonlight and clouds, experiencing a kind of ecstasy of participation.

Life is amplified. The contrast dial is turned up. One senses great splashes of life and lathers them out in bursts of emotion, like the brush strokes of Van Gogh.

The sky is a reverie.

Doctors speak of autistic 'perseveration' – intense concentration – profound attention.

They are not so bold as to mention absorption, as in the ancient Gospel of Philip:

It is not possible for anyone to see anything of the things that actually exist unless he becomes like them. This is not the way with man in the world: he sees the sun without being a sun; and he sees the heaven and the earth and all other things, but he is not these things...you saw the Spirit, you became spirit. You saw Christ, you became Christ...[6]

Six: The Eternal Moment

It is easier for autistics to live in the moment, for their moments can last for hours.

They are born to pause. They may pause to inspect an object or ponder some idea and then go away, only to return to the same thing again and again – for days, for years, for a lifetime, building a world around it.

This is not the way for most non-autistics, who seem to live in the blink of an eye.

The brains of most people are efficiently connected, so that gestures and words usually have no ambiguity. Understanding, as far as it goes, is rapid and automatic.

Most people will look at something – a dog, a sentence, a human, a culture, life – and reduce it, that is, summarize it, or see it *as* something – *as* one thing, without a thought – finished, so they think, before they know it.

And that innate efficiency becomes humanity's approach to religion, ethics, aesthetics, politics, science and life. There is that single rapid characterization; that quick judgment.

…so that even the 'meaning of life' is expected to be a summary.

From the standpoint of this book such efficiency is a most unfortunate reflex – a kind of built in, fast food, gulp it down blindness – a ravenous blur, with no taste.

There is no awareness of other ways of seeing-as, no richness in the moment.

Aspergian creations – stories by Lewis Carroll and Hans Christian Andersen, paintings by Van Gogh and Andy Warhol, theories by Einstein and Bohm, are rich and imaginative to the point of being surreal.

The Aspergian brain *must* be imaginative. It *must* create its own worlds around the smallest moments and the smallest things. To create, it pauses.

An autistic might enter a room and start to imagine a world – a surreal pattern emerging from the sight of a magazine cover, a pencil, or a simple period...

...pausing perhaps to see each period in the world as saying something about thoughts which seem to pause, all on their own.

...or to see periods as symbols – as a part of modern culture...

...or as a part of material existence – as groupings of atoms...

...or as part of 'period perceptions' – as part of life...

...or an expression of many lives – a world in itself.

A savant autistic might notice the positions of all the periods on all the pages, or the sorts of words that immediately precede them.

A science oriented Aspergian might try to imagine the distribution of periods in space in a book and their trajectories through time (an instinct for this author).

An autistic interested in history might imagine a study of human emotions in terms of the shapes and sizes of periods scratched down by monks in drafty monasteries across medieval Europe.

...or feel the chill endured by these ancient periods through a long winter's snow, and from this chill fabricate a story for children.

It is one thing to read for immediate information, another to pause and imagine – to create a period-world and live in that momentary-eternal world...

...to see one thing as many things – to experience a multiplicity of associations – a grand parallel experience – like the experience of a multiplicity of remarks that connect to one another and to life in a thousand ways.

To most sensibilities, continually (even obsessively) pausing to ponder a period or anything else – a color, a table, a star – seems a useless detour into the imagination, the amassing of irrelevant connections and the construction of silly patterns.

At best, the non-autistic may pardon an autistic's distraction – 'Oh, you're stopping to smell the roses.' ...but not for days and weeks and years.

As though the period of a sentence first and foremost had a purpose...for periods are tools...and one must get on with life...

...and the idea of sharing the multiplicity of life of a period, or a color, or a table, or a star – was not only impossible but...pointless.

It is one thing to search for life outside, another to search for it inside. It is one thing to search for a kingdom without, another to search for it within.

When a moment stretches for hours, time disappears.

Wittgenstein wrote: *If by eternity is understood not endless temporal duration but timelessness, then he lives eternally who lives in the present.*[1]

(And that remark feels so strangely superficial – as does its contrary...

...as though any argument about the nature of eternity would miss the mark.)

Imagine a Tibetan monk observing a tourist who wants to take a snapshot of his temple and then quickly move on, as though once she had the snapshot, she would understand his culture.

But she won't understand.

If she belongs to the snapshot culture and the instantaneous mentality, all she will do is report, 'The monk was inscrutable.'

She needs to put aside her camera and live with the monks, for a time.

Imagine the monk (in a moment of dramatic fancy) welcoming her:

> *You are not visiting a different land.*
> *You are not imagining another century.*
>
> *Those are puddle jumps.*
> *This is not some small adventure.*
> *You are in a new world, and no longer using the same mind.*
> *You have crossed the ocean.*

Seven: The Eternally New World

A young autistic man often saw the same woman in an elevator. He spoke with her socially on these meetings.

He also saw another woman in a certain bar. This went on for a year.

He finally realized that the two women were the same person.

He had been confused by the different contexts and had seen different women.

The autistic world is the eternally new world.

In profound autism...

Monday's home may not be Tuesday's home. They may be different homes and different worlds because a chair has been moved.

A car seen from the front may not be the same car seen from the rear.

Someone may be seen as a different person if they change their clothes.

To the autistic, the smallest change may be a tremendous discovery – a tremendous shock – an entirely new world.

We see blueberries as blueberries whether they bulge like grapes or are shrunken like grape seeds. We see blueberries as blueberries in our hand or at the edge of a field. On a sunny day, on a moonlit night, partly hidden behind a leaf, hanging on a bush or lying in a kitchen bowl, we see blueberries as blueberries.

They are what they are. They are never something new.

For a profound autistic this may not be so. There may be kitchen blueberries, forest blueberries, shadowed blueberries, small blueberries, large blueberries...even red blueberries under a red light.

An object that retains its identity despite changing circumstances is called an *invariant*.

Autistics have difficulty discerning invariants, for that is another form of extra processing, beyond the immediate and the raw.

When nothing is the same, the world is eternally new.

It is quite an art to program a computer with a camera to detect invariants. Most computers have terrible trouble discerning that an elbow jutting from behind a wall is part of a human, especially if the elbow is hidden by a plaid shirt and the shirt is illuminated by striped lighting.

…but most humans are terrific at this sort of convoluted thing. They are born to spot invariants – like food – or predators.

In a sense, an invariant is a whole. When someone says, 'Joe,' a particular image comes to mind, a sort of prototype. But *Joe the invariant* is far larger than a single image.

He is a whole consisting of images from every angle and every possible distance, including all partial images, images hidden by clothing, images distorted by illumination and shadow, even images from his youth. He has physical weight, emotional presence, a particular quality to his voice, and a hundred other characteristics.

Profound autistics cannot 'see' the whole because they cannot construct it. 'Joe the invariant' may not exist.

The shoe one sees might belong to a hundred people. It might not be recognized as a part of Joe.

And so the eternally new world is eternally ambiguous.

Autistics have trouble understanding the meanings of words because meanings are wholes. For example: 'Reds' means one thing when yelled by a baseball fan, another when spoken by a communist, and still another when uttered by an artist.

The meaning of a word depends on the word *and* on the context – the *whole* situation, or as Wittgenstein put it, the whole 'language game.'

Autistics have trouble perceiving context – sensing the meaning of a situation (more processing). They are blind to context – for them, social games may not exist.

A Swiss college student with autistic traits offered an illuminating example:

If the conductor in the train says: 'All tickets please,' then I immediately think, 'What does "all" mean? All MY tickets being in my purse? All tickets being used for THIS special train? All tickets of ALL people on the train?…'[1]

Only in comprehending (or better, instinctively absorbing) what the conductor wants – the 'passenger on a train game' – does the request for tickets become clear.

Life in the eternally new world can be confusing, frustrating, embarrassing and overwhelmingly complex. When the game is not perceived, one becomes a search engine – like the raw global mind.

Wittgenstein noted: *It often strikes us as if in grasping meaning the mind made small rudimentary movements, like someone irresolute who does not know which way to go – i.e. it tentatively reviews the field of possible applications.*[2]

Most autistics crave invariants – any structure is good – any pattern is blessed.

Einstein spent his life hunting for invariants.

He wanted to call his first theory of space and time, 'Invariantentheory' (The Theory of Invariants) but Max Planck convinced him to use instead the phrase 'Relativtheorie' (The Theory of Relativity).[3]

The mildly autistic Einstein cared about invariants – the unchanging. He loved to find invariant truths by generalization: 'Look! *Everything* obeys this!'

Zen masters say the only genuine truths are truths of the moment – matters specific to time and place – matters of life – matters of context. In Zen, generalization is a plague, for the world really is eternally new. (And this is not argued for, but seen.)

The anarchy of the eternally new world, can, in just the right dose, be far better than the order of 'invariant world.'

Imagine an autistic describing the many differences between work-Patty and home-Patty; differences to which Patty is blind because she has been raised to see only one Patty.

Imagine work-Patty praying for help and home-Patty changing her mind – do we condemn Patty for her inconsistency, or is the two-Patty world more forgiving?

With multi-people, who would fight? War would be appalled at the lack of invariance.

The world has so many conventional partitions, so many tidy piles of leaves: you and I, the French and the English…and anyone with common sense will protest, 'But we *know* that we are two different people, not twenty…and the French and the English are two different groups, not a thousand, and we certainly *know* that Patty is one person!'

The modern world is the great invariant world, where Patty is Patty no matter what. Her birth certificate proves it.

To scatter the world like a pile of leaves – this is the wisdom of autism.

Those who live in the eternally new world can be like children; innocent and overcome with awe – never bored, never superior, never jaded…like the boy who bursts with joy at his first sight of a bird, and his tenth.

In the autistic mode, one can also feel the transience of the world and the passage of all things, like the ancient observer who silently oversees the rise and fall of civilizations, mountains, and truths.

…who sees himself now and also in a distant future, when his language and his country, and all that is said to be important, have long been forgotten.

The eternally *new* world, in its transience, is eternally *old*. In this unity of creation and agelessness one can be like the flames of a fire that flicker and glow and send out sparks, dangerous and inviting, newborn and ageless…

Eight: Bubble World

In autism there is isolation.

Some Aspergians call themselves 'islanders' or 'Martians,' because they feel that they are living in another world.

In many cases they see themselves as trapped – in a bubble – in a shell – in their own minds – unable to communicate. They speak of prisons and cells, glass coffins and being buried alive.

Each time a bubble is broken, each time one moves to a new level of awareness and makes some new connection with reality, the entire world is remade.

This breaking through seems to correspond to forming neural connections, but the instinct is a call to life.

Breaking a bubble can be any sort of first. In profound autism it can be opening up by painting, talking, getting over a fear or accepting someone new as a friend.

In Asperger's syndrome it can be a rare creative or intellectual realization that seems to turn the world upside down.

Bubble world is also a world of worlds – a mind of bubbles – a foamy mind.

Often the autistic mind likes to simplify and live in just one interior bubble at a time.

Each new 'perseveration' (absorption in some object or sensation) can be a new bubble – an entire world, like…

…staring at the moon for hours.

….or being lost in endless contemplation about airplanes.

…or pondering a pencil, or a confusing remark…

…or thinking about the meaning of the word, 'heat.'

The rest of the world disappears.

Sometimes one can listen just to sounds, and tune out sight.

…or just observe, and tune out sound.

Tuning out compensates for information overload and emotional overload.

Donna Williams called it going 'mono-track.' Most people, she noted, are 'multi-track.'[1]

A decade before I learned about autism, I sketched an outline for a story about a girl's adventures in over 40 worlds. Here are some of the ostensibly disconnected worlds:

…kinship world, idolatry world, blindness world, hairsplitter world, unconscious world, truth as belief world, ultraviolet world, rights world, gift world, tool world, the land of black grass, the land of speaking lions, feral world, memory world, and branch world (as opposed to tree world).

Passing through each world was, for the girl, an adventure and an initiation into reality.

Some of these worlds have slipped into this book.

Worlds are way-stations, as in the autistic child who matures by passing from a purely sensory world to a literal world of objects…

…to a meaningful world of concepts…

…to a significant world of feelings.

Sometimes one can hop back and forth between worlds, revisiting them to clarify and enrich them, so that they evolve and mature.

Each world provides insight and intimations of growth and life, while the great bubble remains…and the desire to escape to something better, something higher:

> *My cocoon tightens, colors tease,*
> *I'm feeling for the air;*
> *A dim capacity for wings*
> *Degrades the dress I wear.*
> *A power of butterfly must be*
> *The aptitude to fly,*
> *Meadows of majesty concedes*
> *And easy sweeps of sky.*
> *So I must baffle at the hint*
> *And cipher at the sign,*
> *And make much blunder, if at last*
> *I take the clew divine. (Emily Dickinson)*

Nine: Detachment

Leo Kanner was the first doctor to note the distinctive traits of autism.

In his studies he included observations by the parents of autistic children. One mother was especially struck by her boy's detachment.[1] Oblivious to others, her son lived without relationships, even with himself.

...as though he could dispense with his ego only at the price of dispensing with his father and mother.

Einstein was detached.

His colleague and biographer, Abraham Pais, wrote that if he had to characterize Einstein by just one word, it would be *apartness*.[2]

One rather noble face of detachment is a kind of judicial dispassion. Dr. Asperger noted his young subjects' unusual dispassion.[3]

Arthur Conan Doyle had Asperger's syndrome, as did his character, Sherlock Holmes.

Apparently Doctor Watson was the thoughtful, caring, non-autistic counterpart to the demanding, rude, but perfectly noble and dispassionate Holmes.[4]

Gabriel Marcel distinguished two kinds of detachment: that of the spectator – alienated, deserting reality not so much by indifference, but by possession and manipulation of all that is separate (including oneself)...

...and that of the saint, detached from the things of the world to be a participant in the highest mystery of reality.[5]

Marcel dreaded the spectator's detachment in himself...the spectator's life...a perpetual audience member, watching a perpetual play.

To strengthen his sense of reality he made a note to remind himself each and every day that he was not watching a play.[6]

Autistics are usually detached in both ways, in the distant mode of the game player and the absorbed mode of life, like Holmes' rapture at the advent of a new, mysterious crime: 'Watson! The game is afoot!'

There is also detachment from society.

Detachment from society means that an Aspergian (or autistic) will construct a personal identity and resist the identity that develops in society.

Aspergians are not, in spirit, members of groups. To put it bluntly, they are not pack animals. Their neural connections are not social.

It is often said that in character Aspergians resemble cats, where neuro-typicals are more like dogs.

Perhaps the independence of Aspergians stems from having to create mental worlds of their own.

The socially defined identity – the tribal mind – the community mind – is formed in relation to a group (Americans, Tibetans, Christians, Jews…) and to a core set of customs and beliefs.

The community mind sees self-worth, in part, as relative to the importance of other selves – creating a neural culture of *status*… and *style*…

…leaders and followers – banners and flags – an entire history – a glorious history some would say, of flowing colors, heroic deeds, kings, kingdoms, servants and serfs…

Aspergians show indifference, humor and even contempt for hierarchy, status and style.

They are careless about their appearance, and they wonder how anyone could be interested in what someone says because he or she has a title or wears expensive clothes, or a uniform, or robes…anything that looks pretentious.

Sometimes Aspergians see fashion as a kind of game…like the runway models who are told to strut and never smile and never eat because only the powerful could do so.

An extreme world of status is an object world – servants and slaves *as things* to be used – *as* domesticated animals…*as* not quite human. Trees *as* inanimate *objects*…

More moderate worlds of status have roles to be played, and often they are played willingly, for one absorbs the *context* of a life and accepts the role into which one has been born.

'But I can't marry the prince!' exclaims the working class girl, who cleans up after her cruel step-sisters…

Yet in fairy tales rules are broken, and objects magically come to life.

The idea of being leaders gave Einstein and Simone Weil the willies. They were neurally blind to class.

…and it would be nice to think that this made them less likely to see others as tools.

Einstein excluded himself as an object of devotion, requiring that his ashes be scattered at an undisclosed location.

…and ancient figures of life often placed themselves at great risk by proclaiming that those of low caste, the poor, the diseased, enemies and criminals alike, were all and without exception, sacred.

The social mind at its most defensive speaks of blasphemy – that which introduces chaos and pain into a community's sacred concepts, sacred institutionalized instincts and sacred social order.

The profoundly autistic mind sees blasphemy, at least initially, in life, for life invites chaos and pain into one's sacred, closed, internal church.

In part, detachment is being able to step back and see without prejudice – to see logically and with emotional distance.

When emotions and logic are separate it is easy to talk dispassionately about religion and politics. It is easy to converse on grounds of logic and evidence; perhaps too easy.

One may treat religion objectively – like an academic toy. This is useful and in a sense oblivious – like an Aspergian child talking for the sake of talking.

At the other extreme, when the brain is too interconnected, logic and emotion can form a tangled mess.

One is incapable of dispassionate conversation about religion or politics because the strings in one's mind are all tied together, and pulling on one string pulls on them all.

Logic tugs too dearly on emotion – communication with others disintegrates.

Connection within fosters disconnection without.

Another form of detachment is detachment from self.

Aspergians *step back*, seeing themselves and others as abstractions, sometimes as deeply and in as much detail as they can.

To the Aspergian detached spectator – the great remote scientist – the large social world is blindly instinctive. The social world follows instincts easily, automatically and without question.

From an Aspergian perspective, customs, covenants and taboos are invisible to the non-autistic world. Conflicts between groups and harmonies within groups are natural and unseen. The contexts of nation, culture and religion are absorbed as effortlessly as a breath of air. The unconscious life does not exist.

Autistics stumble and see their instincts at work – they are more conscious of their subconscious. Aspergians ask 'Why?' until they reach a deep answer or an impasse.

Aspergians take as many steps away as possible…to see some big picture.

Some Aspergians are activists, and they recommend that everyone take at least two steps back and see *themselves* deeply, objectively and from afar.

Doris Lessing wrote a book in the 1980's called *Prisons We Choose to Live Inside*.[7]

Lessing (who may or may not be Aspergian) made the thoroughly Aspergian point that the sciences of human nature are fairly well understood, but not applied.

She noted that subjects like human psychology are not introduced in the early grades and argued that because of this children often grow up to make terrible mistakes…

…they dissolve their better natures in the emotional currents of the group, oversimplify reality, or blindly follow the slogans of leaders without understanding why they or others instinctively do so.

The stereotype is that Aspergians always berate 'group-think' and criticize the religious and educational systems that encourage blind loyalty.

The detachment of the perfect scientist – the careful judge – carries in its wake a rational and stable world, a great deal of useful knowledge, and the distant, autistic life of an eternal spectator.

The best detachment opens a door to pure life.

Mystical detachment is from the illusory constructs of society and the mind.

The mystic says, 'Everything you have learned is wrong.'

Simone Weil wrote: *Attachment manufactures illusions, and anyone who wants to behold the real must be detached.*[8]

She distinguished the 'reality of the world' from 'independent reality.'

The reality of the world is the result of our attachment...the self which we transfer into things. It has nothing to do with independent reality. That is only perceptible through total detachment.[9]

The detachment of the mystic is seeing reality raw. Our concepts, beliefs and desires present an artificial reality that only seems close because it is seen through construct colored glasses...

...concepts we rest upon and use...*seeing as*'s to which we are naturally attached.

There is a progression – from instinctive *one* seeing-as, to a scholarly, detached multiplicity of *many* seeing-as's, to complete detachment – *no* seeing-as.

The medieval mystic Meister Eckhart described total detachment this way:

...*I extol detachment above any love...*

...*God's own natural state is unity and purity and these come from detachment...*

...*I put detachment higher than humility...*

...humility means abasing self before all creatures...but staying in is better still.

...perfect detachment is without regard...

...I prize detachment more than mercy, too...

What then, I ask, is the object of absolute detachment?

I answer, that the object of absolute detachment is neither this nor that.

It is absolutely nothing, for it is the culminating point where God can do precisely as he will.

The man who is in absolute detachment is rapt away into eternity where nothing temporal affects him nor is he in the least aware of any mortal thing...[10]

Ten: Object World

Dawn Prince-Hughes wrote that when she was four or five she had a fascination with kitchen utensils, rocks, mixers, wrenches and tools:

...I delighted in watching my grandparents use these things and perform the same motions over and over...

...I remember feeling like these tools and devices had <u>meaning</u> and <u>perfection</u>. Other objects, such as marionettes, mannequins, and dolls, terrified me.[1]

Donna Williams, another high functioning autistic, wrote:

They (Donna's father and grandfather) had both stopped being objects in my world when I was three...[2]

Things, unlike people, were welcome to become a part of me.[3]

A classic series of experiments was initiated in 1944 by the social psychologists Fritz Heider and Mary-Ann Simmel.[4] They made a movie in which a rectangle, two triangles and a circle moved in ways that were designed to tell a story about humans.

When non-autistic children were shown the movie, they described the moving geometrical patterns as figures playing roles in a story – usually the same sort of story that the psychologists had intended.

Similar animations have been made since then with moving dots.

Autistic children do not interpret the moving dots as people – they see moving dots.

They do not assemble geometrical objects into stories. They see the literal world – the object world of moving geometrical objects.

It is one thing to explain the mechanical motions of objects, another to tell a story.

...and this says something very important about stories; something that we know intuitively, but that now has some meaning in terms of the brain. Stories are closer to life.

Stories carry life, significance and meaning in a way that explanations do not.

Perhaps this is why so many people adhere to ancient religious stories and dismiss all scientific explanations. They find truth in life, so to speak, not in the movements of dots.

Of course, stories lack the standards of consistency and evidence required of explanations, so there are many who dismiss all ancient stories – they find truth in the movement of dots, so to speak, not in life.

Sacred stories and scientific explanations are too grand and royal to be compared to these struggling remarks.

This book is a primitive raft, pasted together with stick and string, built to cross a great ocean to a raw and wordless world of life, and the journey is advertised as therapy for those who feel fine.

In *severe* cases of autism, object world *is* the world:

People seen only as objects are particularly disturbing – unpredictable and frightening...

...objects that make loud noises and suddenly move towards you ...

And there is a spectrum, as they say, of lives in object world.

At one time Wittgenstein wrote:

...How can these gestures, this way of holding the hand, this picture, be the wish that such and such were the case?...

...It is nothing more than a hand over a table and there it is, alone and without a <u>sense</u>...

...Like a single bit of scenery from the production of a play, which has been left by itself in a room. It had life only in the play.[5]

...and later...

There is a way of looking at electrical machines and installations (dynamos, radio stations, etc., etc.) which sees these objects as arrangements of copper, iron, rubber, etc. in space, without any preliminary understanding...

...It is of course an absolutely strict and correct conception; and the characteristic and difficult thing about it is that it looks at the

object without any preconceived idea (as it were from a Martian point of view)...[6]

Einstein, Wittgenstein, Bohm and Weil were fascinated with rational thought and mechanism. Einstein and Bohm drew a lot of grief from their colleagues for opposing the idea that nature is governed by chance.

Spinoza believed that the world was one substance, obeying one set of rules. He disdained chance. Everything in his world was determined.

Democritus loved to discover causes, loved detail, craved dispassionate explanations, and held that nature was nothing more than a complex machine.

Einstein admired the philosophers Spinoza and Democritus for their unencumbered spirituality.[7] Weil also admired Spinoza.

Spinoza was recently diagnosed as possessing Aspergian traits.[8]

I will leave it to someone else to stitch together conjectures about high-functioning autism and the origins and history of science. Apparently the undercurrents of a hidden neural culture stretch throughout history.

Aspergians will often attribute their fascination with science to the beauty and depth of this subject.

But logical thought and science also have stability of meaning. A statement or question will have one and the same meaning by being independent of context.

...like the statements: 'All apples have surfaces' and '5 + 6 = 11.'

These statements are always true. There is no context to worry about. No horror of ambiguity. Object world is autistically, eternally safe.

Object world is a world of rules – contracts, not covenants.

One autistic woman wrote that as a child she saw her friends as things to be used for shared interests, though apparently neither she nor they realized this.[9]

Wittgenstein devoted much effort to understanding the nature of rules and rule following. As he matured, he fell out of love with the power and authority of rules.

Recent research by Pearl Chiu and her associates on the cingulate cortex has revealed that high-functioning autistic brains are built to interact with other people the way normal people interact with inanimate objects.[10]

...so that to some extent the opinions, feelings and existence of others is irrelevant, for others are like buttons on computer keyboards – *its*, not *thou's*.

When *thou* does not register, one is in object world.

Cultures that are hollow, overly bureaucratic, impersonal, contractual or tyrannical are object worlds.

The large, modern world of strangers, laws and even rights is, in part, an object world.

In chapter 43 (The Land of Black Grass) I discuss cultures that are nothing but object worlds, far from life.

Religions that are hollow, overly bureaucratic, impersonal, contractual or tyrannical are object worlds.

Jesus urged his followers to quit the hollow rule following of verbal contracts: *Do not swear at all, either by heaven...or by the earth...or by Jerusalem...(or) by your head...Let what you say be simply 'Yes' and 'No'...* (Matthew 5, 33).

Object world is literal. All statements are expressions of facts.

Imagine a mother who utters out of frustration, 'I'm going to throw this ragged old shirt in the river!' An autistic child might take this threat literally.

All commands are literal – a world of blind rule following.

Once, for example, Donna Williams was told to put buttonholes into fur coats, and she inserted them everywhere, not understanding the larger purpose of buttonholes.[11]

As David Bohm emphasized, literal thought creates a mechanical world – a world of objects, where one is a function.[12]

And the danger is that the dignity of work is lost, for one is not a 'thou,' participating in a mysterious transcendence, or a 'me' helping in a community, but an 'it'...

...a mark in some ledger – a tool in some box.

It takes a tremendous effort for autistics and role players in object world cultures and religions to get beyond object world and object thought – object people, strangers, disconnected points.

Wittgenstein never knew that he had Asperger's syndrome. He never knew about the autistic object world, but he felt it.

In his later years, like George Orwell and David Bohm, he fought object world inside and out, with all his might.

I was surprised to discover that the fight against object world had a link to the history of religion.

Wittgenstein greatly admired St. Augustine.

I wondered why, and searching through Augustine's writings I stumbled upon these lines (which may have nothing to do with Wittgenstein's admiration, but do accord with this book):

...when I wished to think on my God, I knew not what to think of, but a mass of bodies (for what was not such did not seem to me to be anything), this was my greatest, and almost only cause of my inevitable error.

...I believed Evil also to be some such kind of substance, and to have its own foul and hideous bulk; whether gross, which they called earth, or thin and subtile (like the body of air)...

I conceived two masses, contrary to one another, both unbounded, but the evil narrower, the good more expansive.

...I could not conceive of mind unless as a subtile body, and that diffused in definite spaces...

I feared therefore to believe Him born in the flesh, lest I should be forced to believe Him defiled by the flesh...

...But I, conceiving of things corporeal only, was mainly held down, vehemently oppressed and in a manner suffocated by those 'masses'...[13] (*Confessions*, Book V)

Eleven: Picture World

Some high-functioning autistics, many perhaps – are visual thinkers.

Pictures play about in the mind and behave as though they had a life of their own.

Visual autistics think in caricature and image. Temple Grandin wrote an entire book about this autistic mode of thought, called *Thinking in Pictures*.[1]

When growing up, she converted abstract ideas into images in order to understand them.

She transformed the idea of peace into the image of a dove, the idea of honesty into the image of someone returning a wallet, and human relationships into images of windows and doors opening and closing.[2]

Caricatures are sometimes the only means to understanding, like the image that came to the author's mind years ago when he was struggling to understand a debate between two politicians.

The words of the debate were clear, the arguments were clear, but the motivations behind the intense emotions were a mystery until the image of a nest of blue birds came to mind.

The father and mother bluebird were busy building and protecting the nest, adding structure with twigs and instructing the baby bluebird what to do. The watchwords of the parents were protection, structure, stability, family, authority and hierarchy.

Then the baby bluebird grew up, escaped from under-wing, so to speak, and chirped about equality, justice, change, fairness, and the rights of the individual.

The bluebirds displayed their instincts – they did not know them.

Pictures inhabit a large playground, sometimes in object world, sometimes in life.

On the object side, pictures represent.

They are literal – they convey facts but no life.

In object world pictures replace life altogether.

The Lakota Elder Dan complained of this. He said that white men like to make perfect pictures – pictures of facts – pictures without life.

Referring to Abraham Lincoln he reproached the modern world of object-education:

...you teach about him like a dead man. He's not like Jesus to you. He's not alive to you anymore. So you make children learn when he was born and everything about him.

...You teach your children that Abraham Lincoln freed the slaves. Why don't you teach them that he made you all slave-freers and that you are now his children and must uphold his honor?...

...It makes your history thin and ugly because it puts things in boxes on shelves...instead of keeping them alive. I think our way is better. I really do.[3]

In object world the honor of Lincoln need not be upheld – there is no reciprocation over time.

Objects like Lincoln belong to us.

There is no 'living up to Lincoln' for one cannot belong to him – cannot be his child...cannot in any sense be his daughter or son.

Lao-Tzu spoke of the man who knows himself to be a son – the man who does not belong to himself. Such a man, he implied, is not self-important.[4]

He was asked to give advice. He politely refused.

Pictures also play on the large end of the picture playground. They play in life.

In life, pictures are gifts. We connect to life-pictures. We reciprocate.

...like the picture we hold in our memory of someone's sacrifice for us.

The living world and object world seem so far apart.

Pauli (the noted physicist) wanted to construct a bridge between these worlds.

He suggested paying attention to images from our dreams – beholding them, feeling their significance, living them but not interpreting them...not using them as representations.[5]

Dreams are not worked for, neither bought nor sold.

We do not own them. We have no right to them. Valuable, they cannot be protected.

They are not picture-facts of object world.

Dreams are large worlds – they allow us to belong to more than ourselves – they allow us to belong to them.

Dreams enlarge life, like journeys to new lands. Nightmares I don't understand.

Dreams are the last vestige of the free and the wild in a world we have domesticated and risen above.

The English language is misleading. We say, 'Last night I had a dream,' when the reality is, 'Last night a dream had me.'

Long ago in the woods and fields of North America, the custom was to reciprocate for one's dreams – to live them out and honor them, like living out lessons about Abraham Lincoln.

Dreams encompassed the individual, not the other way around.

I once listened to an Iroquois man speak to a group of visitors in the woods.

He told them about his life in the forest, and about his grandmother's life.

At one point he exclaimed, 'Hearing the wolves howl at night – there's nothing better than that – nature at its best!'

It was a wonderful picture – a wonderful gift – a new identity, larger and more humble – something to live, like an image in a dream.

A graduate student responded, 'I beg to differ; I think all of nature is wonderful.'

The Iroquois man then smiled obligingly, as if the student lived in a literal world of opposing facts, and was blind to the larger world of gifts from the heart.

Twelve: Exposure World

Profound autism is information overload – too much connection – too much chaos – too much world.

The result is 'exposure anxiety' – pure stress.

There is no control – no filtering of sights, sounds or touch. It is an intrusive, overwhelming reality, where thoughts are surreal and feelings are raw beyond measure.

Anxiety is in control, not one's self. Reality is a nightmare, literally.

Anxiety becomes a tyrant because it is always in control, and ironically, it is even more controlling because of the addiction to the rush of adrenaline.

When Donna Williams was young she could not tolerate touch. She experienced the absence of touch as respect and understanding.[1]

Scientists explain some of this as a lack of 'sensory inhibition,' for there are cells that normally shut signals down.

But for autistics the overload is unrelenting tyranny.

Donna wrote an entire book about this: *Exposure Anxiety – The Invisible Cage*, which motivated this chapter.[2]

She noted that her anxiety led her to divert all variety of stimuli. For instance, talk about me, but don't talk to me.

The anxiety of over-connection is not limited to autistics. It is also plain to see in non-autistics.

Donna noted that her own self-protective behavior was mirrored in *clowns...workaholics...clinically detached intellectuals*, and *compulsives* of all stripes.[3]

One of the most effective self-protective behaviors is to behave mechanically by communicating with prepared responses – anxiety lines.

Also safe is the world of rules. Blindly following orders is safe.

Another path to safety is to craft a fantasy world and jump in.

Exposure anxiety is more than avoiding the world, it is avoiding one's self. It is running towards non-existence. One tunes out, shuts down and stops being real.

Or one becomes inattentive and indifferent. Calm enters when one refuses to care.

Trying to know, trying to mature, can also produce connection, existence and anxiety, so one shifts responsibility to others – 'Eve told me…the serpent told me…'

Exposure anxiety seeks the smallest possible identity.

By contrast, life seeks the largest possible identity. Life is not anxious. It does not ponder what it might say, how it might respond.

Life loves and understands its enemy within. Life says, 'Have faith,' meaning, 'open up.'

For some, the way to open up is to believe in something – to embrace a life larger than one's own by embracing a larger story.

For others the way is to embrace a life larger than any story one can imagine.

For the young Donna Williams the keys to escape from her anxiety were:

…playing with color and listening to music. (She noted that music gave sub-conscious order to her chaos, and I think her play did, as well. 'Order through play' – a good motto.)

…ridiculous rules, like telling her hand that it had no right to hit itself. (Perhaps rules are tyrants, diminished by humor.)

…being granted freedom to leave her fortress, for instance, scolding her very gently.

Locks on her door included bullies and racists – those who robbed her of power and significance, craving these possessions for themselves.

Life seeks the largest identity. Consider the following story:

An autistic child was asked who she was. She recoiled into a corner and was silent.

Later she was asked again. She whispered, 'You.'

...An American was asked who he was. He gave the name of his job.

...A Japanese man was asked who he was. He offered the name of the corporation for which he worked.

...A Mexican was asked who he was. He gave his family name and the name of his village.

...A century ago, a Native American elder was asked who he was. First he gave the name of his tribe. Then he started with the beginning of the Universe...

Two monks on a pilgrimage were asked who they were. One replied, 'We are God's children.' The other replied, 'Maybe that's a robber's question. Maybe we are deeper than words.' The first monk complained, 'That doesn't sound very humble.'

The two monks then entered into a protracted discussion.

A mystic was asked who she was. She laughed.

This response confused the questioner, who pondered her laughter. The question was legitimate. He did not understand her response.

One day he walked past her cottage. She was inside, watching old cartoons and rolling in laughter.

She laughed at the literal – the baseball that was literally screaming out of the park.

She chuckled at blind rule following, when a thoughtless Elmer Fudd was caught up in one of Bugs Bunny's manipulative games.

She laughed at bodily functions that were beyond control, when a baby bear burped and then blushed.

She giggled at the surprise of an animal wearing a beard and dark glasses, as though for an instant the world was raw and anything was possible.

She laughed at the silliness of the autistic mind.

Thirteen: Detail World

Almost all autistics, high functioning and low, attend to detail – factual detail – significant detail. They see in detail. They look closely.

They care about detail, not about the tribe. They bond to the detail of the world, not to the tribe.

The instinct in some is to leapfrog social life for pure life, and through pure life to find a pure humanity.

Detail world is a kind of raw world – immediate and tactile.

Detail is intensely spiritual. Detail world is the spiritual world. One pays attention to detail.

…like looking someone in the eye…

…or like greeting someone who cannot respond – perhaps an old man in a nursing home. One says to him, 'Hello,' expecting nothing in return, yet acknowledging his presence.

Acknowledgement is a gift – a gesture – a bond – an architecture of life that translates, 'Yes, you do exist.'

The prevalent culture – the culture that bonds to community – asks…

'What is your *opinion* of that nation?' (Just one opinion? For a whole nation? But there are so many people.)

'Then what do you think about this issue?' (The whole issue? Aren't there 10,000 books on that?)

'No, no, where do you stand?'

Oh, I *see* (finally). Yes, I am with you. Don't worry. You're not alone.

And yet this comes out as patronizing, and it isn't meant to.

In social bonding detail is often sacrificed.

In the social world spiritual questions are not questions about one's attention to detail, but about religion – about shared beliefs – about agreement in doctrines and stories.

…and spiritual life is not relation to *every* detail of life, visible and invisible, but relation to a community, visible and invisible.

Autistics often do not realize that questions that appear to ask for the factual truth are in fact soliciting agreement.

It took years for the author to realize that ostensibly scientific questions like, 'Do you believe in God?' are often disguised community questions – 'Are you with us?' or in a more foreboding sense, 'Do you submit to our order?'

But often the hidden meanings are far less foreboding – the questions hide emotional anxieties, like, 'Is there hope?' or they simply express the wonderfully human need for companionship and significance.

It took me much longer to realize that the question about belief in God is asked only by those living in a domesticated world – a world of inanimate objects, where it is not so clear that someone cares.

Autistics see with factual eyes, literal eyes, not tribal eyes, not social eyes, not implicit eyes, not contextual eyes…and their anxieties and hopes have no false covers.

Autistics are taught to reach out to life, hope, and purpose through the tribal, social, implicit mentalities of those around them – to find life in society – not in detail – by ignoring relation to the rich detail of the world.

But the paths to life are many, and trudging through the neurotypical forest is not always best.

Autistics see details in pieces.

They try to assemble pieces into a whole – *without losing the pieces*.

That last part is emphasized.

Non-autistics see the whole and forget the pieces. It is automatic for them. They make names.

They point to a creation and name it a carpet, but forget the threads. They see a tree and name it a tree, but forget about the branches.

Sometimes they speak of nations and forget the people.

The autism scholar Uta Frith put it this way:

> *...for the nonautistic person, fragments, once assembled into a single picture, lose their meaning as fragments and are only meaningful as part of the greater unit they belong to, the whole picture.*[1]

This is a blindness to which non-autistics are blind – a great hidden disability – the significance and meaning of fragments is lost – a world without pieces.

There are tests now given to detect autism where a list of words is presented like: frigid, winter, snow, ice, blizzard. A few minutes later the subject is asked if 'cold' was among the words.

The autistic remembers the detail and answers, 'No.' The efficient neuro-typical remembers only the theme and answers, 'Yes.'

Normal adults build up a world of concepts. They unconsciously suppress details and *see their words and expectations.*

In a sense they see an entire spoon half hidden in a cup of coffee because they expect to see an object invariant to its surroundings, and have been taught the corresponding word 'spoon.'

Autistics are less efficient – as we noted before, they may see a piece of metal above the surface – a detail without a name. They see what they see, not what they expect.

Of autistics one might say, in the spoon they lack faith (as though God was mankind's greatest invariant).

The inefficiency and exhaustion of seeing raw can be a gift. Detail can be beautiful – the raw can be a delight, and in a sense, far truer than any word or expectation.

I once complained to some friends that everyone talks about trees but no one talks about branches – that when I walked down the street I liked to turn off tree-world.

I didn't see trees; I saw branches and trunks. It was inefficient and wonderful; it let me walk more slowly, and pay attention to the different shapes and lives of different branches.

It is one thing to live in 'tree world,' another to live in 'branch world.'

Details like thoughts are easy to retrieve, and they grow in complexity and significance because they immediately connect to other thoughts, and in autistics they often do so *consciously*.

Uttering '2 + 2 = 4' to a neuro-typical person will evoke a simple nod…they understand.

…but to an autistic, this utterance may consciously evoke the entire subject of arithmetic.

…so that '2 + 2 = 4' tries to build a home for itself – it struggles to build a structured, significant world called 'arithmetic.' It *needs* a place. It *must* have a place.

Many thoughts – many expressions – must build their own nests.

In his early days Wittgenstein wrote that the statement *this chair is brown* seems complicated and ambiguous, as though it needed to be infinitely extended.[2]

In one way, this is the sign of a disability – the fact that a mind is driven to create worlds that other minds find unnecessary: '2 & 2 works fine – who needs all of arithmetic?'

In another way, it is the sign of a different path towards life…

Like the poetry of Blake or Tennyson – where the world is seen in a flower…

…or a single letter…or a period…or a single remark.

Imagine a still pond, where each raindrop creates an expanding circle. That is an autistic reality.

In each detail one sees the significance of the world – where it *might* not be seen in some story, or community, or tradition, or collection of beliefs.

…in each detail, in each period, in each remark, in every man, woman and child, one sees the life and significance of the whole.

Wittgenstein once suggested that the following verses could serve as his motto:[3]

> *In the elder days of art,*
> *Builders wrought with greatest care*
> *Each minute and unseen part,*
> *For the gods are everywhere. (Longfellow)*

The contemporary autistic poet, William Julien, wrote:

Everyone is a Shining Star.
Every Character is infinite;
each Letter and Number is unique.[4]

Similar sentiments were expressed in the ancient Gnostic Gospels:

...*Each letter is a complete thought like a complete book, since they are letters written by the Unity, the Father having written them for the aeons*...

...*in this way the Word of the Father goes forth in the all*...[5]

Fourteen: Wittgenstein the Philosopher

Wittgenstein is the most celebrated and maligned philosopher of the 20th century.

He is celebrated for the brilliance and novelty of his ideas.

He is maligned for an apparently superficial philosophy.

In his later years he dismissed the traditional goals and methods of philosophy (analysis of 'the depths' to find 'the truth') and instead described how ordinary people talk in everyday life.

He put aside argument. He put aside theory. He ignored hypotheses and generalizations. He constructed no accounts of truth, beauty, or virtue.

For Wittgenstein, philosophy as a search for the natures of 'deep things' was a profoundly misguided game.

He advised his students to abandon traditional philosophy and to do something useful with their lives.

He noted how ordinary people in ordinary life live and talk…and there he stopped.

The result was a *detailed collection* of observations (a common autistic construction).

Crucially, he placed his observations in the many contexts of life – in the play of life, so to speak, to give them life…and reality.

He recorded his observations in the form of remarks.

Many of his colleagues dismissed his work. They didn't care about the details of ordinary language.

They wanted to build theories to make sense of the world – or at least deep, consistent accounts of things like truth, justice and beauty. What are these things, really?

They wanted accurate pictures (accounts) of these ideas as wholes.

In effect he told them, 'You don't need pictures. You shouldn't seek pictures. You are looking in the wrong place. The nature of these concepts is before you, not hidden. The whole is here, but you do not see it.'

...as though the philosophers he admonished were autistic.

He invented a completely new way of doing philosophy – a 'therapy' as he coined it, for philosophy and for the world.

His long journey towards philosophy-as-therapy began when he was a young man, and his world was completely literal – a world of facts.

He needed a perfect, consistent logic to govern the world of facts. Facts were fragments. They *had* to be organized. They *had* to have a place.

With the help of his advisor (another Aspergian, Bertrand Russell) he wrote a terrifically abstract book called the *Tractatus Logico-Philosophicus* (Work of Philosophical Logic).

Whether the *Tractatus* has value today is difficult to say.

Russell (then the world's leading logician) had run into paradoxes in logic, which he tried to fix.

Wittgenstein found flaws in the repairs and proposed a different way to *connect* language to the reality of fact world.

Language was assumed to be separate from reality, not a part of it. Language *represented* reality – language was an artifice – nouns *named* things, sentences *described* facts.

Language was not a part of life. It was outside. It was autistic.

Today, some people hope to clarify the work of both men and devise a way to insure that computer programs never have bugs...

...perfect languages in a flawless metaphysical reality – heady, otherworldly stuff – rigorous yet strangely vague, for the abstractions are so abstract, they appear free-floating and indistinct, like lights in a fog.

The young Wittgenstein was obsessive about his book – everything had to fit its form.

In the preface to the Tractatus, Wittgenstein summarized the purpose of his book.

...Its whole meaning could be summed up somewhat as follows: What can be said at all can be said clearly; and whereof one cannot speak thereof one must be silent.[1]

The young Wittgenstein cut the world in two, into that which can be said (with perfect clarity – no invisible context, no ambiguity) and that which cannot.

The perfect 'talkable' half of his world consisted of facts governed by logic.

The other half, the perfect wordless world, consisted of ethics and aesthetics. Nothing *could* and nothing *should* be said about them. Only life and art could or should do so.

I think that Wittgenstein intuited that language was a barrier to pure life, so he tried to corral it with logic. I think autistics are far more sensitive to this barrier.

The use of the term 'God' for instance, was seen as a lowering to our level of concepts – a disrespectful utterance – full of pride – self-righteousness…religious graffiti.

The experience of the good and the beautiful was untouchable – sacred and pure.

The young Wittgenstein saw concepts and words as lifeless and therefore profane. Latter, when he sensed that concepts could be lived, not just thought, they were no longer so terribly distant from G__.

The experience of the good and the beautiful was untouchable – sacred and pure.

Language world was not value world.

And so the young Ludwig sculpted his dream of two worlds. For a time he was content with it, perfectly.

The architect and close friend of Wittgenstein, Paul Engelmann, noted that Ludwig was passionate about this division. He mentioned another of his friend's uniquely autistic observations – that values (like the beauty of a woman) are not *in* the world.[2, 3]

Value world is not *the* world. (More bubbles in the foam.)

Consider a painting of a man and a woman, where the man has extended his arm to the woman, offering a single rose.

Most people would describe this painting as expressing a romantic gesture. The emotional content is *in* the painting, *of* the painting – not apart from it.

An autistic would not necessarily see it this way.

First there is a *literal* painting representing two people. The man is holding a flower. The painting is a representation of this fact.

Second, and quite independently, there is an emotional interpretation – a distinct feeling that one can add to the painting. But that cannot be spoken...

Life is not seen *in* the people in the painting – it is superimposed.

...the life mind...the value mind...is distinct and alone.

The life mind...the value mind...is neither of this world nor language. It is apart from us and from the world.

Someone once said long ago, 'Only God is good.'

Later on (in the late 1920's) Wittgenstein changed his approach.

He slowly came to see philosophy as blindly following the model of science. Science was a literal world, where everything was a thing and language stood apart, describing it.

Science was a success. It worked.

Philosophers were trying to construct an even more literal world where *every* philosophical noun (*truth, justice, beauty, joy, pain...*) was the *name* of some *thing*.

Philosophers were asking, 'What is joy?' as if joy was an exotic insect – another *thing* to be held in the palm of one's hand.

...only to be baffled when no thing was found.

Wittgenstein saw philosophy as imprisoned by literalism, ignoring context, figurative speech, and the social life of language.

Ignorant of autism, Wittgenstein was fighting autism, jabbing at object world, doing everything in his power to escape from his literal bubble and trying to convince everyone else to do the same.

He abandoned his devotion to a beautiful, crystalline, context free world of facts because he discovered the nonsense of being completely literal.

He tried to abandon the autistic addiction to patterns. He tried to free himself from the cravings for explanation and generalization

– for conceptual structure – for world building at the expense of reality and life.

He threw away all the conceptual barnacles that had accumulated in his mind and went back to basics – to simple things we say in everyday life, like, 'That brick is red.'

He abandoned, as best he could, arguments and conclusions.[4]

He turned with all his mind and soul to the instinctive perception of detail, the raw and the promise of life.

Many philosophers were outraged and baffled by his methods and his goals. Many remain so.

Even today some of the world's leading scientists and philosophers condemn Wittgenstein for 'retreating' to the study of mere language.

After all, the tradition of philosophy has been to lay bare the foundations of reality – existence, consciousness, knowledge, truth, morality, beauty…

…by argument and concept building – by intellectual battle, not by therapy.

Philosophy has long taken upon itself the great and noble task to penetrate the true nature of reality *in concepts*.

To many philosophers, Wittgenstein was running away from the hard problems.

Inexplicably, he was running away from the task of trying to understand reality.

These philosophers never imagined that trying to understand *things* like joy, pain, life, reality and truth by searching for their 'hidden natures' was evidence of an autistic disability – a literal mentality and a kind of blindness to life.

Bertrand Russell thought that the early *Tractatus* was a work of genius, but that Wittgenstein's later work on language was a disgrace.

Yet Werner Heisenberg (who invented part of quantum mechanics) regarded Wittgenstein's early work as inferior, but thought that his later work was wonderful.

In his later work Wittgenstein reproached other philosophers for looking in the wrong place.

He tried to show them that when we see our language as distinct from reality – as a picture of a world of facts – as dead symbols, not parts of life itself, that we exist in a shallow, confused distortion of the world...a poor gray bubble in an infinite expanse, where language-as-representation (and nothing else) is just bubble love.

He was explicit that his work was not philosophy in the traditional sense, but therapy.

Yet to this day, hardly a single philosopher (as best I can tell) has approached his work as therapy. It is easy to see why – they cannot believe that they are chasing literal phantoms, much less that they are disabled – insensitive to life.

Wittgenstein wrote his thoughts down day after day, for decades. His remarks, they say, could fill an encyclopedia.

He arranged some of his best thoughts in a book, *Philosophical Investigations*, which was published after his death in 1951.

Today his life and work are usually summarized (and over-simplified) by reference to his two great books, the early *Tractatus* and the later *Investigations*.

And accordingly, people speak of the early Wittgenstein and the later Wittgenstein.

These books respectively epitomize his two approaches to philosophy, the first: an abstract, context free, literal, rule based world – the second: everyday life, with attention to detail.

Much of Wittgenstein's remaining work has been gathered over the last 50 years and published in other books such as *Remarks on Colour, Remarks on the Philosophy of Psychology, Philosophical Grammar, Culture and Value, Zettel, Notebooks 1914-1916, the Blue and Brown Books* and *On Certainty*.

He was on the journey from object to life, but for those who are creatures of object world and puzzle over what *theory* he possibly could have sought, his path remains a mystery.

Fifteen: Simone Weil

Simone Weil was a French intellectual, activist and teacher; a clumsy, often pedantic woman who has been called one of the great spiritual figures of history.

Born in 1909 in Paris, she was, as an infant, sickly and weak.

At the age of three, when presented with a ring set with a jewel, she objected, declaring that she did not care for luxury – a characteristic that saw her through the remainder of her short life.

She was solitary, extraordinarily stubborn, and awkward.

She did not dress well, preferring loosely fitting clothes.

She did not like to be hugged or kissed. She found dancing ridiculous.

Her brother, Andre Weil, was a prodigy at mathematics. Despite her brilliance, she was often despairing because she thought that next to her brother she was not especially gifted.

She was always self-critical. She continually blamed herself for her sins just as Wittgenstein instinctively found contact with life through confession and repentance.

She felt that it was crucial to consider how to be good rather than to ask what is best to do. (Rules of behavior can be immature and autistic.)

Her standards for intellectual honesty were severe. Not even she lived up to them.

Intensely spiritual, she wrote:

I did not mind having no visible successes, but what did grieve me was the idea of being excluded from that transcendent kingdom to which only the truly great have access and wherein truth abides. I preferred to die rather than to live without that truth.[1]

She wrote prayers that God would grant her a kind of paralysis so that she would be incapable of movement, incapable of receiving any sensation, incapable of connecting two thoughts.

Weil, like almost every high-functioning autistic, was perfectly intolerant of hypocrisy.

Her early writing was in the style of terse aphorisms and remarks.

People spoke of her intense, hyperactive concentration.

She extolled the virtues of manual labor, feeling that this made her transparent to God.

(The tactile sense is promoted – reality is amplified – like immersion in water.)

Like Einstein, she was attracted to the philosophy of Spinoza.[2]

She often disdained explanations.

In adult life, she suffered from splitting headaches.

She was sympathetic to the poor, the overworked working classes and the unemployed.

Sometimes she saw workers as saints, engaged in the purification of suffering and work.

She spoke of what was hidden as an infinite and perfect good. She suggested that we see each human being as a bottle containing a genie.

She imagined a future science where participation is never interrupted – wonderful!

Weil spoke highly of detachment.

She opposed attachment because she saw it as a form of possession – of grasping to compensate for a weak sense of reality.[3]

She regarded pure attention as the true path – attention that is silent, open and receptive, not grasping and attached.

Attention is what seizes hold of reality, so that the greater the attention on the part of the mind, the greater the amount of real being in the object.[4]

Attention defeats blindness to reality, like attention to an isolated remark.

She was afraid of her weakness of character – she felt that if she were surrounded by Nazis she might become one – but her community of friends helped her.

She detested community idols:

In chapter three we noted the tendency of non-autistics to *listen to bond*. This is the innocent kin of *listening to a group to create an agreed reality*.

Simone Weil warned of listening to others so as to find a stronger sense of reality in their soulless abstractions – the 'Great Beasts' of materialism, atheism, Marxism, patriotism, capitalism...every ism that is worshipped and obeyed – every idol.

She noted that a Pharisee was someone whose virtue was obedience to a Great Beast.

She accurately understood Pharisees, but was blind to the domesticated paths to life.

She was afraid of prayer for its hypnotic power of suggestion, until learning the 'Our father...' which she then repeated and repeated, for it removed her body and mind to a place without perspective.[5]

Education and tradition, Weil felt, should cultivate attention. They should not encourage thought but suspend thought, make us detached, empty, waiting and receptive, so that we may see values in others beyond rights and truths beyond words.

She was appalled by the tendency of human beings (including herself) to *think* in terms of absolutes – abstractions without any notion of proportion.

She felt that we fight over words like 'nation,' 'property' and 'democracy,' having been raised to think in terms of slogan absolutes, not in terms of more complex realities like 'democracy to the extent that...'

(And of course that sounds heretical to anyone raised in slogan world.)

Her desire was to silence in herself *all* opinions and desires...as though concepts were misguided...looking in the wrong place.

She extolled the highest impersonal virtues of love and justice.

She tied justice to the 'mad love' of mercy and forgiveness – not to judgment – not to anything that might fortify the lower, mediocre notion of 'myself.'

A modern philosopher wrote that the issue of 'justice over time' is and always will be intractable. For example: the injustice of slavery in the past cannot be undone without doing injustice to many in the present.

To similar seemingly intractable cases Weil imagined the parties involved not worrying about who loses more, but instead actively applying mad love.

She spoke of the difference between visible and invisible religion.

She called for a new type of sanctity – attention intense and pure.

In her last years she regarded the truths she had discovered as gold, and desperately hoped that others would ignore her intellect and read her works to recover the gold.

She created her own theology – God and Jesus had emptied themselves; God to allow the creation of the world, Jesus to allow the creation of a new order of the world (…both counterparts to the mystical path.)

Eventually only the ideals of emptying and purification guided her life.

She died in 1943 at the age of 34, refusing to eat more than those on rations in France.

Weil's friend Gustave Thibon wrote many years after her death that he was at first quite uncomfortable with her…

…that she was impossible, argumentative (very political and far-left) and spoke in an *inexorably monotonous voice.*

He continued,

…it needed much time and affection, and a great deal of reserve had to be overcome, before she showed what was best in her…

…a limpid mysticism emanated from her…

…Such mysticism had nothing in common with those religious speculations divorced from any personal commitment which are all too frequently the only testimony of intellectuals who apply themselves to the things of God.

…She actually experienced in its heart-breaking reality the distance between 'knowing' and 'knowing with all one's soul', and the one object of her life was to abolish that distance.[6]

Sixteen: Wittgenstein the Autistic

Wittgenstein confessed: *It is humiliating to have to appear like an empty tube which is simply inflated by a mind.*[1]

His sister Hermine observed that when he was a boy, he found the world alien and painful, just as his schoolfellows found him.[2]

When he was a little older, she noted that philosophy (logic) became an obsession – for a time part of a psychological transformation, very much *against his will*.[3]

Wittgenstein exhibited autistic characteristics throughout his life.

This has (in the last decade or so) become well known in autism circles, but it's not well known among philosophers. It may not be known at all.

One psychiatrist, Michael Fitzgerald, noted Wittgenstein's Aspergian traits:[4]

Ludwig was interested in the object world of mechanical engineering.

He was often absorbed in his own reflections.

He was sometimes timid of people.

He felt that he was apart from the world.

He was obsessive about his philosophy.

He was hypersensitive to change, criticism, art, music, politics, literature…

He used pedantic language.

He was extremely self-critical, blaming himself for perceived sins like literalism.

We tend to think of being literal (seeing an object rather than life) as almost comedic, like searching for a dump when someone says 'down in the dumps.'

But imagine ignoring an injured man by the roadside, as if he was just another pebble. Or imagine seeing a category – an *abstract object* like a Samaritan – instead of the truth – a *good* Samaritan.

Then imagine drawing a conclusion; that is, seeing literalism – the generic, abstract object – as a sin...or seeing some other 'ism' as a sin...rather than perceiving the manifold truths of life.

Sometimes he was hurtfully frank – distancing himself from friends and colleagues.

A closer inspection of Wittgenstein's writings reveals subtler traits.

At one point early in his life, he seems to have played with the idea of 'going normal.'

He tried to imagine the big picture in a non-autistic way – without the details.

Is it imaginable that—e.g.—we should <u>see</u> that <u>all the points of a surface are yellow</u>, without seeing any <u>single</u> point of this surface? It almost seems to be so...[5]

...complex spatial objects, for example, seem to me in some sense to be essentially things...And the designation of them by means of names seems to be more than a mere trick of language.[6]

In his hesitancy we see that he failed to fully see the whole without the parts.

Like most Aspergians, he could not stand pretense.

He once commented that every time he heard the word 'wisdom' he felt there was only vanity behind it.

On a visit to New York in 1939 he liked only one person – a shoeshine boy – because the boy was sincere.[7]

He saw significance in the *use of* words where most see nothing at all because, tragically, he was blind to the *life in* the words.

An example of one special use of words noticed by Wittgenstein:

Flowers or animals that people find ugly always strike them like artifacts. 'It looks like a...', they say. This illuminates the meaning of the words 'ugly' and 'beautiful'.[8]

Only an autistic would notice this, and only an autistic would need to.

He spoke of 'solving philosophical problems' not by traditional analysis – but by arranging remarks. And the solutions he compared to magical gifts and the enchantment of fairy tales.[9]

Autistics exhibit special styles of life and of writing.

They prefer, in general, short factual remarks over long flowery sentences. They prefer more commas, more periods, more dashes, fewer contractions, more associations, and more idiosyncratic emphases. They like to assemble pieces and circle the problem.

Their style may be a subconscious means towards structure…or life – or both…

…or a path away from some terrible obsession, like feeling perpetually empty or incomplete or fearful of change – like obsessively hunting for *the final* verbal meaning of a word – *the* definition for all possible contexts – when what they really need is the deeply felt, non-verbal life of the word.

…so that a style of writing can be like biting one's arm.

In the predominant culture, one does not read philosophy for the arm biting. (But one may listen to certain kinds of music or smoke cigarettes *just* for the arm biting.)

Wittgenstein seldom wrote, 'therefore.'

What could be wrong with connecting two thoughts? Can no inference from a single thought be trusted? Does inference rob each thought of life because it ties one to a world of abstraction?

The plentiful dashes in this book allow sub-remarks – phrases that are more than clarifications or examples of other thoughts – associated fragments of thought that merit a life of their own.

(The later) Wittgenstein wrote that style was crucial to his philosophy.[10, 11]

Judith Genova devoted an entire book to Wittgenstein's style – the intense remarks that circled each issue without the usual generalizations of philosophy.[12]

…remarks that stayed in the immediate thought, obstinately refusing the fatal next step into theory.[13]

Marie McGinn also picked up on this: that Wittgenstein's philosophy was a method, not a doctrine.[14]

(These two women emphasized Wittgenstein's style. Male scholars, as best I can tell, seem to attend almost exclusively to interpretation and argument.)

Wittgenstein's style is no ornament, no pretence. He thinks and sees and lives this way.

We are being asked to understand a cat not by its meow, but by its life as a cat.

We are free to interpret. But instead of interpreting the small world of content, we are now free to interpret the larger world of style and its associated form of life.

…the remarks that may be like a row of crayons at which a child endlessly stares, or a succession of bites on an arm…

…resolutions from the depths of the soul to connect to life.

Aspergians are in various ways perfectionists. It is not unusual for their high standards to fall upon themselves.

Wittgenstein blamed himself.

He blamed himself for being unheroic, cowardly, untruthful, vain and sinful.

He blamed himself for outbursts of temper.[15]

He blamed himself for literalism – for seeing every statement *as* a factual truth and every noun *as* the name of a thing; and for confusing constructs of the mind – language, mathematics and science – with reality.

He blamed himself for fear of the truth and a lack of faith.[16]

His fear was emotional and spiritual – fear of touching *the world* – fear of letting *his world* touch *the world*.

Emotional and spiritual fear of reality was the flaw that he saw (or projected) equally in the modern world…expressed at various times and in various ways by University life and Western culture.

…at its worst, devotion to the fantasies of bubble world – and the incessant striving to blow larger, more secure bubbles – with all their wonderful symmetry, power and beauty.

He tried to control his temper, he tried to have faith, he tried to be true beyond any measure.

Temple Grandin recalled that it came as a tremendous relief to discover that her problems with society and life were not due to flaws in her character.[17]

Wittgenstein never learned that he had a form of high functioning autism; he was never blessed with this revelation.

The autistic world *must* be organized.

Everything must have a place. *Everything*...even things that are neither something nor nothing.

In his mature years Wittgenstein observed:

...One would like to say 'I see red <u>thus</u>', 'I hear the note that you strike <u>thus</u>'...or even '<u>This</u> is what one feels when one is sad, <u>this</u>, when one is glad...'

...One would like to people a world, analogous to the physical one, with these <u>thuses</u> and <u>thises</u>...[18]

The autistic mentality never left.

...the desire to organize the barrage of disordered experiences by placing each one in a visual space.

Wittgenstein's words also needed places. Autistics fear replacement.

Suppose I wanted to replace all the words of my language at once by other ones; how could I tell the place where one of the new words belongs? Is it images that keep the places of words?[19]

Time itself had to be pictured and filed away in his mind. When he spoke of time he had to take out his watch and make an image in order to understand.[20]

There are coincidences in reading Wittgenstein's life story and the stories of other autistics. (They may be nothing more than coincidences – still, they are interesting, for they carry a touch of neural magic.)

For example, Temple Grandin recalled that as a girl she enjoyed playing with kites and model airplanes, and she devised various ways to improve their flight.[21]

But when Wittgenstein was a young engineer, he expressed his utter delight at having to improve the performance of kites.[22]

Rocking and twirling seem to be common autistic traits, helping to reduce tension.

Dawn Prince-Hughes, in the introduction to a collection of essays by autistic college students asks:

What would make a student get up from her library chair every five minutes and twirl in a clockwise direction three times, only to sit down calmly again?[23]

In describing a kind of instinctive therapy in her autistic childhood, Donna Williams recounted that she gave herself whizzies – spinning in circles with arms outstretched.[24]

Temple Grandin also spoke of continually spinning as a kind of therapy – a way to release pressure.

With Wittgenstein one cannot but help note the following:

He tried to make an airplane engine which spun the propeller by releasing, at an angle, the pressure of the engine exhaust.[25]

After this, he worked on propeller design.

The significance of propellers may reside not only in the fact that they are mechanical and spin, but that in observing them one sees a regular flickering light.

It was reported decades ago that some autistic children instinctively wave their fingers back and forth in front of their faces to relax, and today flickering lights are sometimes used for therapy.

Beyond these coincidences, Wittgenstein's philosophy was the idiosyncratic expression of an autistic life.

Autistics tend to be obsessive, and Wittgenstein was certainly obsessive – he threw his life, blood and soul into his work.

His early work *had* to fit a certain form – it *had* to be logical and precise.

Every expression *had* to have a *precise* meaning, and language *had* to have precise limits.

In his later work he criticized obsessions and told his students that obsessions, at times, are almost impossible to recognize.[26]

He was talking about the obsessive literalism of philosophy.

The philosopher keeps asking, 'What is consciousness?'…searching for its mechanism, for its scientific pieces, for some invisible object world *thing* that will explain *it*…and fails.

Almost every philosopher and scientist today continues to think this way, and I believe that many would be horrified to contemplate that this mentality might be limited.

They would see its abandonment as a return to the dark ages, not as a step forward.

They would argue, 'Our method is right – science will prevail – we have failed for the last two thousand years only because of a lack of imagination…

…perhaps quantum mechanics or quantum gravity will explain these mental *things*…some*thing* must.'

Well, at least now we see the outline of how Wittgenstein had the insight to dethrone part of his autistic mentality…and put object world on the back burner.

And we see the difficulty of presenting this view to a culture which has ordained the object mentality king.

Finally, there is a mystical aspect to Wittgenstein.

He once said that he saw every problem from a religious point of view.

But *his* religious point of view was far from the ordinary religious point of view – the conceptual view that explains the mysteries of life – it was in fact (as Philip Shields first realized) the opposite of explanation.[27]

In explanation, one fits an anomaly into some familiar pattern. Wittgenstein urged himself (and us) to do just the opposite – to accept and even celebrate mystery.

Everything is astonishing.

This is the point of view that joyfully leaps into the wordless ocean that underlies the worded froth.

Wittgenstein, Bohm, Weil and Marcel say this again and again – concepts and theories are superficial – life is deep.

The direct experience of reality was evident in Wittgenstein, as his friend Bouwsma related:

…when he reads, what he reads is in bright gold and shining and it is for so long imprinted and ready in his mind.[28]

Bertrand Russell was surprised that Wittgenstein had become a mystic, but thought that this helped the young philosopher cease his incessant thinking.[29]

The great logician, Rudolph Carnap, described Wittgenstein's attitude and approach to life as artistic and inspired – like a seer. Problems were not solved by analysis. After intense concentration, an answer was revealed.[30]

Like a playwright guided by an invisible muse, Wittgenstein participated in the creation of miniature worlds. He was the main character in the cast.

When characters are puppets, only in the play are they alive.

Seventeen: Association World

The autistic mind has been called a pin-ball mind.

It thinks by random association – by bouncing from one thought to the next.

By contrast, arranging thoughts in a sequence is difficult and unnatural.

> *I felt a cleavage in my mind*
> *As if my brain had split;*
> *I tried to match it, seam by seam,*
> *But could not make them fit.*
>
> *The thought behind I strove to join*
> *Unto the thought before,*
> *But sequence ravelled out of reach*
> *Like balls upon a floor. (Emily Dickinson)*

Dawn Prince-Hughes commented that *autism spectrum people… constantly see divergent possibilities (and at a staggeringly fast pace)*, and that this associative thinking affects sentence structure and word choice.[1]

For example, commas often appear in order to pause and stop – to consider possibilities – new associations.

Dashes seem to link associated thoughts.

(After reading about the autistic proclivity for commas, the author deleted perhaps a thousand commas from this book, but he retained most of the dashes – *they* seem right.)

Donna Williams recalled an episode where her teacher asked if her essay was a joke.

Donna explained that she put in periods every few letters in order to help the reader breathe.[2]

For how could one absorb a full sentence and breathe – all at the same time?

Periods. used. in order. to breathe.

…as though each phrase was a world in itself, and one had to pause to take each one in…

…as though breath was important…

…like the ancient Eastern writings about breath being the path to the sacred.

Short strings of verbal information – even this book is written in remarks.

It is quite natural that concept cultures (and concept minds) see the excessive use of commas and periods as symptoms of a disability…

…not as a form of sight where every phrase merits attention…

…not as a form of life where every word breathes.

Emily Dickinson was criticized for putting too many dashes in her poetry.

…and in a sense, or one might say, within a sense, her critics were right.

Here is a fictitious little 'story' I've written to convey how much fun the Aspergian mind can be. (Luckily I am able to turn this creative, associative urge on and off.)

(No name – that would tie it down):

Imagine an old-fashioned Western with cowboys, villains, shoot outs and a sheriff, in a scrubby little town.

It begins with the sounds made by all the hammer blows on all the nails that built the buildings that constitute the town.

Now squeeze all these sounds together into a single concussion, as though the town were built at once.

Consider the footprints made by all the horses and people, night and day, rain or shine. Watch as they overlap – as one footprint in the night covers one made in the day.

See the wet, shiny footprints at night, slanted towards the heels, and a thousand full moons in their reflections.

Consider the number of layers of paint on every barn, shed, and saloon. Like brushwork geology.

Did the paint crack because the paint cracked, or because the wood cracked underneath?

Inside the saloon – the intricate pattern of stains on the floor – different sizes, different colors, different shapes, with preferences for location and tendencies to flow, so that the floor is a terrain unto itself, with hills and gullies, scraped and cut by every boot and chair, decorated by every spilled drink – as mesmerizing as any natural landscape.

Reflections are glimpsed from the end of a rusty nail. Did the hammering change them?

The End.

You may have noticed that this Aspergian 'story' (or stream of consciousness) was intensely mechanical and caught up in sensations – noises of hammers and reflections of light.

Aspergian creations can be filled with life. Life flows in tales that not only associate details, but display different priorities. Animals are favorites.

…Like the Hans Christian Andersen tale of the little girl and her mother who busied themselves all day sewing the finest and most beautiful dress…

…and when the mother praised the dress and exclaimed how everyone would admire it, the little girl gleefully added… *what will the dogs think…!*[3]

Temple Grandin wrote a book called *Animals in Translation* about the similarities of autistic and animal thought, including associations.[4]

Elsewhere she described her autistic thought processes as starting with specifics and generalizing by nonsequential association.[5,6]

The pin-ball mind explores. The sequential mind looks for conclusions. It expects everything to resolve.

The pin-ball mind searches for opportunities – for new connections. It is forever breaking down walls to connect to the world. It wants to journey. It wants to create and destroy new worlds of thought and significance.

It is a blessing to be able to move with less constraint among worlds, and to more easily abandon primitive, temporary mansions of thought.

The sequential mind wants a quick summary. It wants to be done.

It asks ancient-modern questions like, 'Who is my neighbor?'

It builds walls – it draws lines.

The random mind is never done. It erases lines so that life can step in.

Eighteen: David Bohm

David Bohm was born in 1917 and died in 1992. He was a superb physicist.

Bohm was extremely creative, and Einstein spoke of him as his intellectual successor.

Bohm's work was deep – it provided entirely new insights into the quantum nature of reality.

F. David Peat wrote a penetrating biography of Bohm, yet only hinted at Bohm's autism, probably because when his book was written, the autistic spectrum was little known.

Many anecdotes in the biography reveal Bohm's autistic traits.

Bohm was often shy and withdrawn. His niece noticed that his body would instinctively pull away when he anticipated the contact of affection.[1]

Bohm was uncoordinated, so he studied the movements of other boys and planned his moves ahead.

(His niece Ruth)...*came to think of him as a spirit come to earth, that had been forced to inhabit a physical form in which it never felt at peace.*[2]

He loved books and had little interest in team sports.

He loved to wander alone and dream.

He was mesmerized by the dappled light and shadow of the forest.

As a youth he had *dreams of light, power, control and transcendence.*[3]

...Had he lived in an earlier age, he might have spoken of communicating with gods or making compacts with the energies of the universe...[4]

...Bohm yearned for contact with the transcendent...for moments of 'breaking through.'[5]

Like Einstein, he preferred the depths of physics to more modest problems. (Einstein chided those who 'drilled a lot of holes where the wood was thin.')

...and when a problem arose, Bohm, like Einstein, often internalized the phenomenon, becoming a kind of human simulator.

Only later would the simulation be translated into mathematics.

The simulations were not visual but quasi-muscular, and involved tensions that were combined and manipulated.

Bohm described himself as participating in some movement that was analogous to the physical system he wished to understand.

He found the idea of movement and flow irresistible.

He believed that he contained (in some sense) the laws of nature within his body.

He was naïve about politics and was described by one of his doctoral students as being free from guile and competitiveness.

He was often caught up in his own anxieties.

He preferred to study a subject from all angles: A colleague of his (Basil Hiley) noted that Bohm was like a helix, moving forward by constantly circling the issue.

Bohm wrote a textbook on Quantum Mechanics that treated the understanding of phenomena as primary and abstract theory as secondary.

He wrote a science fiction story in which alien beings *encased in protective layers...(communicate)...through their deep understanding of the way the brain operates...*[6]

He rewrote this work in the 1970's. The aliens fell into a state of insanity...

...Despite their advanced science and absence of self, deeply buried forces that they had previously failed to acknowledge remain within their minds...

...Only by going into this dark area and transcending it are they finally able to emerge from the ships and transform humanity.[7]

He spent a great amount of time in dialogue with the teacher Krishnamurti, and they discussed the importance of being free from mental conditioning.

Bohm described ordinary consciousness as rigid and brittle. (These are the same terms used by critics of rule based artificial intelligence.)

Bohm was excited by the idea of context-dependence in art and science – how qualities of a brush stroke could be defined by the surrounding painting, or an electron could be defined as a particle or wave depending on how it was measured.

He believed that we need to perceive a *concrete,* immediate world.[8]

Understanding reality was not a sporting contest.

Physics, he felt, was fragmented and confused, and language was at fault.

Nouns were the problem because they isolated objects – a language of verbs was felt to be the solution.

Even in object world this idea is now a respectable fad. People are pursuing new forms of science that are more verb-like and less noun-like...

...relational quantum mechanics (where properties exist only in relation), category theory (all about relations) and quasi-set theory (where things are not individuals and cannot be identified by names.)[9, 10, 11]

With respect to life, Bohm's instincts were right – a verb language is another means of escape from object world – another pin to burst the autistic bubble.

When giving is pure in heart it is more important than the gifts or those who give or receive. The verb is more important than the noun.

A world of givings is a world of pure life.

There is another way to think of it. Imagine a little girl who is pure in heart. Wishing only to give, she is blind to the gift, blind to herself as the giver and blind to the recipient.

A world of 'being blind' is a world of pure life, if one is blind in just the right amount, and just the right way...to objects...to things...to nouns.

There is no verb in English for 'being blind' or for 'not seeing.' The closest might be, 'ignoring.'

It is a pity, for in feeling empathy with another we are blind to the difference between 'my suffering' and 'your suffering,' or 'your joy' and 'my joy.'

...and in that blindness is life.

Bohm met with a group of Native Americans, interested in their verb-based language.

A friend of his was dubious about the value of such a language and suggested that Bohm read Wittgenstein's *Philosophical Investigations*. Bohm refused (I don't know why).

He studied the poetry of Coleridge.

Coleridge, some believe, had Asperger's.

Coleridge's poem 'Kubla Khan' was dissected many years ago into a network of associations of words, images and sources, and is now a hyper-poem on the internet.

I don't know if Coleridge really had many autistic traits. But he coined the word 'selfless,' which is a nice thought. And his writings are full of hidden currents and strange worlds.

...and in the 'Rime of the Ancient Mariner' he penned the famous line, *Water, water, every where, nor any drop to drink*, as good a metaphor for autism as pen will ever put to paper.

When asked about the mental illness of another, Bohm, projecting his own failings, seemed to regard it as a moral failing on the part of the sufferer.

In his later years he conceived the idea of the implicate (enfolded) and explicate orders.

All that there is – consciousness and matter – is enfolded in each part...

...the entire world is contained in every tiny piece – in every detail.

In his last years Bohm worked with dialogue groups, hoping to transform human consciousness. He spoke of the need to find order in reality, and like Einstein and Grandin, he rejected all notions of chance.

He hoped that dialogue would slow down the process of thought and make it less prone to religious and political conditioning.

His ideas came randomly and fast and formed a vision – a whole – a gestalt.

Booth Harris, a teacher who knew Bohm, believed that...*Bohm's concern with wholeness arose from his deep need for connection to the world.*[12]

David Peat summarized David Bohm's life with singular empathy:

...Bohm's world was holistic...

(He) *remained a scientific rebel. He rejected the current fashion of seeking closure in some 'grand unified theory,' in favor of a vision of nature's inexhaustibility...*

...Bohm lived for the transcendental; his dreams were of the light that penetrates...

...He never achieved wholeness in his own personal life, and the fruits of that life, which are still with us, were gained only at great sacrifice.[13]

Nineteen: From Eternity's Point of View

Very high functioning autistics seem drawn to the universal and the eternal.

Centuries ago the Aspergian Spinoza suggested that we should try to see the world *Sub Specie Aeternitatis* – from eternity's point of view – the sublime, *detached* standpoint from which one beholds timeless truths.

He solicited this delightfully remote standpoint as a way to contend with the whims of nature and man.

Eternity's point of view is more than a retreat from chaos.

…and more than the forgiveness and bonding that can flow from a detached understanding.

The need is to feel a larger existence – if possible, a majestic existence.

Einstein wrote that his life *as* an individual – as a fragment of an entirety – felt like a prison, and he wanted to experience the world as a whole.[1]

He found this experience in grand theories and universal laws.

He exclaimed in a letter to his friend Grossman how wonderful it was to explain…and unify…and generalize.[2]

In an interview with a poet in the early 1920's, Einstein described his breathtaking point of view:

The laws of creation interest me, and not whether God is made in the image of man, with a long white beard, and has a son. I am a part of infinity: I see everything in specie aeternitates.[3]

Einstein's dream was the goal of centuries of Western science – a dream devoted to assembling all phenomena under the glow of a single physical theory.

When you sweeten this ideal by a series of successes, it becomes a religion.

For Einstein, curiosity was holy. He *saw* science *as* a religion…

…a unifying structure of beauty and integrity, to which he could devote an essentially creative life.

He lived in heady times – nothing seemed impossible.

The mysterious and disparate phenomena of electricity, magnetism and light had just been unified. In a single theory, the unconnected were connected.

The periodic table was born – chemistry had a single foundation – a single pattern.

Atoms were discovered – a small number of tiny objects were responsible for the incredible variety of object world.

By 1916, space, time, energy, gravity and matter were, to an astonishing extent, unified by Einstein, Minkowski and others.

Swept up by their successes, scientists started to dream about unifying all of science.

The historian of science Gerald Holton noted a deluge of papers calling for the creation of a single picture of reality.[4]

There was even a manifesto published in 1912 to advance a *total conception* of the world.

It was signed by the leading scientists and mathematicians of the day: Ernst Mach, David Hilbert, Felix Klein, Albert Einstein, and Sigmund Freud…among others.

Einstein insisted that a simple, unified picture of the whole constituted the scientist's *supreme task*.

For any scientific high-functioning autistic, the prospect of a world of objects obeying a handful of simple rules was heaven.

Standing behind this magnificent edifice was the desire for *simplicity*.

Einstein remarked:

My desire, or shall I say my mission, has always been to simplify human life by simplifying human thought.[5]

…and the way he proposed to start was to construct a world based on tangible, simple objects.[6]

Einstein believed that attaining this godlike view was heroic. One abandoned the petty and subjective – the merely personal – for the sublime and objective.

It *was* a kind of heaven. Yet Einstein didn't deal with sensations or consciousness. He doubted that they could be treated by science; they were 'problematic.'

They were not a part of his great unity. They were stranded, outside his great scheme.

The young Wittgenstein also loved eternity's point of view, but in contrast to Einstein, he regarded science as superficial (wonderful – useful, but *as* reality, superficial).

He pointed out that one will stop taking physics seriously – as reality – when one takes note of its equivalent theories – different theories describing different realities, but giving the same results.

In Wittgenstein's time there were half a dozen completely different ways to express mechanics – Newton's way, Euler's way, Lagrange's way, Hamilton's way…

And today there are easily a dozen interpretations, formalisms and reconstructions of quantum theory – each with different object worlds – different realities that give the same results.

Some people have called this the reality crisis. They expected science to serve up *one* picture of reality, not a buffet of confusing but tempting choices.

How much freedom does reality need?

For Wittgenstein, the good and the beautiful were deep.

When he was young he believed that *seeing* an object *as* a work of art, and *living* life *as* a good person employed the same detached, eternal eyes.[7]

…being aloof so as to sense the beautiful – being aloof so as to be good…

Einstein and Wittgenstein loved to stand back and see it all, feel it all, and especially sense the unity comprehended by it all.

It is easy to imagine in these men two egos on the road to megalomania, but the autistic ego seeks to stand in heaven more often for the sake of serenity than power.

Einstein once shared in a letter that his life in the quiet town of Princeton was a refuge from the chaos of society, that the music of Mozart was beautiful and comforting, but that in the end only the contemplation of eternals could bring peace.[8]

Neither Einstein nor Wittgenstein found life in the pure sense spoken of by mystics.

…but at least Wittgenstein eventually recognized his mistake and erased his pictures.

He fought generalization – he fought the oversimplification and distance of concepts and searched for a raw, pure world of life.

Einstein's instincts, like those of many Aspergians, were less ambitious. He struggled to find patterns – to generalize and make sense of the world – to amass better concepts – to grasp reality with a simple universal model.

He was born to paint equation-pictures of the world.

In his later years he joyfully confessed that his theories were mere toys, but he never relinquished them.

He held onto his toys, and cherished them till the day he died.

Twenty: Reddish-Green

There is a little book by Wittgenstein called *Remarks on Colour*. The remarks in this book are as odd as can be:

...couldn't there be people for whom there is...reddish-green?[1]

Someone who is familiar with reddish-green should be in a position to produce a colour series which starts with red and ends with green...[2]

Everyone is familiar with reddish-orange or bluish-green, but Wittgenstein was attracted to the impossible color of reddish-green.

The idea of seeing two supposedly mutually exclusive colors at the same time, in the same place, is wonderful.

Ignore the conceptual probings of philosophy.

Why not try to see reddish-green? Try with all your might to see something that you can't see, or feel something you can't feel – that is an autistic idea.

...and these supposed impossibilities include *parallel perceptions* – seeing, hearing or sensing several things simultaneously.

Most people listen to music and hear only a mash of harmony.

But some few hear every instrument. In a symphony say, the horns, the clarinets, the violins, the violas – every 'voice' is distinct.

Years ago the author (possessing very mild autistic traits) heard only an overall harmony in music.

But a friend recommended that he put aside popular music and listen instead to a symphony by Vaughn Williams.

The author listened to this piece once or twice each day for weeks. This went on until one day he listened to it over and over, filling every moment of the day with this music.

That night, he could not sleep. He could not remove the melodies from his head, and then all in one moment, each instrumental voice was clear and distinct, and he could recall each independently.

This clarity was a great joy – the confusion of the whole was removed.

He soon lost this ability but gained another: he met a young woman at school, and as he studied her face he saw her as young, middle aged and elderly – all at the same time…and this he could sometimes see in other women, yet this ability also faded.

To see the life of a face in a face may be like deja-vu; being there in the present and the past – all at once.

Parallel perception is a royal road to clarity and life.

It is akin to associative seeing – seeing many possibilities, one immediately after another, but in a clump – like hearing the hammering of many nails all at once.

…or like the aged man who stands before his childhood home and sees himself a boy, running in the yard, while aware of himself now, observing.

There is poignancy, depth and reality in parallel world.

It is like the mystic who pondered the notion of love until he sensed *in parallel* the love of father for son, son for father, mother for daughter, daughter for mother, grandparent for grandchild, and grandchild for grandparent.

The Sufi author Idries Shah noted that to most people a word has only a single meaning, and an experience only one significance.

But one should try to see and experience a multiplicity – a divinely beautiful woman should be seen as divine *and* beautiful, separately, distinctly, at the *same time*.[3]

Simone Weil also understood, but only partially – in conceptual terms – in terms of grasping and interpretation:

Conscience and reality are proportional to the multitude of simultaneously grasped systems of a single operation of the mind.[4]

Whatever is real enough to allow of superposed interpretations is innocent and good.[5]

The 14th century German mystic, Meister Eckhart, described parallel perception in religious terms:

The active intellect…cannot have two ideas together, but first one and then the other…

...What though light and air show multitudes of forms and colors all at once, thou canst only observe them one after another...

...And so with thy active intellect, which resembles the eye...

...But when God acts in lieu of thy active intellect he engenders many images together in one point...

...Suppose God prompts thee to some one good deed...all thy possibilities for good take shape and come into thy mind collectively, focused to one point...

...Clearly this is not the work of thine own intellect which has in no wise the perfection nor plenitude for it; rather it is the work and product of him who has all forms at once in himself.[6]

Twenty-One: The Well Adapted Concept World

Verbal autistics will often ask 'Why?' in an endless chain of whys. Their minds are never done – their pictures are never complete.

Aspergian perfectionists ('philosopher-kings,' 'know-it-alls,' 'little professors,' 'Vulcans') are like this. They see flaws *everywhere*.

They are forever busy painting some 'perfect picture' or hammering together some unassailable argument.

They are not comfortable. They are not well adapted to the world.

Consider the idea that the Earth is round. (Everyone knows that.)

A normal, pragmatic teacher would teach this fact to her young students and stop.

But an Aspergian perfectionist would continue…

'The Earth is not perfectly round. It bulges a bit around the equator, and besides, it has mountains and valleys…

…The ocean surface has waves and tides, and even the land is deformed by tidal forces, floods and erupting volcanoes…

…Lakes and oceans are always growing and shrinking from rainfall and evaporation, and also, nobody really understands space at very small distances, so on a very small scale the idea of an object in space is probably entirely wrong, much less a round object.'

An Aspergian child might complain, 'The teacher lied to us today – she told us that the Earth is round.'

…and a parent might respond, 'Don't take things so literally. Try not to be so exacting. Your teacher lives in a good-enough world and most of her truths are good enough.'

Aspergians see a primitive, chaotic and inefficient world.

Like Einstein, Wittgenstein and Weil, they dislike oversimplifications. They are annoyed by half-truths being received as whole truths.

The good-enough world is not good enough.

They want everything to be rational. They are little professors.

Imagine listening to a performance, hearing flat and sharp notes throughout, but everyone else smiles and applauds…or watching a baseball game, and after one inning everyone is satisfied and goes home.

To the Aspergian perfectionist, the world is brimming with people who strangely *stop* asking questions – people who agree with their friends, 'The problem is…partisanship…crime…indifference…' and then stop.

Most people don't *continue* to ask why.

Perhaps they are comfortable with certain thoughts, and because of this thinking comes to an end. (A comfortable thought – what is that?)

Perhaps conversation bonds: 'Oh, yes, we *agree* that *that* is the problem.' – and pursuing the issue would be impolite because one might disagree. (Impoliteness? What is that?)

Perhaps human nature is too hard to understand – the subconscious is too far away. (Really?)

Perhaps most people feel that their role in the world is not to pursue such things. They have a place in society. (What is that? Like a room in a building?)

Perhaps an enquiry into human nature would make the participants feel like dissected worms, and the taboo is a protection to significance and life. (This is object world – what is a taboo?)

Perhaps it is too hard for people to walk about all day reminding themselves, 'Our words are misleading; our ideas are incomplete – the Earth really isn't round.' (Hard *not* to trust your thoughts – what could that be like?)

Perhaps it is too distracting to value integrity over common sense and stumble about, awestruck at the failure of one's concepts every minute of the day. (Isn't everyone distracted?)

For most people the Earth is round. They learn this fact as children and write it down and use it on a test. The answer is marked correct. The picture is somehow final.

In the well adapted concept world, the concept *becomes reality*. It feels that way.

The round Earth is real.

We live with our images and care for them. Life connects through our intermediaries – our images and concepts – our filtered pictures of life and reality.

For most people that is fine. They love the subconsciously structured, conceptually filtered invariant spouse, not the raw spouse, not splotches of color and touch.

'I love you dear; you're conceptually filtered and invariant.'

David Bohm wrote that representational thought is dangerous.

It creates the impression that it is our servant, but actually it controls us. It gives us pictures of reality as it erases the knowledge that we are picturing.

Bohm attributed this hidden control to the nature of thought and to conditioning by a scientific culture.

And the scientific culture he felt, worked with an ideal of absolute non-participation…the idea that thought is doing nothing whatsoever – that thoughts don't represent – that concepts *are* reality.[1]

But the thought of the table is *not* the table. And here one almost feels the need to bang one's fist upon a table…

…to wrest an unfathomed reality from a deceptive, invisible brain toy.

Perhaps Bohm missed one vital element. Our minds erase the fact that our concepts and images (husbands and wives) are only brain toys, because our 'toys' are alive and real. For autistics that may not be entirely so.

It is a blessing and a curse to know that one's pictures are incomplete.

One is blessed with the sense that concepts, *as they are thought*, are just plastic toys and not full realities. The round Earth is just a model.

…reality is far subtler – far more mysterious – filled with magic.

Yet one is cursed with the sense that concepts, *as they are lived*, are just plastic toys and not full realities. The round Earth is not real. Concept-reality is a ghost.

When *every* concept seems to be complete and fully real, one's journey towards life has stopped.

One has signed a contract.

The autistic boy who sees his sister as an object has stopped. The man who sees another as an instance of a category – a Samaritan, say, and nothing more, has stopped.

The concept is complete. The concept is real and alive…not the man.

In an argument, both parties may play roles not as humans, but as categories:

'What? Are you calling me a…?' – as though argument induced category world, and the instinctive, invisible tendency was to *see* the other and oneself *as* opposing categories…living, real categories.

No wonder Wittgenstein was squeamish about argument.

Even the polite sensitivity of diplomacy can be a tight poverty. One is 'French' – branded – seared – a hollow box inside a box.

Lacking the multiplicity of being 'French *plus* richly human' one becomes the box…

…and the box alone is real.

One's soul dissolves in the comfortable eyes of the labeler and the abstract, benevolent games of the well adapted concept world.

Twenty-Two: If You Complete It, You Falsify It

Autistic paths to completeness are often dead ends...as in the autistic boy who feels incomplete and asks, 'Am I alive?'...and then sets off to study philosophy.

Philosophy shares the autistic prison of object world, for the completeness it craves is most often *in* object world.

'What is feeling? What is life? What sorts of *things* are these?'

The elder Wittgenstein warned that this sort of obsession was misguided – that philosophy needed to mature – all of it.

He used the analogy of a collection of colored pieces where one imagines that the pieces *must* be assembled into a coherent picture.

He urged us to leave the pieces as they are.

...*Here is the whole. (If you complete it, you falsify it.)*[1]

An example: we know what pain feels like. We say, 'Ouch!' Others say, 'Ouch!' We live a life – listening, exclaiming and understanding these exclamations.

Wittgenstein would observe, 'We're done – we understand pain. That is the whole.'

The philosopher immersed in object world would argue: 'No. We're not done. We don't know what pain *really* is. What sort of *thing* is it? Why can't we point to it? We don't understand the nature of pain. Every*thing* has a nature. We may feel pain, but our understanding of it is far from complete. We don't understand sensations like these at all – we're only beginning.'

Wittgenstein believed that we are finished, living our feelings. We do not need philosophy to pursue the fantasy of theoretical completeness. Science may find more correlates to pain – structure, but not content.

He said that our conception of pain and other sensations *as things* was an illusion.

Or in the terms of this book, that we are trapped by the ideal of object world – the ideal that all of reality can be stuffed into the framework of things.

Trying to conceptualize our sensations distorts and diminishes reality. It makes the many dimensional one dimensional.

…and the craving for a literal world of nothing but objects is the real problem.

Only by seeing experiences *as* living and whole will you find the real – this is the autistic mind heeding raw life…

…and warning of the damage done to reality and one's soul, when one struggles to force fit the living pieces of reality into the remote perfection of object world.

Twenty-Three: The World Seen from Every Angle

We seem to live in a world of things with names.

There's a tree – that's the sky – there's a stone.

However, *named-thing-world* (object world, fact world) is rather threadbare. From a personal perspective, that this is not the only possible world, is a great relief.

There is also a rich and living *metaphor world*, where the sky is the arch of heaven, the firmament, the azure canopy, the starry sphere, this friendly vault, and Shakespeare's 'majestical roof fretted with golden fire.'

Poets grace us with this multiplicity. We live their metaphors.

…and this frees us from a gray, literal world.

Yet there are many other worlds. I shall discuss two.

First there is a marvelous autistic world – the *World Seen from Every Angle*.

Autistic children collect and arrange things – cards, crayons, stones…

I think they want to see a *genuine whole*, a 'something seen from every angle' – far better than a *disguised whole*, a 'something seen in only one way.'

They want to see all the variations – all the detail. By having every instance before them, they begin to feel the whole – the *full* nature of card, crayon, and stone.

An autistic child might inspect a toy car for hours, days or weeks, working on it, turning it over and over, gazing at it, feeling its outline, absorbing its nature – gaining more than just a felt understanding – gaining reality and life.

When I was a student in a class on ethics, the discussions often seemed misguided and abstract, as though the participants were hunting for just *one* angle – the 'right angle,' whatever that was, and not for the parallel life of every angle.

It was odd: The class was hunting for some general principle – utility, the greatest good, consensus, the least harm – *some rule*.

At one point the professor observed, 'We all agree that as a foundation to our ethical decisions we should place equality,' to which the class heartily assented.

But I replied, 'No!' and a shudder of horror reverberated through the room.

'Well,' I noted, 'Everyone in this class was allowed to enter this University on the basis of inequality: on merit, not equality. Maybe what we believe in is something like fairness.' Everyone paused for a moment and then reluctantly assented to this revision.

But later I wondered how the class (including me) could so easily be blinded by virtue words. Fairness is a poor foundation for virtue…

…when it excludes a noble responsibility (taking a burden upon oneself as opposed to portioning it out)…

…or heroism (taking a great risk upon oneself)…

…or fun (at *someone's* expense)…

And fairness can be a horror when it is completely rule driven – a blind and rigid algorithm with no suppleness or humanity…no innocence.

Each principle – equality, fairness, duty – seems sacred. A shudder of horror reverberates through us when any one of these is questioned.

…and the idea that principles might need each other or conflict with each other is not seen. We worship each of them without qualification – alone, powerful and unbounded.

…as though the rough edges of principles were never felt or imagined, for we placed them on pedestals and bowed before them, and *never* touched them…

…as though they were special *because* they were disconnected and alone.

Men and women (as distinct concepts) seem to be like this: sacred domains, with purely emotional identities.

In the women's suffrage movement, the slogan at first was 'Equality!' A shudder of horror reverberated throughout the male nation. It did not work.

But when the slogan was changed to 'Women are superior!'... that was a success.

Men readily admitted the superiority of women in many ways – women were special, worthy and unique, just like men...just like guiding principles.

The ethics class did not care for the disorder, complexity and paradox of life. They did not want to see each issue from every angle. They did not want to live each issue, they wanted to grasp and resolve each one with a policy-rule based on principle.

...as though the *need for a rule* – despite the damage done – superceded reality and life.

Wittgenstein tried to inspect reality from every angle:

Each of the sentences I write is trying to say the whole thing...it is as though they were all simply views of one object seen from different angles.[1]

If I am thinking about a topic just for myself and not with a view to writing a book, I jump about all round it; that is the only way of thinking that comes naturally to me. Forcing my thoughts into an ordered sequence is a torment for me.[2]

Simone Weil pursued every perspective, for it conveyed to her a sense of reality. She wrote: *...if one is not sure about what one sees, one shifts one's position while going on looking (for example, one goes round the object) and the real appears.*[3]

She did the same with time; shifting from moment to moment (angle to angle).

When a toy car or a person or a dog or a principle like equality is seen from *every* angle, it becomes magical and sacred and more than thing-real. It becomes far more than a thing.

It is too rich and significant to be disfigured by a name.

A world seen from every angle is filled with the nameless.

The Lakota Elder Dan, raised in a world with the nameless, lamented:

...We didn't see that you had to name everything to make it exist, and that the name you gave something made it what it was...

...Without even knowing it, you made us who we are in your minds by the words you used...

...You are still doing that, and you don't even know it is happening...

...There was an old man who told me when I was a boy that I should look at words like beautiful stones...

...He said I should lift each one and look at it from all sides before I used it...

...Then I would respect it.[4]

The meaning of the simplest words may be traced in the autistic way, slowly and from every angle.

...like the meaning of the word 'game.'

To me, this apparently innocuous word signifies a turning point for the modern world, because Wittgenstein turned this word over and over, and discovered something remarkable.

He discovered that we do not live in named-thing-world.

Imagine someone who asks for the meaning of the word 'game.'

We reply with two examples: basketball and baseball.

This response is sufficient for any non-autistic. The questioner understands the answer – he gets it. He has a feeling inside – a sense of completeness, like the stomach being full. The two examples suffice.

He does not feel the need to examine the meaning of 'game' closely and from every angle. That seems pointless.

Wittgenstein was autistic; two examples did not suffice. He needed many examples; he needed to understand every possible meaning – to see games from every possible angle.

He urged the readers of his work *not to think* about the meaning of the word 'game,' but to *look* at examples of games and see if they had anything in common.[5]

OK – we'll look. Football, basketball, baseball, golf and tennis all have something in common; they use a ball.

But chess and badminton and poker don't.

Hockey has teams, but golf and poker usually don't.

All of these games are played between people, but tossing a Frisbee can be played with a dog, and two dogs can play keep-away with a stick.

Perhaps all games involve play in the sense of having fun, but war games can be deadly serious.

Perhaps games are imitations of something – a kind of practice for something later on, like a kitten playing with yarn – but what does golf or badminton imitate?

Most games are won or lost and involve competition, but not leapfrog or 'fetch'.

Most games have rules, but not fetch, and not the game a cat plays with a mouse.

Wittgenstein discovered a complicated network of similarities, but no common feature.

He called 'game' a *family resemblance* term. There is no characteristic activity – no common *thing* that bears the name 'game.'

Such a simple discovery – a word that is a noun, but that doesn't refer to some *thing*.

In a specific setting (like baseball) 'game' refers to a specific thing – but in general, it doesn't refer to a general thing.

We have been taught that nouns are names for things – but apparently *not* all nouns are names.

Some people who know a little Wittgenstein will often mention their appreciation of the family resemblance concept, but still they conceive of 'game' as referring to a thing.

To them, 'game' previously meant a single clear thing – a kind of activity.

And with Wittgenstein's admonition, 'game' now refers to a loosely related cluster of activities, and still, that *cluster* of activities is a thing – a vague thing out there in object world.

And when you ask them to describe that vague activity, they'll admit that 'game' is used in many ways, but it *must* still refer to something. How could it not – it's a noun.

They commend Wittgenstein for pointing out the richness of language.

Yet in a way these people are like autistics in the grip of literalism.

They have not seen family resemblance as a clue – as a stepping *stone* – that one might escape object world altogether.

…that one might find the meaning of 'game' by simply speaking the word, reading the word, listening to the word as spoken – living its use directly, not hunting for a hidden, corresponding thing.

…and that other nouns like 'joy,' 'pain,' 'hunger,' 'reality' and 'life' might find their meanings *not* by referring to something hidden, but by being lived.

…so that the meanings of these words are whole – and 'completing' them by finding things to which they refer only falsifies them.

A 'game' is a name in name only.

To see each word only as a symbol that represents, only as information and not as a part of life, is significance lost.

Perhaps the most enlightening game is to stare at a glass, hold it, contemplate it, and list one hundred of its properties.[6]

It may take some time. By nature one starts with isolated properties, of which there are a handful, like weight, size and reflectance.

But then, if one persists, there follows a long list of properties in relation, like the image of a window in the glass, or the emotion it conveys in some setting…

…every detail, every angle…multiplicity…the life of the glass…

…like a stone turned over in one's hands…

With days or weeks of effort, the richness of what had been only a simple object is revealed – a new world – a better world – a world seen from every angle.

What is so special about pondering some object or some topic from every angle – every perspective?

What is so special about exhausting the meaning of a concept?

There is also a world that, with far more effort, sometimes follows. I shall leave it nameless.

Wittgenstein wrote about looking from all angles, but in a sense he never completed his inspections – he seemed to leave himself and the reader just hanging in air.

...like the Sufi mystic who wrote about his material from every possible angle, but left it to his reader to finish...[7]

...like a collection of paintings of cans of Campbell's soup.

...like the succession of worlds encountered by a little girl named Alice.

...like a succession of interpretations of koans – paradoxical thoughts presented by Zen masters.

...like a collection of remarks, suspended on a page.

Zen students are instructed to puzzle over their koans with great intensity in order to awaken and discover life.

Kenneth Leong described the traditional Koan of One Hand Clapping.

The idea is of course silly if understood literally. Zen students puzzle over it for weeks, turning it over and over in their heads, like a magical object whose shape can never be grasped...[8]

Even Zen is not everything. Long before Zen...ages before Zen...

When Buddha was in Grdhrakuta mountain he turned a flower in his fingers and held it before his listeners...Only Maha-Kashapa smiled...[9]

Twenty-Four: Parallel Angles

There is an ancient story told by the people of a native tribe:

When the Great Spirit created the first man, he also created the first dog, but the man and the dog found themselves separated by a ravine. The earth began to shake, and the ravine began to widen into a canyon. The dog did not hesitate; he leapt across to be with the man, and together they remain to this day.

This story conveys a personal and loving truth. It conveys life in a way no record of facts could.

Simone Weil believed that we should run the risk of taking such stories too literally so as not to diminish their reality.

…she suggested that first we interpret these stories and images as purely literal, then take them in less literal fashion slowly and by degrees, abandoning the literal for a pure, unmediated contemplation, and then return to a literal view again, back and forth, using all forms of contemplation, all angles, in order to *drink in the light.*[1]

Seeing literally true facts – then abandoning their truth to contemplate them for significance? Manipulating an ancient story for the purposes of life? It seems almost sacrilegious…

We feel that we should believe these ancient stories as matters of faith or else resolve them as matters of historic fact – but not use them as tools…not jump around with our seeing-as…seeing in all ways…or worse, seeing in parallel – not even for the sake of life.

Seeing in parallel is too indifferent…too dispassionate…too manipulative. Or perhaps it is too innocent…too vast in its multiplicity – like the Great Spirit.

Twenty-Five: Theology

An autistic boy may see his little sister first *as* a toy but later learn to see her *as* a person, as evidenced by not trying to put her in a box.

His new way of *seeing-as* opens a new world.

We feel that this advance is good.

We appreciate new perspectives, new ways of seeing-as.

...like seeing a triangle *as* solid, or *as* translucent, or *as* a mountain, or *as* a folded napkin, or *as* a symbol that represents an organization, or *as* a geometric figure with three angles and three sides.

We feel that this multiplicity is good – it opens the mind.

But sometimes concepts aren't available, and all our confusion is prior to concepts – in the basement of the mind. There is not even one seeing-as. And this is terribly uncomfortable.

Like the autistic infant who sees only patches of color when he looks at his sister. He has no idea what he is looking at.

There is great multiplicity in the colors, shapes and movements, but interpretations don't reach him. The concept of a bodily object does not reach his world.

He is immersed in a flowing cascade of raw sensation. Shape and color shift with every movement – even his own movements. His world is more chaos than world.

The multiplicity is too great – the richness of his uninterpreted world is overpowering – he craves structure and order.

To survive, multiplicity must be diminished. All that is beyond reach must be organized and simplified. The child is starved for stability. He must see *as*.

Theology beckons.

But is it the aloof intellectual theology of coherent theory, or the deeply felt theology of living stories, or the vulnerable, painful, often incomprehensible theology of autistic therapy?

Twenty-Six: Bewitchment by the Literal

In the 1920's and 30's Wittgenstein discovered that philosophy was bewitched by language.

He discussed many forms of bewitchment, but the most important form was literalism, the language of object world.

For thousands of years philosophers have searched for the true natures of joy, pain, seeing, feeling…

Implicit in this search is the notion that these are all mental things – ghostly things.

Wittgenstein discovered that language deceives with nouns. We take these nouns literally, as though they *always* refer to things.

And in the case of sensations and feelings – hidden, invisible things.

Wittgenstein diagnosed philosophy as being ill – as being caught up in the fruitless search for phantoms. The world, he feared, was being carried along in this search, and being transformed into the mirror image of the object world it adored.

This was certainly an instance of self-diagnosis, for Wittgenstein saw his own mentality as bewitched by literalism…and of course it was – he was autistic.

The word mind deceives. It creates false pictures.

For instance, language creates the picture that life is a thing. 'Life' is a noun, so we feel it must be a thing until we find that there is nothing to point to: no substance…no invisible stuff…just physical objects that laugh and cry.

And of course nothing could be more real than life – and we feel baffled because our minds and our language have taken object world too seriously.

The autistic child asks, 'Am I alive?' and *our* arms flail about, searching for a proof – searching for an object to point to – a thing to support an object world argument.

Language invites us ask the wrong questions – it invites us to be literal.

'What is life…*really*?'

It takes a huge leap to see that questions like these are not questions of fact, and not really questions at all – just misguided uses of language – bewitchments of language.

Philosophers have been enchanted with object world for twenty-five centuries.

Think of Wittgenstein's discovery as subtracting false, bewitching structures from the world – removing shackles from reality and oneself.

…removing certain concepts; removing the fantasy parts of 'concept-world' in order to find reality.

Reality with fewer objects is a new world.

Twenty-Seven: What is Joy?

If you utter the phrase 'I'll make some time' to an autistic child, this may only confuse them. How can one possibly make time?

Autistic children are taught that when asked, 'How are you?' they should not reply, 'How am I what?'

Wittgenstein was terribly literal when he was young.

Even as a young man he was aiming for a literal ideal – that *every* noun should have a clear meaning by being a name of some thing.

For instance, the word 'joy,' like any other noun, would mean something by naming some thing.

It didn't matter what the 'some thing' was, only that it existed. It didn't matter that 'joy' might refer to something invisible or intangible, as long as language could be literal and used to represent.

But when he was older he tried to teach everyone – especially philosophers – not to make the same mistake.

He tried to teach them that when they cry, 'I'm filled with joy,' that this should not be taken literally.

We're especially susceptible to this view when we do science and philosophy, whose business it has been to uncover the nature of *things*.

We are embarrassed when we point to some chemical process or molecular state when speaking of joy, for they are only physical correlates.

It seems that the only alternative to object world is medieval superstition, for if we can't point to *it*, the *mysterious thing* must be invisible.

By becoming philosophical it looks like we have become deep thinkers – hunters of mysterious and invisible things…

…but all we have done is to leap into object world, into our literal minds and literal language, where it is all a puzzlement.

We feel puzzled about joy because our minds are built on the object metaphor – first feeling and then seeing ourselves as objects, then building a language and a world of objects, and then being puzzled when not all of reality conforms to object world.

There is no discovery to be made. The depth of philosophy is an illusion, or as Wittgenstein put it,...*nothing is hidden.*[1]

The philosopher Marie McGinn places the blame squarely on the shoulders of abstraction – where the *power* of language to represent has blinded us to its other uses – as when a child in a moment of spontaneous exuberance shouts, without depiction, 'Joy!'

The belief in object world, the whole-hearted devotion to our invisible thing-selves, our invisible thing-sensations, is akin to a powerful instinct.

And this is not to deny the feeling of joy or the behaviors that express joy, only to deny that our language lets us speak of this reality as an invisible *thing*.

What is joy? Only in object world does this question exist.

Twenty-Eight: What's for Dessert?

Bewitchment by the literal is made worse by similarities in language.

Wittgenstein was the first to note this, but in a rather scattered and idiosyncratic fashion. The Wittgenstein scholar, P.M.S. Hacker, organized these remarks with the clever use of the word pair, 'pin' and 'pain.'[1]

I am grateful to both these men, and have condensed these ideas even more, placing them in the context of object world and using an equally valid but tastier pair of words.

Consider some common expressions with the words 'dessert' and 'desire.'

…'I have a dessert' and 'I have a desire.'

…'I noticed your dessert' and 'I noticed your desire.'

…'Your dessert is like mine' and 'Your desire is like mine.'

These formal similarities make desires appear to be *things* – mental things.

But consider other uses of language; other expressions.

'I have a plane to catch,' 'We have to go,' and 'They've had it with him' do not involve the ownership of anything. There is no *thing-one-has* in 'I have to do it.'

The word 'have' in 'I have a desire' seems to say that we possess some *thing*, but it *might* not say this. This is one of Wittgenstein's clever but rather weak observations.

Another pair of expressions opens the door from the literal cell a little bit wider:

We might say, 'I have a dessert and I'm going to give it to you.'

But not, 'I have a desire and I'm going to give it to you.'

A devotee of literal language and object world would respond, 'Desire is an unusual object; an internal object that we can't control. We can't transfer it, but it's there.'

Fine. But there are other expressions that are more difficult to explain in terms of objects.

We might apologize for an error: 'I was wrong – yesterday I thought I had a dessert on this shelf, but it was something else.'

…but not, 'I was wrong – yesterday I thought I had a desire in my head, but it was something else.'

What would an object worlder say? How would he defend this?

It would have to be something like: 'Desire is a *very* unusual *thing* – it cannot be misidentified.'

Could there be such a thing?

We try another example, 'I doubt that I have a desire.'

No one says this, but when an unexpected guest arrives, they do say, 'I doubt that I have a dessert.' The object worlder must claim that desires are things that cannot be doubted.

Or imagine exclaiming, 'How would I know if I have a desire?' No one says this. There is no ignorance of one's own desire.

Yet there is plenty of ignorance of objects. 'How would I know if I have a dessert?' is easily plausible if someone else did the shopping.

The object worlder must create a surreal world of things to explain these expressions as referring to things.

If desires are things, they are things for which there is no possibility of ignorance, doubt, or misidentification – strange things indeed.

Perhaps Wittgenstein was wrong.

We can work in other ways against the idea that sensations like pain, joy and hunger are hidden, mental things.

Wittgenstein suggested that saying 'I have a pain' is not a description of some internal invisible stuff, but a *substitute* for pain behavior.

Consider an infant crying. This is behavior, not a description.

Later the parents teach the child to say, 'Ouch!' This is a substitute for crying, not a description of anything inside.

Later the child is taught to exclaim, 'I'm in pain!' – again a substitute for crying or saying ouch, not a description.

Eventually the child shouts, 'I have a pain!' – the final substitute for crying, and the apparent description of something inside – the inauguration of bewitchment.

The philosopher James Edwards asked why we would believe that sensation words are the names of things in the first place.

He attributed this not so much to human psychology (such as a literal mentality) as to a mindset that he calls *rationality-as-representation*.[2]

This mindset says that to be rational is to represent – rationality consists of representation. Not to represent is to be irrational.

The idea is far more engaged than object-world. It is a program for all mankind.

It is an idea that has been endorsed throughout Western history.

If science were a man walking down the street, rationality-as-representation would be the dog on the leash dragging him along.

All that science needs is a second dog, to help the first adjust (perhaps Edwards used this phrase: rationality-as-presentation).

'I have a bruise,' and 'I have an ache' seem so close.

'I have a bruise' denotes, points to, pictures, represents or re-presents *a physical thing* – a bruise.

'I have an ache' manifests, bodies-forth, embodies or *presents* an ache. There is no corresponding thing.

No corresponding thing? We resent this. We point to our arm. We say we are pointing to our ache. We did this as children, with great success. We do it now.

Well, what color is the ache? Is it transparent? Is it textured? Does it glow?

Our words are body language in disguise.

Yet an ache is certainly not nothing.

Wittgenstein said sensations do not fit our language of things and non-things.[3]

To even speak of them as 'them' is misleading, for we attach all the structure of things to the term 'them.'

In a way, Wittgenstein was like Galileo, peering through a telescope. He simply looked at our language, where others didn't.

And by making the world more than objects, he made us into more than spectators.

We can now imagine *presenting* our life, participating in a reality that is more than things – and more than facts *about* things – a reality that is itself life.

As in Zen...

> *Has a dog Buddha-nature?*
> *This is the most serious question of all.*
> *If you say yes or no,*
> *You lose your own Buddha-nature.*[4]

Twenty-Nine: Not Object World

'If this is not object world, what is it?'

It?

'Well, we need to call *it* something – *it* needs a name.'

Some people think we began by domesticating plants (agriculture)…

…then proceeded to animals (livestock), and dogs – who they say are bred to be perpetual teenagers.

…then the spiritual world (religion)…

…then the physical world (science)…

…and finally language (information) and people (civilization).

In the English language there seems to be no antonym for the term 'domesticate.'

Imagine it is winter. A tape recorder is carried outside and turned on 'play.' The machine cries out, 'It's cold – let's go back inside!'

This has meaning but little significance. We understand the cries, we understand their meaning. But it is just a machine.

Isn't that what so many people think they want: understanding as information gain?

Compare the cry of a newborn – significance but no meaning.

Thirty: Logic Fills the World

For the young Wittgenstein, logic was no mere tool of reasoning. It was a safe and ordered world in which he could escape the ambiguity and confusion of his autism.

Logic was his world – not his experiences – not his life.

Logic was his reality – an artificial, transparently conscious, book-taught set of rules.

That it was conscious was essential. Nothing was hidden – nothing subconscious – nothing that weaves in the shadows, like the part of the brain that silently and without rules automatically gives one the ability to walk…

…nothing messy, weak or untrustworthy.

Wittgenstein asserted:

…*Logic <u>precedes</u> every experience—that something is <u>so</u>.*[1]

Logic fills the world: the limits of the world are also its limits.[2]

Why was the rigid mental framework of logic so important to him?

Facts: *The facts in logical space are the world.*[3]

For many autistics, facts are the content of the world. Autistics are infamous for collecting and absorbing facts – and for driving others batty with their endless recitations of facts.

Facts are details. Facts are fragments. Logic is the glue that binds them.

Facts are expressed by clear assertions like, 'There is a book on the table.'

Facts of logic are either true or false.

The young Wittgenstein minimized assertions of problematic truths like, 'This candy cane is red,' as he ignored uses of language that expressed humor, irony, sarcasm, status, context and emotion.

He ignored the social world of language because in a sense, society for him was irrelevant.

In fact, in a sense, the external world was irrelevant for the young Wittgenstein because the external world did not exist.

He denied the external world. He said so.

(Out of sequence, the preceding remark has the power of connection, for it *may* refer to anyone. Alone, it radiates.)

The young philosopher was a solipsist – only he existed. The merely apparent external world consisted only of logically ordered facts.

He was, one might jest, a good philosopher.

Logic filled his world. It was anti-raw – protected, safe, reliable – a flawless gem.

Facts about England were more real to him than England.

The fact that his hand had four fingers and a thumb was more real to him than his hand.

The fact – the idea – the representation – was more real than the experience. Life was an almanac.

At one point, Russell expressed his astonishment at Wittgenstein's adamant denial of external reality – allowing only facts within the framework of logic – representation *as* reality.

Perhaps somewhere in Wittgenstein's brain the connections that granted life were weaker, more painful and more incoherent than the connections that formalized those experiences.

Perhaps most important to the young autistic, logic was independent of the facts.

Logic must take care of itself. This is an extremely profound and important insight.[4]

Logic 'took care of itself' by providing a foundation for reality *independent* of reality, disconnected from it, as though the only trustworthy foundation for the world *had*, in some sense, to be disconnected from the accidental, the contingent and the chaotic...

...to be disconnected from life...

...like God.

Logic may have relieved Wittgenstein from the deeply felt insecurity of autism – the writhing distrust of a surreal world. Logic could always be trusted (Sherlock Holmes knew that).

Logic was also pre-built and largely complete, relieving him from the immense strain of continual personal world building.

The young Wittgenstein saw the mental *abstraction* of logic as something *so real* that in his later years he confessed to this mistake as a sin.

Referring to his youthful logic as a crystal, he wrote:

…But this crystal does not appear as an abstraction; but as something concrete, indeed, as the most concrete, as it were the <u>hardest</u> thing there is.[5]

Part of the appeal of logic comes from exact rules that allow one to replace one expression by another.

Autistics are known to fear change and replacement.

One such autistic was a boy named Zachary.[6]

Zachary was terribly anxious about the prospect of the death of his relatives – not because he anticipated grief or sadness, but because of the change and disorder it might portend.

His obsession was not about their loss, but about who would replace them.

Wittgenstein created a world momentarily safe from change, for his logic consisted of perfectly clear rules in which replacement was always safe.

And as the young philosopher created his system of logic – a style appeared: the struggle to articulate, the irrelevance of the reader, extraordinary integrity, and a world dictated by obsessive order – a world to which all must conform.

Zachary's style of speech was much the same:[7]

The listener was ignored. There was no conversation…no idea of conversation…

Zachary's words were the commands of a director in a play, and every listener was a cast member – a human tool, expected to play a part.

His use of language was a form of pattern making – a source of comfort and order.

Language used in this way is a kind of 'logic-light.'

Zachary could not abstain from anxieties about death. He could not lie to himself.

He hungered for the past.

He had been expelled from Eden, and the only path he could distinguish to return was through the order of language and ritual.

He was condemned to endlessly ask questions and to direct a succession of momentary utopian worlds.

In his later years, Wittgenstein grew away from autism. He came to see logic as an abstraction; as a creation of the mind, not as concrete reality.

The youthful mistake of reifying logic was caused by a blindness induced by the overpowering light of a sublime ideal.[8]

He was not aware of the autistic attraction to fantasy – the tendency to create mind-worlds more real than experience.

The Wittgenstein scholar, Judith Genova, described the error of fantasy as due to the lack of applications – or the preference to create theories without boundaries…[9]

…allowing bubbles to grow indefinitely – an infinity of creation.

As noted by Ray Monk, Wittgenstein did struggle to defeat the lonely, formal solipsism of his youth.[10]

In the mature Wittgenstein, 'I' and the world were finally accepted as real.

In the young Wittgenstein, only 'I' was real.

At an even earlier stage there is only a distant abstraction called 'you.'

It is well known that autistic children often refer to themselves as 'you.'

According to Donna Williams, it is because they do not interact with the world.[11]

Complete detachment.

'You' (and 'she' and 'he') are comfortable terms. In their 3rd person detachment these terms defeat the terror of connection.

'I' requires too much – a social place – manners – interaction – clarity – decisions amidst ambiguity – a thundering social waterfall that overwhelms any coherent identity.

Here we should not relax in the comfort of knowing that Wittgenstein and Donna Williams suffered from autism (but 'we neuro-typicals' or 'we very mildly autistic' are fine).

We should *not* feel self-assured in our ability to sense 'the world.'

…as though our identities were as close to life as could be, and our sense of reality was complete…

…as though nature had finished with us, and our minds were perfect.

…as though 'I' and 'the world' were the best we could ever do, and no other terms superior in maturity and sense of life could ever flourish.

If others sensed reality and life more deeply than we, we might be baffled by their words, and deny their participation in this greater reality, as the young Wittgenstein might have denied our reality, or a young autistic might deny their own 'I.'

We might be baffled by Zen monks, who dismiss all 3rd person knowledge and speak not of their own identity, but of the all consuming Buddha identity…

We might be confused by Christians who speak of the participation of man, spirit and God in one.

We might be puzzled by Tibetan mystics who admonish us that 'I' is an immature term, denoting an individual who experiences only distinct external and internal worlds.

We might not understand the story of the little girl who asked if she could marry her doll when she grew up, and her mother replied that for the few who really grow up, marriage is far better.

Our words (and their logic) often set the boundaries to what we allow as our experiences.

Whether we are an autistic girl, a mature autistic philosopher, or a mature neuro-typical reader, our logic, whatever it may be, fills our world.

Our words and stories are our loosely logical patterns and our homes. They are consoling and healing. They provide what some have called the meaning of life.

It is said that a group of South Pacific islanders were psychological wrecks after the deaths of their relatives, but that a Westerner gave a name to their malady, 'grief,' and after this simple act their health improved greatly.

With a simple word they knew what plagued them. They could deal with it once it became a concept, once *it* had a *name*. A meaning had been granted to them.

For millennia people have been pulled towards the healing nature of metaphysics and worded theology for the same sort of reason – the fact that words provide a safe and healing conceptual home.

The defeat of suffering and alienation by pattern fitting oneself into the verbal world is like the story of the woman who was unable to depart Earth until she realized that she was a ghost...

...and like the tale of the man who loved badly – who could not escape hell until he realized that he was in hell...

...and like the young woman who once told the author that she decided to study philosophy because her parents had divorced.

Conceptual patterns (like those accompanying the words 'team,' 'nation,' 'science,' 'religion,' and 'philosophy') may be of value for more than finding a home in a strange world; they may allow one to better feel life and reality.

Raw is not everything. Statues, symbols and stories are the best paths to life for those who *must* sense life through concepts.

Some Aspergians report that to *feel* an experience they must first locate it and put it in the right context. *First* the experience is labeled and understood. Then it is genuinely felt.

It has to make sense in order to be real – as though only interpreted feelings were real – as though 'representing connections' in the brain were the only pathways to allow 'experience connections' with the world.

It must be named in order to exist.

It is not only among autistics that a feeling must be represented *to be* a feeling.

Here resides the foundation for an entire culture. The fact of the hand allows the reality of the hand:

…like a malady that is real *only* if one can give it a name…

…or a spiritual experience that is real *only* if a religion can locate it in its imagery…

…or a sense of self worth that is real *only* with a teacher's star…

Yet some ancient figures of life refused to name the nameless – they refused to apply concepts – refused to hunt for them.

They participated in that which is nameless.

They felt that the attempt to gain control of '*this*' by naming was wrong – a diminishment *of this and of self* – missing the mark – a sin…even for the sake of finding a safe home.

Their participation (in autistic terms, their 'resonance') was their home, and they felt that their raw, large, pure life should not be spelled out and the parties should not be labeled.

They felt that their covenant should not become a contract. Language could only distort and diminish.

For them, the reduction of confusion and stress with concept-structures was not always beneficial – not always right – logic did not fill their world.

The mediated path to life – the path of names – was not their path.

The story of Rumplestiltskin was said by Wittgenstein to be deep…the idea that one can be saved from a terrible fate only by discovering a secret name.

Wittgenstein was right – the power of names is deep – far deeper and more dangerous than my simple musings…

…as with the words 'game,' or 'joy,' which are tempted to be *names* of impish, hidden noun-creatures.

I looked into the story of Rumplestiltskin.

It seems there is also a French version of *Rumplestiltskin* called *Ricdin-Ricdon,* where the beautiful young heroine Rosanie spins beautiful patterns, but terribly slowly.

She has difficulty with figurative speech and forming letters into words...and her father is reserved and dislikes small talk...

...but she loves ribbons, birds and dogs.[12]

Thirty-One: Raw Math

Wittgenstein wrote a great deal about the philosophy of mathematics. In his later years, he disputed the idea that math has to be interpreted, justified and given a special, independent foundation.

Consider a simple expression like '2 + 2 = 4.'

'That's always true,' most would contend, 'if not, the whole system of arithmetic would collapse!'…which is true enough.

And yet some philosophers in Wittgenstein's day tried to prove this truth not by internal system collapse but by means of an external logic.

They tried to prove arithmetic by going outside of it – by finding special, hidden rules – the deep and hidden laws of arithmetic.

This is an autistic idea – nothing is trusted on its own – everything must fit some deeper pattern – some larger, hidden context.

…there must be hidden laws everywhere – laws of behavior, laws of relationship, laws of rudeness and courtesy.

There *must* be social rules one can obey – invisible foundations one can unearth and put into language and formalize. Watch for the patterns. Watch closely.

Ask for the rules of behavior. They *must* exist – they *must* – how could they not?

…and do the same with arithmetic.

To many, the rules of religious faith are the larger context of life.

And some say this is just a small, insecure fish in a tiny pond, dreaming of a great invisible ocean, while others say the fish knows what it knows.

But both are debating the rules, which are hidden. 'But there *must* be rules,' they say.

Wittgenstein imagined what we'll call 'raw math.' He imagined teaching a group of special people to continue different series of digits, like continuing 0, 2, 4…, or 1, 2, 3… and teaching this only by example.

No rules are given – and in these remarkable people, no rules are intuited. For these people, learning to continue a series is like learning to walk.

Doing well with their series, the people find it absurd that rules would be needed to justify their efforts.[1]

For the elder Wittgenstein, mathematics, like social behavior, is a part of life, not a remote collection of rules…

It is a part of life with more breadth and depth than rules obeyed by abstract objects…and the possibility of raw math simply highlights this observation.

There seems to be a strongly felt need to *interpret* math (and joy and pain and morality and science and the sacred…) and stand it (and them) more securely on independent foundations of rigorous laws and structure.

An Inuit once prepared to tell a story to a white man. Before starting he said, 'Now don't think like a white man; don't try to interpret the story. Think like an Eskimo; try to wear the story.'

Thirty-Two: Bubble Gum in the Storm

We sense our life – we sense our joy and pain. What are these things?

We are modern – we have been educated. We know that science is powerful. We can look through microscopes at our brains. We can see neurons at work and lots of chemicals moving around.

How do we get joy from neurons and chemicals? No one knows.

We can point to a pill that gives us joy – a pill made of molecules. The molecules enter our brain and join with other molecules. How do feelings arise from the joining of molecules? No one knows.

We look more closely. We look at physics. Neurons and chemicals are made of particles and fields.

How do we get joy from particles and fields? No one knows.

It is a fabulous, bizarre mystery. It may be beyond mystery, beyond fitting to a pattern. It makes absolutely no sense. Do we stop? Do we give up? No! We ask the big boys – the experts on small things – the creators of quantum mechanics.

We ask Niels Bohr. It baffles Bohr.

He says that just talking about consciousness removes it from experience.[1]

...as though our attempt at standing back and explaining were somehow self defeating.

...as though the action of representing consciousness was the wrong action.

We ask the great theoretician Dirac. He likes math – he loves object world – but he doesn't like philosophy. He has nothing to say.

We ask Heisenberg. He doesn't know.

Concerning sensations he says, ...*there can scarcely be any doubt but that the concepts of physics, chemistry and evolution together will not be sufficient to describe the facts.*[2]

(And for Heisenberg this is not an instance of religious literalism pitting its miracles against science, but simply puzzlement at one of the apparent limits of science.)

We ask Schrödinger. He notes that modern science, inherited from the Greeks, insists on an objective view where the personal and subjective – the mind – is ignored.

He suggests incorporating elements of Eastern religion. He says that the conscious mind is a stranger to the world of substance, but he warns us not to abandon the precision of science on our strange journey beyond.[3]

What about Einstein? He should know. Einstein smiles like a child, like it's all a big game. He's says that science is a child. It has just started.[4]

He advises us not to bother with theories – the connection between a feeling (of hunger, say) and the corresponding concept (of hunger) is not scientific – not a matter for logical analysis, but something intuitively understood.[5]

…as though we could only live our feelings, not understand them, and life were deeper than theory.

Wolfgang Pauli doesn't know, but he does have some interesting advice.

He looks to his pre-conscious and to his dreams, and advises us to do the same (perhaps because dreams are not literal – not autistic, but part of the 'life brain').

He urges us to pay attention to our dreams – images of geometry and emotion – images of significance.[6]

We ask ourselves, 'Do dreams explain?' Not in words. Their task is not to explain. Images, metaphors and stories are freely given – they are dream gifts – they connect.

Jesus – Buddha – Lao-Tzu – Rumi.

Ancient figures of life are like living dreams – seldom explaining in words, presenting only their actions, stories, poems, parables and metaphors – presenting forms of life.

We look to our dreams and to these living dreams of the past.

If we are patient, that may suffice. But if we are impatient, we continue asking questions.

How about a philosopher of science, like Hilary Putnam?

He says that people typically explain consciousness by talking about signals going from our eyes to neurons in our brains, and then there is this mysterious 'connection' that gives us a *sense datum* or a *raw feel*...

But he thinks that this sort of explanation is a kind of hand-waving joke, and that the scientific picture of the world that we inherited from the 17th century (Newton and so on) – is *disastrous* and needs to be replaced. He says, *it is high time we looked for a different picture.*[7]

Do we stray in hunting for yet another picture – more distance? Perhaps we commit the great autistic error – searching for more literal pictures...worshipping, for the sake of a safe home, the literal, visual story more than the felt life that the story conveys.

We are tempted at first to agree with Wittgenstein that joy is not a thing, but then retreat to object world. Perhaps joy is a thing in another world – a different dimension that intersects ours. We are gasping for air.

How else could we discuss joy? We feel that the world must fit our object language or fall to pieces.

Our mental construct, object world, seems to be such a small bag. Like our poor head, it can only hold so much. We reach into this bag and find some equations, some beautiful pictures, but not joy, not pain, not life – certainly not the pure life revered by saints.

Few people worry that joy and pain are mysteries. They don't much care. They *feel* that their workaday pictures are everywhere and always true. They feel that their sense of life is complete. They don't feel caged by their concepts.

Perhaps only cities under repair really care about truth and life. The well adjusted don't feel the need for such perfection.

Feeling trapped, we go out on the ocean. We invite others along – passengers all, on a long voyage.

We rent a nice sloop, and find a fresh breeze, and relax in the sunshine and the open air.

We abandon the problem of grasping the natures of joy and pain and life, and resign ourselves and accept these 'almost-things,' whatever 'they' are.

Our non-linguistic mind knows – in its own way. Our linguistic mind will have to get used to its ignorance and poverty, and be humble, receptive and silent.

The day goes well, but near sunset a storm arises – the same old mystery of sensation, the mystery of life.

The passengers begin to worry. 'What is joy, really? What is life, really?' The connections feel weak. Whitecaps grow and waves begin to crash against the hull.

The passengers are afraid. The captain – a weathered old salt – advises, 'Faith is what you hold onto in a storm.'

The passengers hold onto the mast.

The first passenger, for whom *religion is faith*, tries to reassure herself and the others: 'Joy is spirit and love is spirit...and pain and life and God...they are all ghostly, sacred *things* in the invisible world of the spirit.'

The second, for whom *mystery is faith*, cries out, 'Joy is a miracle – the world is a miracle! Joy is beyond knowledge, beyond the language of words, beyond us all. It is beyond your religious, invisible world. Humble yourself. Enjoy the storm! Enjoy your awe!'

But he clings to the mast.

The third, for whom *science is faith*, admonishes his fellow voyagers, 'Don't give up the hunt; joy is neither a miracle nor some ghostly thing in some make-believe world – the bag is bigger than we think – it is limited only by our imagination. We need better concepts and tools – we need to *imagine*! Maybe some future meta-bag will be big enough to contain joy. Maybe when someone truly clever is born we'll finally understand, or maybe when we evolve into more intelligent beings the *concepts* will become clear!'

As the wind rises, the fourth voyager, for whom *unity is faith*, shouts above the gale, 'Don't draw a line between the mind and the body – that distinction is only an illusion. We need to *ascend!* There is something more than the world we perceive by our five senses, and more than conceptual bags, more than a separate spiritual world, more than miracles, more than objects, something radically different, a deep and hidden participation that unifies the qualitative and the quantitative – after all, the Universe is one, and we are all one, and we participate in the great Cosmic creation!'

The fifth and final voyager, for whom *language is faith*, shouts above the wind, 'You do not see your language! It has mesmerized you. Look and you will see that not every word refers to something – we manifest life and joy, they are not *things* we have. You grant structure to the world that does not exist – there is no mystery to joy – it is not a mystery because *it is not an it*! Your need for explanation is an illusion. This storm is an illusion! Your worries and theories are obsolete!'

The captain hears this all and shakes his head.

'Blast ye all – Miracle! Meta-bag! Cosmic! It is not an it! *Big* words...*Big* ideas! You landlubbers are really somethin!... Look about. It's wonderful to be human – to steady your legs on a heaving deck over a furious sea, battered by the lash of wind and wave. But you cling to that mast and blow up great big bubbles, and then you pop them, getting gum all over your faces. And then you start all over again!... And all the while the spray of the salty sea stings and chills, leathering our skin, showing that we have truly lived.... Look to the ocean, ye lubbers. Someday ye've got to swim.'

The captain's small daughter, accustomed to her father's blustery nature and the fears of passengers on many prior voyages, overhears it all. She then approaches the frightened voyagers and reassures them that the storm will soon pass:

'Don't worry – my father finds his life in the sea. But you find life in the stars and in all that is hidden by the storm.'

Being pure in heart, she then offers them some more bubble gum.

Thirty-Three: Lumps of Dough

Figures of life who speak of life teach love, mercy, faith, honesty, humility, piety, silent contemplation, prayer and the abandonment of the ego.

They offer many recipes, but each recipe contains the same ingredients, more or less.

…as though we had to be sprinkled with a dozen virtues, kneaded, shoved into a container and baked just to get something decent.

The beginnings are so inauspicious, the process appears to be filled will travail, but the scent of the finished product is delicious.

If humanity as a whole is truly autistic, then these are not independent ingredients. They are all means to a common end – opening the autistic door.

There is a common thread: courage, especially the courage to be vulnerable. It is only a single thread among many in a rich tapestry, but it is a good thread.

The autistic bubble is punctured especially by love, courage and faith.

To profound autistics, the vulnerability required by any of these virtues is too much to endure.

They are far too vulnerable at the outset. Like monastics, they retreat from the world.

They seek a haven where vulnerability is diminished – a world of silence, trust, ritual and serenity.

Others are told that they need a recipe for life.

Consider the dissolution of the ego.

Is there a recipe for this?

Aspergians steer their own ships.

A ten year old boy, writing about his Aspergian life, was adamant about the strength of his identity. He knew exactly who he was. He chose his own path, and would brook no interference.[1]

Einstein was like this, and Bohm, Weil and Wittgenstein.

They could not be tampered with. It is unthinkable that they would ever follow some recipe suggested by another – for life or truth or anything.

They were not inflexible. It would be more accurate to call them determined. They had, after all, constructed their own realities.

They followed their integrity – their personal identity – not the dictates of society.

Referring to an article she had written, the Aspergian Jane Meyerding cogently described this contrast:

The seeking individual, I implied, has a much greater chance of finding and holding to the truth than has any formal organization...

...personal (individual) integrity must be the basis for action, rather than, for example, loyalty to the group, theory, or dogma...

...The responses I got to that article, which had a much broader focus, all took exception to this single point...

...They tended to say something along the lines of:

'I really liked the article. But you're wrong about individuals being better than groups for finding the truth... Only in the context of the group was I able to begin to understand the kinds of things you wrote about in your article. Individuals are really self-centered. It's being part of a group that socializes us.'...

...Hmmmm. That conflicted so entirely with my own experience that I had to come up with my first major division in humankind...

...Some of us are solid core, I decided, and some of us are hollow cores. The hollow cores need outside help to find the proper center of gravity that will allow them to orient themselves in society.[2]

Like compass needles in a magnetic field, Aspergians orient themselves in their interests. Their identities merge with their interests.

At their most open and vulnerable, they dissolve their egos in their interests. The needle dissolves in the field – it becomes the field – the *interest* is the key to life. And if the interest is purity of heart, they find pure life.

Non-autistics orient themselves more in their families, their nations, their ethnic groups, their religions, their teams...

Their identities merge with the group.

At their most open and vulnerable, they dissolve their egos in the group and the beliefs of the group.

The needle dissolves in the field – it becomes the field – the *group* is the key to life – sacred and inviolable.

...and if the beliefs are pure in heart, they find pure life.

Are these different recipes? Not really. We are simply pointing to different paths.

This is not a cookbook, and the reader is more than a lump of dough.

Imagine a lump of dough with a recipe within.

Thirty-Four: Sighted Ethics

A man named Lee Stringer was interviewed on the radio. He had been a homeless drug addict and had written a popular and insightful book about his life on the streets of New York titled, *Grand Central Winter*.[1]

For a decade he had helped other homeless people.

At one point he was asked about his *policy* towards the homeless.

He resented the question and responded indignantly, 'I don't have a policy; I'm not a government.'

He was a human being, not a government! (I cheered when I heard this.)

He was more than a book of rules...he was alive!

He was not opposed to policy – he wanted good policies – he was opposed to surrendering part of his humanity. Give unto Caesar what is Caesar's...

Stringer went on to explain that from his perspective, each homeless person was different, and each situation was different.

To substitute a generic policy for the personal courage and energy needed to attend to every *detail*, to every human *as* a human, would be to sell his soul.

To substitute rules for a soul – a profoundly autistic error.

An expensive gift was lavished upon Jesus. A bystander complained that it would have been better to help the poor.

But Jesus valued the selfless act of giving. He valued purity of heart over a policy of compassion. In effect he responded, 'Don't you get it?'...as though his critic was autistic; a compassionate logician blind to the life bestowed by a gift.

...as though a gift was only an object, and carried with it no other gift – invisible, tangible and pure.

In the ancient parable, the prodigal son, whose highest freedom was adolescent independence, abandoned his family. Eventually he returned, repented and was forgiven. His brother resented this.

The brother was blind to the value of a life reborn, and spoke only of rewards for rules well followed.

Lao Tzu believed that the affairs of men would be in far better order if only they followed the natural course of the Tao, rather than the artifice of continual problem solving.

Consider the autistic boy for whom dinner is a collection of problems in etiquette. He *consciously* tries to solve the problems that arise from eating together, for he cares about his family.

The boy is a table activist. Distinct problems exist – saying 'please' at just the right moment and 'thank you,' and not grabbing for food.

…caring autism as a kind of policy ethics – caring remotely, caring at a distance, caring dispassionately – with rules.

…having a heart but seeing in abstractions…like drawing a stick figure of one's beloved.

Consider the infant who picks up language from her parents, naturally and *without system*, versus the adult who is taught language using explicit grammatical rules.

Consider the self-destructive neighborhood, gnawing on its wrist to find life, and policies are instituted to help, versus the street where neighbors know each other as friends rather than strangers.

In the former, one tries to repair a consciously articulated system. In the latter, no formal rules or descriptions are needed, for everything works.

There is neither instinctive dogma to assert a solution nor advanced systemic science to argue for one. There is no need. The notions of 'problem' and 'system' are irrelevant.

Consider the uncrowded man who cares for the stream where he fishes versus the four inch thick 'environmental impact' rule book that the crowded man must consult.

Consider the small group of primal people who gather to reach a consensus. They don't vote, for they find voting *within their group* to be a divisive, oversimplifying activity.

Are we nostalgic here for an idealized past? Perhaps. We are pointing to less autistic forms of life.

Insofar as one's times *demand* wise policies, they must be autistic times – abstract times.

…distant connections…articulated forms…a host of rules…and words like 'functional,' 'system' and 'impact.'

As Stringer fiercely observed, the desire to help requires the courage to be vulnerable – a requirement that escapes policy.

There is at least one exception.

In Westerns, the good guys fight the bad guys *and* the vigilantes.

Justice – real justice – is hard, courageous work. The law says that one *must* be vulnerable, for the evidence may be weak, the jurors may be foolish, and the bars of the cell may not hold. One *must* pay attention to detail and pause to inspect. One *must* live a covenant (innocence before guilt), not a contract (guilt before innocence).

Hanging an object-man without a trial is cowardly and easy. To substitute fear for a soul – a profoundly autistic error.

Policy connections are not flesh and blood but rules. Do eyes make contact? Do ears listen? Is there touch?

Sighted ethics makes eye contact. It listens. It touches.

Temple Grandin emphasized that kindness is taught not by formal lessons but by gentle touch…and that touch is also a path to reality.[2]

This *shows* itself. It is an ethics of experience, not thought.

It is connected, not apart…tangible, not abstract. It presents itself – it is not represented by principles.

According to Bertrand Russell, Wittgenstein was by nature good, and though he might lash out in passion or a fit of temper or ego, he was free from what he regarded as silly, unnecessary moral principles.[3,4]

Russell, at first distressed, eventually came to understand that Wittgenstein happily relied on his innate sense of the good, not on rules.[5]

Sighted ethics is concrete, not abstract.

(An example follows: in this world, it is impractical. The trick is to imagine a world where it is as common as pumpkin pie.)

As an autistic, it was very difficult for Donna Williams to communicate with people. For a time she created a protective alter-ego named Willie, who *was* able to communicate.[6]

Willie had a strong sense of right and wrong.

Donna enrolled in a college philosophy class where the professor and the students criticized the ideas of famous philosophers.

Willie was outraged! To Willie these poor philosophers weren't there to protect themselves.

He argued against anyone who tried to criticize the absent philosophers.

Long deceased humans were not allowed to be treated as abstractions. To Willie they were significant and deserving of respect.

Donna (Willie) saw life where others saw only tools. And her sight (as far as I can tell) was not a policy or a rule, but simply the unwavering instinct to escape from an immature, object-world cell…

…to avoid becoming an object herself.

Now my favorite example of sighted ethics: a true and heartening story whose origins I have forgotten, but which stuck when I heard it long ago – and despite its deceptive simplicity, it is still throwing off sparks.

A Native man (from a Northwestern tribe, I think) one morning asked his son to bring the family's flock of sheep out to pasture.

At the end of the day the son returned, but one of the sheep was missing.

Something had gone awry.

He said to his son, 'One of the sheep is missing.'

This story made my head whirl. When I heard it I paced about and about, wondering why it felt so significant.

This (I think) is why:

The man did not order, 'Go get the sheep' – as though his son was some *thing* to be commanded – some object in object world, some tool.

He did not judge, 'You're in trouble' – as though judgment was justified – for judgment is an abstraction – a single seeing-as that may be blind to other realities. Maybe the sheep had been struck by a car – maybe it was ill.

The father did not invoke a rule, following some ancient 'Shepherd's Commandment' that says losing sheep is a sin and therefore punishable...

...allowing for himself the cover of being moral in the lowest way – doing violence to his son without feeling regret...

There was no quick interpretation, no easy pattern, no armored invocation of authority or principle, no safe autistic distance.

There was a fact – a sheep was missing – and an implicit duty for the son.

For both there was a connection to the world and to one another, deeper and more mature than simple rules – deeper and more mature than the tool world of language.

In their simplicity and trust father and son transcended the immature *abstract* world of morality, and manifested instead the mature *living* world of morality.

...their ethics was sighted and alive.

...and so their ethics was not really ethics at all, but life.

Thirty-Five: Mystical Views

Mystics are spontaneous hearts. They often ignore moral rules.

They are not always just. Mercy is not just – grace is not just – unconditional love is not just…

…as between mother and child or a dog and his master. Unequal burdens are invisible. Imperfections are invisible – beyond forgiveness.

One mystic may embrace religion with all her heart. Another may be far removed.

The mystic who has 'fallen into living waters' is as close to religion as a castaway on a raft is to an ocean liner.

Such a life is lived, not organized. Words present more than they represent.

The Tao is Great…The Tao cannot be spoken… These words present. How can one argue over them? Argument has no place – it is the wrong language game.

Like the words on the back of a box of cornflakes, Lao Tzu's words are very straightforward. They manifest the world in a living sense.

The word 'Tao' is no more mysterious that the word 'red' is to the color blind.

In the mystic's raw pure life everything is sacred – *everything*, without exception. And in a way this makes it terribly inhuman.

And because everything is sacred…like rotten apples, or the cliff from which one falls, or the eyes that warn of the cliff, there is nothing exclusive in the mystical world – no 'Only you are sacred,' or 'Only your people,' or 'Only your religion.'

…only the torment, dangers and joy of life on a raft, tossed by the waves of a great ocean.

The nature of pure life is not so much to solve problems as to dissolve them.

Imagine two trees arguing about whose leaves are more important. The mystic responds, 'Think of being the soil.'

The soil is always tempted to become a tree: There is an ancient Buddhist story of a man who discovered a bit of truth. The God of ignorance and evil was delighted, for he knew the man could not resist eventually turning it into a belief.[1]

…like the raw perspective from an ancient garden, where an apple is plucked from the tree of knowledge with the whisper, 'Eat – nothing is lost…nothing is lost.'

Imagine a non-autistic child, bursting with life, enthusiasm and chaos seated at a dinner table with ten autistic children, also bursting with life, enthusiasm and chaos.

The non-autistic child knows exactly how to behave – how to be quiet, how to say please – how to respond to the question, 'How are you?'

Sometimes he actually does behave, and then the others marvel at his innate skills and ask for his rules.

Thirty-Six: Sufism

Traditional Sufis are Muslim mystics.

In recent years 'non-traditional Sufis' have emerged who identify only loosely with Islam.

Sometimes a Sufi will remark that most believers don't know what religion is – they have not experienced it.

Sufis find truth in their own experiences, and express these truths in poetry and parables. They often educate with poetry and parables.

Sufis, like the parents of autistic children, teach new ways of seeing – seeing with the heart – seeing life.

The facts they teach are often secondary – a means of removing one's blinders.

Sufis insist that many people are not ready to be taught the living nature of Sufism – they can't absorb its lessons (lessons towards life, not facts).

Sometimes those who cannot learn carry too much baggage from their culture or religion, conditioned to look in the wrong places for answers that fit their *expectations*.

…or the real motives are subconscious and unknown to those who say they wish to be taught.

Sufis note that it is all too common to be blind to one's motives, and that this is one of the greatest obstacles to being able to learn Sufism.

For instance, some people travel great distances to find a 'guru' or 'wise man.' They think that they want to devote themselves to a larger and greater life, but in reality they desire something else…

…relief from pressure, friendship, community, escape, adventure, a feeling of significance, bolstered prejudices, or worst of all, secrets and powers for 'me' – possessions craved out of complete self-interest.

One lesson of Sufism is to step back and dispassionately look at oneself so as to change enough to ask the right questions.

Some Sufis identify God with all of reality.

Some identify God with love.

Some express no views, only poems or parables or funny stories.

They are concerned with insight and transformation more than consistency.

Because they understand and experience themselves as manifesting reality, their need for ultimate conceptual truth eventually dissolves.

Though they do not see the world as a collection of objects, they praise correct and deep understanding – even understanding in terms of *things*.

Understanding is, in part, a path towards life.

Sufis see the rest of humanity as sacred but uncivilized – underdeveloped – lacking understanding – lacking eyes to see.

…like children…sacred barbarians.

The journey is away from explanation (trying to grasp reality – making nature yield its secrets). It is towards purity of heart.

This theme is constant – the abandonment of conditioned thought.

The ancient Sufi Nasrudin rejected pattern-thinking (conditioned thinking), and accordingly acted in odd and humorous ways. He was a pattern breaker; a comedian who showed us our raw selves.

There is a continuing use of metaphor and simile among Sufis.

Sufi poets were the chief disseminators of Sufism – they used a secret language of metaphor.

Historically the use of multiple metaphors may have been a way of deflecting the literal mentality and protecting Sufis from accusations of heresy.

Sufis do not care for argument. Rumi said that nothing important could be taught at the level of opinions and disagreement.

Sufis believe that argument cannot induce certainty – where there is language the possibility of doubt remains.

For Sufis the idea of poverty does not mean that one should necessarily be a beggar (vulnerable in body) but that one should be free from attachment and desire – free, for instance, from wanting to *possess* the truth.[1]

Sufis believe that the mentality of the predominant culture is confining but can be overcome – that life has far more significance than we commonly see.

Sufism is said to be built not on rules of conduct, but on comprehensive detail.

For many Sufis the great sin is inattentiveness. (Concepts are often disguised means of inattention – half-truths dressed up as whole truths.)

And so there is the idea of wearing a story – living the detail of the world – feeling it rather than interpreting it.[2]

Sufis speak of the prevalent culture as being blind to true reality, but themselves as being blind to practical concerns.[3]

For Sufis reality precedes theory.

Sufi life is largely religious ritual...

...like the instinct of autistic ritual...a calming, invariant means towards life.

Sometimes Sufis encourage withdrawal and detachment from the world, but only if it is useful on the journey.

They regard the mentality which seeks withdrawal and spiritual intoxication for the selfish experience – spiritual self indulgence – as useless and out of touch with human life.

Silence is encouraged – practicing the art of silence.

Intense concentration and contemplative practice are encouraged.

Idries Shah wrote a fable about the Sufis which reads like an Aspergian travelogue:[4]

In this fable there lived a group of people whose perceptions were richer and slightly different than those of the people in the predominant world.

They moved away to an island to undergo a painful transformation.

However, their island became a kind of prison, for the lives of the other islanders were combative and complex, and these other islanders wrote books arguing for the value of their world, founded solely on emotions and reason.

The Sufis say pure life is subtle.

The Sufi and East Indian mystic Inayat Khan wrote of the great struggle of finding pure life, that is, of becoming love.[5]

Thirty-Seven: One Night in the Sistine Chapel

> *What god has not been made a mere term
> of a need in search for better explanations.*[1] *(William Julien)*

Imagine entering the Sistine Chapel – it is midnight – the lights are off.

So much above is hidden. So much beauty – so many ancient stories.

Our eyes gaze upwards, despite the darkness.

Each story is a gift of meaning and significance.

Each story gives one a place in the world. Each story offers a pattern of life.

Paul Dirac loved scientific explanations. He was the purest theoretician of the 20th century – a great mathematical physicist – the man from whose mind fell a completely abstract and general formulation of quantum mechanics. He was truly an artist of science.

Dirac said he disliked religious myths (sacred stories) on principle, because the stories of different religions contradict each other.

He saw each story literally.

For Dirac, each story was a tale told in object world.

…*Life,* he said, *when all is said and done, is just like science*…[2]

He preferred modern explanations over ancient stories.

Imagine this great scientific artist, entering the Sistine Chapel at midnight, gazing upwards, contemplating the ceiling, thinking about repainting.

Explanation can give us such marvelous things…unity, coherence, predictability, beauty…understanding.

…yet also a distant, autistic reality…a one-dimensional world…a strangled heaven.

When an autistic child asks, 'Am I real, am I alive?' we are pulled to autize ourselves – to become philosophers or scientists – keepers of object world. We try to do more than answer 'Yes!'…

We try to explain, to search for some*thing deep* in object world like *reality* or *life*, some essence we can point to or grasp and hold before them.

We look for scientific answers in object world when the child's questions are not scientific; they are not about objects, not about things.

It is better to play some music for the child, tell her a story, give her an artist's brush, immerse her in water, get her a dog, or share her interests – share her world.

The child needs contact – gently – and a place in the world – a pattern of life.

It is a hard thing to relinquish the power of explanation, even when this power is limited.

Explanations are the organizing tools of object world – they settle our lives and our thoughts and create wondrous, reliable pictures of objects and things (things imaginary and real, visible and invisible, tangible and evanescent, earthly and heavenly).

Explanations in science, philosophy and religion offer a grand buffet of object worlds – there are multitudes on the menu.

Imagine it is sunrise in the Sistine Chapel, and Dirac has been at work all through the night.

Sunshine bathes the chapel. The colors are gone.

Every image – every story – has been replaced by an explanation, every image but one.

One painting has not been painted over – it has merely been altered.

…the image of Michelangelo's Adam, his arm gloriously outstretched, no longer touching the finger of God, but pressing a button on a remote control.

Thirty-Eight: The Wheels have Come Off

As a tense and exciting contest between two extraordinary athletes was nearing its climax, one athlete faltered and the commentator cried out, 'The wheels have come off and he has his teeth in it!'

Metaphors add life, even when mixed.

A no-nonsense general, medals and all, was once asked for the meaning of a very 'poetic' poem. He responded, 'It doesn't mean a damn thing!'

In a way, he was right. But we should expect the metaphorical style of writing when the instinct is towards life.

…and the intent is to break through some shell, not to convey literal information.

We should expect abundance of metaphor if the goal is not to inform but to transform.

…as when an ancient figure of life speaks of immersion in the living water – a lived, felt experience as real as immersion in the water one can swirl with one's hands.

Metaphors and similes seem obscure to those who expect the literal. Jesus spoke of the kingdom and his disciples expected a place.

But the kingdom was like the man who…and the king that…and the maidens who…and the shepherd that…and the leaven that…and the mustard seed that…

The kingdom was like these many forms of life – a multiplicity of life – not a place.

Yet metaphors do not always point towards life.

Sometimes metaphors dump us in object world. They take us straight to it; there is no waiting. They do so when the *only* metaphor is the physical object.

Much research has been done on the psychology of metaphor over the past few decades, and it shows how powerful the physical object metaphor can be, because we feel and see ourselves first as bodies – as physical objects.

Lakoff and Johnson wrote a thick book on the subject, called *Philosophy in the Flesh*.[1]

They reported that we (humans) use hundreds of metaphors for our key philosophical concepts: understanding, knowledge, time, mind, causation, morality, love...

(That is no surprise – just read any novel.)

The surprise is that most of these metaphors arise in one way or another from the physical body – from body movement or body control.

For instance, we ask someone if they understand what we've said with the metaphor, 'Do you *get* it?'

...or we complain: 'It's difficult to *grasp* that concept – that subject is *over my head*.'

Here a body metaphor is unconsciously and instinctively applied: understanding is grasping – comprehension is holding an object.

Lakoff and Johnson believe that our concepts are 'embodied' – that they are woven into the brain's sensory and motor systems – body systems.

They believe that we are wired this way, and have little control over our metaphors.

They think it is likely that the brain structure of concepts is similar to the brain structure that controls the body – a natural outgrowth.

Here are some examples of body metaphors:

The mind is an object: 'His mind *wandered* just then.'

Thinking is (some *thing*) moving: '*Where are you going* with that thought...Can you *go over* that again...My thoughts are *racing*.'

Ideas are locations: '...*returning* to the topic...*straying* from the topic...*approaching* the topic...How did you *reach that conclusion*?...*Where* are you in the discussion?'

Ideas are objects (so that thinking is object manipulation): 'Let's *play around with that* – I'll *toss it over* to you...maybe you can *turn it over* in your mind...There can be many *sides* to an issue.'

Lakoff and Johnson think that philosophy tends to emphasize one metaphor at the expense of all the others, taking that single metaphor as the final, literal truth.

If they are right, the greatest such metaphor seems to be the object metaphor – everything is a thing – including joy, pain, desire, humor, fear, hope, justice, life and reality.

How ironic that scientists of all stripes battle the many intrusions of religious stories while blind to the overreaching literalism of their own object metaphor.

Scientists are, as it were, taught to be blind to life…

…taught to see every ounce of reality and life through the body metaphor.

There is no intention in science or religion to desiccate reality and life.

The body metaphor is so intertwined with life; it may be the only way to make experiences that are deeply felt, real and alive.

Perhaps sensations must be significant *things*.

Perhaps the Kingdom of God must be a sacred *place*.

Standing back, one could almost begin to conceive of humanity as autistic.

Are we on the *wrong track*? Maybe we're *full of it*! Is our argument *circular*? Where's our *foundation*?

There is a history of the coming to power of the object metaphor.

Among primal peoples, truth has long been a *multiplicity* of metaphor, lived and experienced, not a philosophy based on a *single* metaphor.

For primal peoples, justice is the sun, a light shining equally upon all…

…justice is the wind, a force of nature, toppling the tallest of trees, leaving the humblest untouched.

…justice is the water, strong and impartial, giving and kind.

Philosophy changed this. Socrates complained that he was not satisfied with the 'primitive' notion that justice was the sun.

It was not enough to live the metaphor of a light shining equally upon all, and it was incoherent to welcome the richness of a host of other lived metaphors.

He wanted a single coherent concept, not the disorder of life.

He wanted justice to be a well defined thing, like an object with distinct edges. He wanted virtues to be objects in object world, even if they were remote, abstract, perfect objects, never to be touched.

He wanted to *figure it out*.

…and so began Western philosophy, when the rich multiplicity and experience of life was no longer truth.

…and the domesticated, singular world of objects and tools rose as mankind's shining star.

Today perhaps the most popular metaphor is: 'The mind is a computer.'

…and this metaphor, like all metaphors, like all statues built and eventually torn asunder, is to be worshipped, for a time.

Thirty-Nine: From Faulkner to Harry Potter

Subjects of the psychological studies of A.H. Maslow in the 1960's who were found to be most 'fully human' described their peak experiences in words like these:

> I could see that I belonged in the universe and I could see where I belonged in it; I could see how important I was and yet how unimportant and small I was, so at the same time that it made me humble, it made me feel important.[1]

Many years before, William Faulkner wrote a novella called *The Bear*.[2]

Old Ben is huge, powerful, living deep in the forest, so much a part of nature he is nature.

Sometimes he is there when you do not see him.

He is hunted by the young boy, Ike.

Ike's Indian guide, Sam, teaches the boy the ways of the woods.

The hunt for Old Ben is an initiation into manhood; a vision quest.

One day, deep in the forest, Ike senses the presence of Old Ben. Hearing only the tapping of a woodpecker, he knows that he is being watched.

Holding his gun, Ike stands motionless, but the bear vanishes.

To see Old Ben – to meet Old Ben – is everything to the boy, but time passes and he searches in vain.

Sam instructs Ike that he hasn't 'looked right' – that he'll have to choose whether or not to keep the gun.

The next morning Ike sets out without the gun.

He is no longer the hunter.

But leaving the gun is not enough.

Ike is still tainted. Leaving behind his watch and compass, he wanders until lost in the depths of the green forest – in the *markless wilderness*.

Finally he sees the bear. Old Ben pauses to look back at the boy, acknowledging his existence, only to turn and fade again into the wilderness.

The boy is initiated into humility and pride.

Only in humility is he allowed to see the bear – putting aside his weapons and tools of orientation. Only after being seen by the bear does he merit the reward of pride.

The boy does not kill the bear or possess it. That is impossible.

He does something far more dangerous – he participates in its greater existence.

The boy *receives* power; he does not grasp it.

Gabriel Horn (White Deer of Autumn) spoke of this same distinction in the contrast between the lives of primal and civilized peoples:

To primal peoples, the Earth is a living entity – a mother that helps connect everyone to life.

To primal peoples, language is also a living entity – sacred and respected, for it connects everyone to the living and to life.

To the civilized, language is a tool: *...language becomes a technological achievement used to acquire power rather than receive it...*[3]

To acquire power one must use something as a means to an end.

To receive power one must seek not to use something, not to stand above it, but simply to *be* with it.

...like seeing a remark not as information but as part of a shared reality (as *thou*, not *it*).

...or as the wise and kindly headmaster explained to young Harry Potter,

You see, only one who wanted to find the Stone – find it, but not use it – would be able to get it, otherwise they'd just see themselves making gold or drinking Elixir of Life."[4]

Forty: Abstraction

Abstractions are more useful than fire and more efficient than wheels. They are humanity's most powerful tools.

Abstractions are powerful because they ignore details.

The concept of an Inuit is an abstraction; a conceptual whole without conceptual parts.

Imagine Canadian ministers having to write legislation about the Inuit with only the names of hundreds of thousands of individuals.

Imagine living in a world where each tree was unique, so that there was no word 'tree' and no summary concept to simplify and erase.

Abstractions are wonderful because they give us such big pictures – encompassing views, finished and complete.

Abstractions carry two dangers: they oversimplify and they ignore life.

The linguist Hayakawa wrote a book that warned of the dangers of oversimplification – of living in one's own linguistic fantasy world – *Language in Thought and Action*.[1]

An unwitting slave to abstraction, one may live not in reality, but in a world of categories – a world of 'who is my neighbor?'

Sometimes the term 'autistics' distinguishes a group of people as a rich entirety. One beholds the entirety like a painting. Variety and detail are preserved within a frame.

Sometimes variety is ignored. One beholds the entirety not as a painting, but as a small, hollow square with a check mark.

Awkward phrases like 'people with autism,' attempt to compensate for category induced disrespect.

They attempt to break the chains of category thought by emphasizing that first and foremost, autistics are people.

Imagine a conversation between sensitive diplomats that begins: 'On this issue the *people* with Britishness disagree with the *people* with Frenchness...'

In an odd way, in a way that would make a Martian shake his head, it might work.

The necessary remedy for dehumanizing the world with detail forgetting abstractions, Hayakawa felt, is *consciousness* of language as the construction of over-simplified pictures.

David Bohm offered the same prescription – *awareness* of one's almost invisible, automatic tendency to abstract.

For the philosopher Gabriel Marcel, *thou* is the remedy for abstraction. *Thou* is a partner, *it* is an object. Thou world is not object world.

Marcel's way comes closer to addressing abstraction's second problem: hollowness.

Abstractions are apart. They refer to something. The letter 's,' the word 'sparrow' and the drawing of a sparrow are all abstractions of a real sparrow.

According to Arthur Versluis, Native Americans draw images that we would call pictures of animals, but they are *not* pictures of animals.[2]

Their symbols and images are not representations of things, but living reminders of spiritual realities – living reminders of life.

The image of a hawk *presents* the spirit of the hawk…

…the image manifests hawk spiritual energy and reality, as does every living hawk.

In the Native American world every work of art is the living manifestation of the invisible, living truth for which the world exists.

Art is alive and real…

…as in our world a smile is not a mere picture – not a photograph – but a *living presentation* of joy.

In the Native American World, stones and water, sky and Earth are alive and real – all presenting their spirits – not representing. They are all living works of art.

Perhaps that is why in most Native languages there is no word for 'art.' The closest translation is 'life.'

Perhaps that is why modern artists splash out colors and shapes that cannot be interpreted – cannot *represent things*…

…but that *can* evoke a sense of spirit and life in a world raised to see images as copies of objects.

When the first photographs were taken of primal peoples, they were afraid that their souls were being stolen. The photographers reassured them – 'Don't worry, they're only pictures.'

Seeing with living eyes is difficult in a domesticated world.

Perhaps a more modest remedy for the loss of detail and life – the side effects of abstraction – is consciousness of social pressure…

…so that when someone asks for your opinion on *this* issue (this condensation of reality) you respond, 'But *this* is so many things and it depends on so many circumstances.'

Maintaining your integrity, you confound the questioner and pay the price of relegating yourself to a social limbo.

You side neither with the questioner nor against them. You abstain from the instinctive oversimplifying, territorial world of with and against and choose instead, reality.

…and in this way, you are more 'with' them than they could ever imagine.

Forty-One: Free from Pictures

The simplest possible ideal permeates the writings of mystics – to be free from pictures.

Often called the father of German mystics, Meister Eckhart sermonized on this theme.

According to one master, many people arrive at specific understanding, at formal, notional knowledge, but yet there are few who get beyond the science and the theory...

...yet one man whose mind is free from notions and from forms is more dear to God than the hundred thousand who have the habit of discursive reason...

...God cannot enter in and do his work in them owing to the restlessness of their imagination...

...If they were free from pictures they could be caught and carried up beyond all rational concepts, as St Dionysius says...[1]

One way to climb beyond all rational concepts is to 'reject the grammar' of those concepts:

As in the *Philosophical Investigations*:

(Pain) is not a <u>something</u>, but not a <u>nothing</u> either! ...We have only rejected the grammar which tries to force itself on us here.[2]

Or the *Upanishads*:

...I do not think I know it well, nor do I know that I do not know it.[3]

Or in Zen:

...place yourself in the same freedom as sky. You name it neither good nor not-good.[4]

Or with Simone Weil:

The capacity to drive a thought away once and for all is the gateway to eternity. The infinite in an instant.[5]

Forty-Two: Idolatry

In ancient days idolatry was the worship of false Gods. The term 'idolatry' was used as a kind of staff to shepherd together followers of the same religion.

Over time this term lost its force, for humanity discovered other religions with different Gods.

Eventually, idolatry seemed more of a tribal artifice. Today the term is hardly used.

Yet there is a deeper and more interesting meaning to idolatry:

They that make them are like unto them: and so are all such as put their trust in them. (Psalms 115)

In 'deep idolatry' one becomes one's own concepts.

And this is something good to know.

In an otherwise calm book on the spirituality of autism Abe Isanon launched into a tirade against turning reality into a collection of mere abstractions and objects for selfish purposes.[1]

Why was he so insistent? He noted that autistics live in a society of tool users who too often discard or ignore those who are not useful…especially those who show no progress with verbal language (humanity's preeminent tool).

But there is more. Today, in large part, the linguistic mind *is* the mind.

The great deep idol is the language mind.

It is more than a devotion to education. It is devotion to representation over presentation – to models – to being about more than being.

That sounds so philosophical – soft – like cotton.

Consider: sometimes people burn flags. Are the flags sacred or are they representations of something sacred?

People in advanced societies have, in some sense, become their linguistic-representing minds: art is interpreted, life is dissected, work is thinking *about*, decisions are elaborate algorithms and rules – quite aloof and professional.

There are millions of books *about* religion.

Is this a form of wealth and progress, or more akin to Wittgenstein's endless, obsessive remarks…

…the wrist-biting of the world?

Perhaps one could equally say of primal peoples, 'Their great deep idol is the intuitive mind.'

Autistics like Wittgenstein, Weil, Marcel and Bohm feared the literal worlds that their minds created, for they saw themselves becoming literal things – object-people.

Autistics, more than most, are truly in danger of becoming objects – machines that respond in a monotone – tool users who become tools.

Owen Barfield devoted an entire book to what we have called deep idolatry and to its history.

He saw idolatry as tied to literalism, and saw idols not so much as images that one falsely values, but as images within those on their way to becoming those images.[2]

Imagine worshipping gold only to become shiny and dead.

…or worse, worshipping gold only to transform oneself into gold…protected, hidden, eternally alone.

Among primal peoples, meat must be shared before it rots. Honor is crucial to those who give and those who receive. Gold does not rot.

In a way, (deep) idolatry has taken this book full circle – we began on the journey from object to life, and now it has taken us from life back to object.

Yet the mentality of object world does not make one into an object when this part of human nature is recognized.

Conscious of the natural tendency to treat concepts as deep truths, we may dig out these unconscious idolatries, admit them, and joyfully abandon our 'forms in thought' – dissolving all forms in ourselves.

His form is vanished…He is neither this nor that…

…he is void of form…Nothing is seen in him but the reflection of another.[3] (Rumi)

Idolatry is neither a simple thing nor a bad thing.

Only in object world is idolatry a thing.

In life, idolatry is neither good nor bad, both good and bad, not a thing, but a part of life and life itself.

Sometimes idolatry is sacred.

Children draw pictures of God every day, but none are false.

Forty-Three: The Land of Black Grass

To understand autism is to understand culture, for in autism one sees in the starkest possible contrast, connections and disconnections among people.

There are many kinds of cultures – nations, cities, states, groups, businesses, marriages, families...

A culture, like an autistic child, may be innocently overwhelmed...

...frustrated and confused – as though nothing it does works. Connections are not organized and filtered. Complexity is winning the battle.

A culture may be surreal – like the morning newscast of an impending disaster, and 'Next, Jane will show us how to make cookies'...

...a fragmented world of distant stories...a drama with a thousand disconnected acts.

Yet worlds like these are not thoroughly autistic-raw. There are empathy stories, silly stories and serious stories – stories that connect to the social world and carry life in broadly human ways, because they are stories.

A culture, like an autistic child, may be tyrannical – driven by unyielding demands.

There is no trust, no faith – nothing that works invisibly of its own accord...

...the world outside is too hard...too unpredictable...

A culture, like an autistic, may be obsessive – trapped in the vortex of some 'ism,' for *the ideal* has wrested control from the real.

A culture may be impersonal and bureaucratic – artificial in its soul.

...a rule world...a game...

...fences and schedules for the immature, who must be directed and guided.

Ray Bradbury created a fictional world like this in his 1950's novel, *Fahrenheit 451*.

…a future world where life is some *thing* that society arranges for the sake of peace and order.

…and a kind of super-domestication is fostered through benevolent control and the maintenance of perpetual immaturity.

Civilization means domestication of the human animal, nothing more.

The world of Fahrenheit 451 is a city under repair – a city whose past was dysfunctional, for the people were eternally at odds, hypersensitive, disconnected, fragmented…

And so now its present is a bubble – it has shut down and withdrawn from its painful existence.

Yet connections are even weaker in this withdrawn society. People stare through one another. Reality is pale. Life is dim.

The hero of Bradbury's story breaks through society's great bubble, discovers spontaneity and love – of books, reality and life.

Defending life, he commits a terrible crime. The chase of the criminal is broadcast.

His apprehension brings relief.

But in truth, he escapes.

His death is only apparent. (Bradbury did not include a cross.)

In the end, the hero comes to the woods (to his true nature, one might permit) to a tight knit community (not an indifferent world) where each man and woman puts a *story* (a source of life) to *memory* – as ancients used to do when stories were lived, not written down.

Some years ago I studied what the world looked like in ultraviolet light.

In the world of ultraviolet light (and no other light) almost everything is black.

Only a tiny portion of this light reflects.

Our teeth are black and the whites of our eyes are the blacks of our eyes.

Our hair, our skin (of every race), our clothing, our rooms, our houses – all black – with slight variations in shade. Only the sun is bright, and reflections from mirrors and metals.

At first I called this world the land of black grass. It was beautiful to imagine, in a way...hills of black grass, blades flowing in the wind – reality, in ultraviolet world.

But in a different sense, a profoundly autistic culture is the land of black grass, where all light is absorbed. It is cultural autism at its most extreme.

In the land of black grass, the highest wisdom is to be jaded – to have suffered through a storm of falsehoods and survived.

Pride and humility are opposites.

Everything is a thing. Truth, freedom, joy, religion, men, women... all are territory.[1]

...objects to be guarded, fought over, staked out and owned.

The world is power world, category world and name world.

Every neighbor is a stranger, guilty until proven innocent.

One's greatest strengths are one greatest weaknesses – concepts, beliefs, instincts, loyalties...

Existence is paralysis punctuated by violent outbursts – victims all and purely self righteous, they cannot control their instincts. They speak in erratic monologues. They interrupt and never listen.

...exposed – thin skinned – acting out at the slightest touch, and then utterly insensitive – dull and inert. It is the best they can do.

The land of black grass is not inevitable – indeed, the tendency to crave a future collapse is too easy – too mechanical – too fated.

Life and humanity of spirit are abundant in everyday selfless gestures...as the author discovered when a young man volunteered to help rebuild a damaged home a thousand miles away, and a religious community dispensed with home insurance, agreeing to repair and rebuild anyone's damages within the community.

Seemingly trivial policies can easily carry the spirit of life, as when Colleges *personally* interview each of their student applicants, and charities send thank you notes for contributions with *no* requests for further donations.

Even small gestures can carry an enormous significance, as when someone, wrapped in their own concerns, decides to *pause* and listen...

There are selfless gestures like these everywhere, every day. They are gestures of respect and maturity, of love and fullness of life. They are gestures of civilization.

A civilization will value the covenant over the contract, the unwritten over the written, the personal over the impersonal and the humane over the inhumane, but be mature enough to know when the language and powers of contracts, rules and laws must be applied.

In her book, *The Echo of Greece*, Edith Hamilton described ancient Greek civilization.[2]

She understood that great freedom requires great *unwritten* bonds.

The infant democracy of Athens flourished because of its *unwritten laws* – its *covenants* between state and individual. For example, at first, politicians and jurors were willing volunteers.

But some volunteers lived near and some lived far, and some were wealthy and some were poor. The covenants were unfair. Compensations had to be made.

Athens fell because of war and because the unwritten, unseen covenants of responsibility and devotion became contracts of fair pay.

Fairness was mechanized. Justice was mechanized, as in the autistic object world.

Unwritten, selfless compensations could have been made. They were not.

Laws were written. Athens soon became a city of employees with rights, with no larger sense of identity or obligation. The bonds between citizen and state were broken.

Their highest, most vulnerable and most unfair identity, identity within a covenant, fell to an identity that was small and fair and seemingly secure: 'I have my rights.'

Democracy was no longer a bond, but an autistic game with players and rules.

Unwritten to written – covenant to contract – life to object… for the sake of a justice that was neither love nor obligation, but equality of burden and reward.

Forty-Four: Mountains and Desert

In the early 20th century an extraordinary European woman named Alexandra David-Neel journeyed across Asia, visiting Buddhist monasteries and studying Buddhism.[1]

She settled in Tibet for over twenty years.

There she discovered people who followed their instincts to lead perfectly detached lives, seeking a complete mastery and understanding of the origin of all their thoughts, appetites and desires.

These 'sportsmen' went into the mountains and either found masters to teach them the science of enlightenment, or lived in solitude and meditated – sometimes for an entire life.

They regarded themselves as engaged in an arduous battle against spiritual obstacles.

In their terms, they were not finding religion, but making it. It was dangerous, hard work.

The idea of a purely solitary spiritual adventure has long vanished in the West, or perhaps fallen into the quiet, hidden shadows of monastic life.

Even St. Bernard of Clairvaux's vision – that the world is a place of banishment and men are but strangers and pilgrims – seems antiquated today.

But the solitude, the danger, the personal revelation and the banishment – all are elements of the autistic path to life.

Traditional paths involve the poses and breathing exercises of yoga – singing, dancing and ritual – means of living in the moment, away from the conscious mind and its worrisome life of past and future.

Meditation is encouraged – concentration on imagery, on breathing, on feeling, on divine themes. Intense concentration is encouraged – perseverance.

Purification is encouraged – poverty, solitude, repentance, fasting, silence, penance (walking barefoot, skipping meals), a simple diet, abstinence from the world and from fleeting desires.

Every purification – every form of going without, every sacrifice, is a way of opening a door – of being vulnerable to the world – of making oneself receptive.

...and of connecting more resolutely to a dimly felt reality.

Centuries ago mortification was encouraged, though not biting one's hand.

In the East, paradoxical expressions – koans – are still contemplated.

A concept is contemplated until it is de-reified – made unreal.

...like erasing an image by continually staring at it...

In the West, Simone Weil proposed what she called a *proper method of philosophy*: to concentrate on impossible problems for years, exhausting the intelligence and the will.[2]

In the East mandalas are created – intricate, colorful pictures filled with detail and ornament – and then erased – reflections of the koan process.

One mystic contemplated the nature of faith for months.

A response eventually came in the form of a question: 'Is it better to have faith or to be faith?'

'What's the difference?' he asked. The response was immediate: 'What's the difference between wearing a coat on a cold day, and being that coat?'

Later, in abandoning concept-beliefs he noted the sense of being the truth, not having it, and the sense of being love, not having it.

And still later came the question: 'Is it better to have life or to be life?'

...and after all of this I think the immediate and the raw finally sank in, and the fact that his questioning was answered only by questions showed that the answers had to be lived.

For some there is more than simply becoming life. There is the wonderful and terrible obligation to pass it on.

In the ancient Gnostic 'Gospel of Truth,' it was written:

Jesus was patient in accepting sufferings...since he knows that his death is life for many.[3]

Forty-Five: Celebration

The experience of truly seeing:

Observing her autistic son Elijah, Valerie Paradiz was mesmerized by the poetry of his extraordinary perceptions.

Elijah laughed at the sound of the wind, and how it rounded him as it flowed about his body.[1]

Wittgenstein, as his friend Bouwsma noted, read in *bright gold*.[2]

Autistics who work with animals perceive subtleties in these animals to which others are blind.[3]

They celebrate the reality of the animals. They look at the mysterious reality before them with joyous eyes.

Jamake Highwater noted that Native Americans use images to celebrate reality, not to explain it.[4]

Awareness to Native peoples is not a matter of observing, but of knowing some reality by celebrating it and becoming it.[5]

In joy one transforms.

Donna Williams described the 'resonance' of her autistic childhood:

I learned eventually to lose myself in anything I desired—the patterns on the wallpaper or the carpet, the sound of something over and over again…

…I was too happy losing myself to want to be dragged back by something as two-dimensional as understanding…[6]

The phrase *two-dimensional* is apt – the origin of the term 'explain' is 'to make plain – to make flat.'

Perhaps understanding really *is* just a surface.

The novelist Iris Murdoch observed that we celebrate reality through great art, like the characters of Shakespeare.[7]

She noted that his characters are portrayed with detachment, clarity, multiplicity, justice and compassion.

Hamlet is not presented from one person's view, but in his rich and startling reality – his entirety.

According to Murdoch he is important to us – and celebrated – because the drama of his life penetrates our self importance and proves to us that he is more than a thing.

Zen practitioners celebrate seeing reality.

They do not interpret. They do not generalize. They do not argue.

They try to see without belief.[8]

Forty-Six: Wittgenstein as Human

There is a tendency to see Wittgenstein's work as so inimitable and his personality as so intense, that the man himself becomes an abstraction.

In a philosophy book especially, there is the tendency to think only of the object man.

…the target of thought, the source of a view, the name on a page.

This is wrong. This chapter is compensation.

It is important not to abstract away his humanity.

Wittgenstein liked to talk about works of fiction. He admired *A Christmas Carol*, by Dickens.

He said he didn't understand religious languages, and that he was particularly puzzled by the gospel of John.

In 1913 he went to meditate and work on logic by a fjord, north of Bergen.

Wittgenstein perceived a host of personal shortcomings. He tried to compensate.

Despite a medical exemption, he served (heroically) during WWI, motivated more by the danger and the opportunity to stop thinking about logic, than by patriotism.[1]

As a prisoner of war in Italy, where thousands were dying of disease and starvation, he refused to leave until the last of his men were released.

His friends were understanding. They knew him to be naïve, extraordinarily sensitive and all too often extraordinarily irritable.[2]

Naively convinced that he had solved all philosophical problems in the *Tractatus*, he went away to teach children…

…and then for a brief time he worked as a gardener in a Benedictine monastery near Vienna.

During the second war he worked as a hospital porter and helped to conduct research on wound shock.

Wittgenstein once remarked to a friend that his philosophical work was only for people who could not leave philosophical questions alone.³

He was practical. He wanted his philosophy to accomplish something.⁴

Wittgenstein enjoyed the English countryside. He spoke of the marvelous colors of the fields and roads.

He once stopped to enjoy the expression on a child's face, and instructed a friend to take more notice of people's faces.

He wrote thousands upon thousands of remarks in an effort to conquer the temptations of perfect conceptual structures – the fantasies of metaphysics – the supposed 'true natures' of math, life, games, rules, joy, pain, beauty, meaning, color…

…but to his friend Maurice Drury he offered this observation one day:

*Don't think I despise metaphysics. I regard some of the great philosophical systems of the past as among the noblest productions of the human mind.*⁵

At one time, Wittgenstein expressed doubts about his status as a philosopher to the point of writing to his friend (Drury), suggesting that the two of them enter medical school and practice psychiatry.

According to his sister, despite his demanding nature, he was always ready to help – he had a *big heart*.⁶

Wittgenstein was always a misfit, and in his later years his spirit was not at all the modern spirit of devising more ways to structure the world.

He loved clarity as one might love a window – for the sparkle of the glass, not as a means to protect oneself from the weather.⁷

He did not care for the modern world.

Wittgenstein's biographer, Ray Monk, also mentioned this spirit. In the light of autism, it carries a unique significance.

*A picture that intruded upon him, he wrote, was of our civilization, 'cheaply wrapped in cellophane and isolated from everything great, from God, as it were'.*⁸

He felt himself to share exactly the faults characteristic of our age, and to need the same remedy: faith and love.[9]

His life was filled with joy and anxiety.

Near the end, when Wittgenstein was dying of cancer...

He talked about thunderstorms...

...One of his sisters was very fond of them, and they were terrific in the Alps where his father had a summer home...

...Another sister was frightened of them and used to hide...

...She was cured once when she and a friend were walking through a forest in the mountains, and were overtaken by a storm. After that she did not mind.[10]

Forty-Seven: Gabriel Marcel

The 20th century French philosopher Gabriel Marcel wrote in long, flowery sentences.

He was flexible, kind and good natured. He was quite social. He joined the Catholic Church.

...and he distrusted the detached philosophy of Spinoza. He did not want to risk diminishing himself only to be lost in the drifting clouds of some amorphous high reality.

I have no idea if Marcel had Asperger's, but his instincts and experiences were close to those of Wittgenstein and Weil...and that is more relevant than any half-understood label.

He wrote dozens of plays to make his philosophy 'concrete' – dramatic and real. His plays were part of his philosophical writings; passionate first person *dialogues* rather than detached, academic monologues.

Dialogue is advanced. One must listen and weave an entirely different point of view into one's own...a new thread in every phrase – a new world – exhausting.

Monologue is much easier than dialogue; more primitive, more autistic. Speeches, books, broadcasting – ignoring the other's circumstances entirely. With respect to the possibilities of life, one might as well be wearing a fur skin and dragging a club.

In one of his dialogues Socrates complained about books. How could books explain anything decently? They don't listen. They don't respond.

Socrates never wrote anything down. He discussed everything in dialogues.

His young student Plato wrote all the dialogues down. They were too good – they had to be preserved.

In the early 1920's an American radio station was going bankrupt and desperately needed a way to raise money. Someone suggested that along with music, sports and news they could broadcast advertising.

At first the owner angrily rejected this idea, 'You don't enter people's homes and try to sell them something without their permission!'

But eventually he relented. The world was growing, and distant connections were eagerly desired and much needed…and a little bit of civility could be sacrificed.

In a short autobiography, Marcel spoke of the *incessant anxiety* of his youth, and noted that ideas and abstractions provided a *shelter from these wounding contacts of everyday life*.[1]

In childhood his greatest joys were to explore and to imagine exploring, and his greatest desire seems to have been to carve out a larger life.

He recalled that his childhood world seemed lifeless, vague and abstract.[2]

Marcel passionately loved music, for listening to music was *real* in a deep and fulfilling way that his other experiences were not.[3]

His childhood reality was like the space under a shroud, but with ear-holes.

When he was older he longed to connect to others without having his thoughts and feelings about them relate *always* to himself. That was a small world – a confining prison.[4]

Marcel wrote volumes to pull himself out of his self-centered world. But how?

Einstein remarked that the objective detachment of science freed him from the merely personal…

The detached, mechanical part of his mentality, packed with an extraordinary array of models, concepts and theories, freed him from the prison at the center of the Universe.

For Einstein, object world pierced the autistic bubble.

Marcel emphasized the importance of attention.

His instinct was to circle each theme, seeing it from every perspective.[5]

He regarded attention as the measure of his freedom – an embodied, participatory freedom – a kind of dissolving absorption in which his small self vanished.

He measured his freedom not by the power to do more, but by the ability to be more.

His mature work, *Problematic Man*, was unusual, even unique.

It was devoted to the notion of uneasiness as expressed in the New Testament, the writings of St. Augustine and others.[6]

...uneasiness – not worry, not anxiety, not any sort of pathology – but the sense that one should not be content with oneself, for something in life is deeply askew and requires grace.

Marcel wrote plays that analyzed the spiritual by starting from relations among human beings and working towards something higher.

He contended that the greatest freedom comes from being able to see through another's eyes.[7]

This empathic freedom was readily extended to considerations of communion with God (seeing through the eyes of pure life, so to speak).

As Marcel matured, the protective shell of abstraction diminished.

The more he aged, the more he demanded the concrete – the momentary experiences and details of everyday life.[8,9]

While appreciating and even lauding the merits of technology, he often condemned the spirit of abstraction. He did not care for a technological view of human life.

Imagine a child's bad behavior – lashing out with a fist – injuring someone.

A parent might react in kind...by tongue lashing...

Or she might take a more detached view, seeing the behavior as a disorder (a mechanical malfunction)...

But Marcel suggested communion – empathy – entering the world of the child, and the world of the injured party – communion on both sides – on every side.

...communion from every angle.

Marcel's work was a struggle against the systematic spirit, against the spirit of abstraction, against the tendency to give primacy to analytic knowledge...

...and in a complementary way, as the struggle *for* the concrete...

...the struggle to recognize others...to recognize one's own faults...to sense that humanity is sacred and has a capacity for the sacred.[10]

For Marcel existence cannot be reduced to anything else – 'man' cannot be reduced.

He identified the experience of participation with a richness, plenitude and totality that cannot be divided or fragmented.

For Marcel, life is a whole without parts.

Marcel was deeply worried about the modern world; about the tendency of the modern individual to see himself...*more and more as a mere assemblage of functions*...[11]

He wrote...*passers-by look like people who have retired from life...this world is empty, it rings hollow...on the one hand riddled with problems and, on the other, determined to allow no room for mystery.*[12]

Anyone familiar with the large and modern world will understand Marcel's observation...

...it is a world of...*innumerable technical problems, bound up with the difficulty of knowing how the various functions, once they have been inventoried and labeled, can be made to work together without doing one another harm.*[13]

...like an artificially intelligent computer built as a collection of thousands of rules, that must *struggle* to coordinate an infinity of combinations of these rules...

...like a government that functions with a mass of independent laws...

...like an awkward Aspergian teen who lives in a world of conflicting social rules rather than a smoothly automatic world, ordered and calm.

In a revealing grouping, Marcel expressed his hopes for the vanishing of *technocrats, statistic worshippers, tyrants and torturers*.[14]

...as though hyper-sensitive to being treated as an object.

As an example of a concrete totality, he offered orchestral music. Here he felt, the whole precedes the part. The whole is composed – the parts are secondary.

...Like the idea (Einstein's, I think) that the connectedness of space-time and its distance relations form an inseparable whole – an idea to this day that defies mathematics, which creates one structure (connection) and then adds another (distance)...

...whose abstractions are from the outset, disconnected fragments.

Marcel wanted his philosophy to be drama – embodied philosophy.

His metaphors would evoke life, not be literalized into theories.

He wrote a great deal about participation and communion, urging the reader to regard them as forms of life.

Existence, in Marcel's eyes, can never be analyzed. It is not a thing to be analyzed. It cannot be doubted.

It is better.

...existence is not only given, it is also giving...[15]

He was disheartened that Sartre could not understand the nature of gifts – blind to the fact that *genuine reality* is governed by our capacity for openness.

He spoke of fidelity and integrity, often hedging and confessing that it was difficult to speak about such things – that doing so inevitably degrades them – for one substitutes images and ideas for essence.

He felt that philosophy should be far more than an intellectual game – that it should ceaselessly work against man dehumanizing himself.[16]

On one occasion he presented the following example of being dehumanized: animals in cages – outside their natural context...

...like an autistic child behind invisible bars...

...like a word used not in a real setting, but abstractly defined... as in philosophy.

He felt that judgment is always betrayal (for the other is thou, never the object, it).

He valued the human over the partisan: there is no 'Marcellian system' of philosophy.

He renounced the idea of building a system.[17]

A system is used – it requires exploitation and management. It places one at the center.

He wrote about the incredibly vague term, 'being' which in many cases (I think) is what I have called 'life.'

The 'being' of which he spoke, he flatly contended, was meaningless if it was compared in any way to an object. He went so far as to treat it as a verb, not a noun.

He was especially grateful to the philosopher Bergson for pointing out that human language is modeled on things.

He often distinguished between mysteries and problems – a mystery, like the meaning of one's life, cannot be conceived as an abstract problem – a problem of modeling. Life is *repugnant* to the modeling mentality.

Marcel loved the idea of life.

He collected, arranged and wrote volumes about concepts like participation, communion, fidelity, and mystery.

He felt that they could never be fully analyzed – never be reduced – only lived – and lived to depths the modern world could scarcely imagine.

Forty-Eight: Creatures of Abstraction and Creatures of Life

Science is a great and noble cause – sometimes heroic.

Rene Descartes is often credited with initiating the modern, scientific world view.

Growing up in the early 17th century, a world of superstition, religious fanaticism, war, famine and plague, Descartes defended the necessity and worth of science – the mind always open to threatening new theories, yet always skeptically attentive to the facts.

In a world where hardly anyone imagined that a discipline like science could exist, he believed in the power of abstraction curbed by facts.

He devoted years to the study of medicine.

The 'Cartesians' who came after him were those who shared his belief in the rigorous, rule based world of science. In fact, prior to about 1950, a Cartesian was thought of as someone who was vaguely Aspergian; overly pedantic and logical.[1]

The concepts of science are limited by facts, but the facts are always incomplete, and so strictly speaking, all concepts are incomplete.

Yet almost no one speaks, thinks or lives strictly. They live in a casual, everyday concept world, where their shared, useful concepts are complete and true.

As an example of two concepts taken too far – trusted too literally – space and time have long been footings for our notions of the world. But today, physicists are working on theories that derive space and time from more primitive things.

Scientists like Percy Bridgman and Albert Einstein warned against trusting our concepts and theories too much and extending them far beyond the measurements that confirm them.

They did not carp against theory; they knew that we have to make conceptual leaps.

They simply wanted science to have as strong a foundation in fact as possible.

But even they were not as adamant as Zen masters, who continue today to instruct their students to trust none of their concepts in any ultimate sense.

Of these Zen masters one might say, they take science seriously.

Science – so beautiful, trustworthy and strong, the great shining workhorse of the modern world, suffers from a kind of autistic literalism when it holds to its fiercely won concept worlds…accurate theories and trusted laws…as *more* than useful tools…

…treating *every* aspect of life as *represented* and remote, as an object or thing…

…creating a world purely distant and mechanical…always at arms length…that of which symbols speak…

…a half-reality, where life is a dance of mannequins, robots and toys.

For non-autistics and those with only mild autism, science is not *that* cold or mechanical; it is moderated by an unconscious, unspoken empathy.

Life and significance – intrinsic value – is somehow seen in bodies we otherwise describe as mere atoms in motion.

But the purely mechanical view *is* (one) stark raw world of severe autism, *and* the tendency of a tool based culture whose livelihood and understanding is founded on the use of things.

Imagine a brain with two halves – one half connected to reality, the other half at a distance.

When the two halves connect, they help to form a human who writes books with observations like, 'Everything I say is superficial – I can't describe the taste of an apple to one who cannot taste – but at least I know this.'

Imagine the clash between a creature of pure abstraction and a creature of pure life.

This is a clash of worlds.

A vast paraphernalia accompanies the creature of abstraction – laws, theories, explanations, models, the need for more depth, more answers, the idea of reality as an object or a collection of objects, the primacy of logic and mathematics, axioms, theorems, the spirit of construction, clarity as a means to an end, philosophy as super-science, and the largely unconscious desire to understand by grasping.

By contrast, the creature of life tries to lose this baggage or put it aside:

There is life – life is deeper than theory…this is experienced, not argued for…

…language is not always used as theory, nouns are not always names of things, logic and mathematics are not hyper-independent abstract systems, but obtain their meanings by being lived, explanations come to an end, reality is far more than an object, purported objects like the mind are just confusions, clarity is sought as an end in itself, and the largely unconscious desire to understand is achieved not by grasping, but by letting go.

Dramatically opposed as these worlds may be, the wall between them is paper thin.

Both creatures are devoted to some sort of truth, and both are careful and attentive.

There is contemplation, not instant analysis. There is dispassion and openness to reality.

There is depth of understanding.

There is devotion to something larger than oneself.

The wall is paper thin, and may be pierced as easily as a bubble.

Forty-Nine: Silence

Imagine a world where religion is never put into words.

…like a farmer silently hoeing a garden…

…showing, not saying…

…a world where religious truths are of the whole – not one dimensional, like language.

To silently *see* the truth in others…and let their words drift by.

Silent religion is crucial for those who feel that words are just abstractions (unmixed with significance).

Silence can be calming. The prayer of a young autistic man named Adam was meditative and calming. It slowed down the incessant barrage of images and talk that overwhelmed his mind.[1]

Silence is a language of gesture and emotion, a language of belonging, a language just right for many autistics, including Simone Weil, who regarded silent attention as prayer.[2]

The spirit of religion seems to say:

Look at the Gods of Mount Olympus. They have all the power, beauty, independence and freedom of the world…

…They are all that humanity seems to desire…

…They fly through the heavens, they rain down bolts from the sky, they see all that transpires, they indulge in luxury, they command the devotion of mortals, and they themselves are immortal.

…Look at them closely. They have pride without humility. They have passion without love. They lack contentment and grace – they lack gratitude and kinship. You call them gods but they are phantoms of life.

People listen to this spirit and take it to heart.

Then follows vulnerability, solitude, and silence. Some succeed – the silent success stories.

But for others the silence is too much to bear…and so some structure is sought in concept world, and some structure is found.

It is like the inverse of an autistic, who seeks community and communication with the world – and that is too much to take, so silence and solitude are sought, and silence and solitude are found.

In his book on Native Americans, Vine Deloria describes an undomesticated faith – a faith without concepts, theories or beliefs – a raw faith – a silence that *is* faith.

It was not what (Native) people believed to be true that was important but what they experienced as true... Religion for them is an experience and they have no reason to reduce it to systematic thought...[3]

...no reason to create worded connections when ties exist without them.

Primal peoples and profound autistics share this: both live in worlds of wonder, mystery and awe. They share fidelity to a silent, wordless world that is immediate and near.

Gabriel Marcel loved the wordless world, for it was free and real. Prayer was not a verbal request – not even a silent request.

It was the opposite of a request – a giving and devotion of oneself.

One participates in a transcendent reality by making oneself open and *disposable* to that reality. Hands are joined to symbolize the absence of grasping.[4,5]

Mystics like St. John of the Cross say that we can participate with our entire being in covenants; that God is not an object to be grasped, but the substance of faith.

It's doubtful that the silent religious communion of some autistics would even be called religious or spiritual by others. Autistics live on their own islands. The interior life is more beautiful.

For these islanders the interior life *is* the church.

They are singing life silently.

Fifty: Talk

Native peoples say talk is sacred. Words have power. Words connect – they strengthen reality…they give life.

In the 1990's a writer named Kent Nerburn recorded the observations of the Lakota elder, Dan.

Recalling his early education in a white school, Dan remarked that he was often called on to talk.

He thought it was disrespectful to talk when he had nothing to say.

Dan had been raised to think about what he was going to say before he spoke, and whether his words would be of value to others.

Dan's days at school must have been disorienting.

He said that the teachers at his school wanted everyone to connect by words. They didn't like silence.

Silence was uncomfortable – it made them nervous.

Nothing changed over the years. The 'white people' continued to talk whether their words were of value to others or not.

As an adult, Dan was still annoyed with this alien culture. At one point he vented his disapproval: *They don't even let each other finish sentences. They are always interrupting and saying, 'Well, I think…'*[1]

Here is the tale of a journey from one world of talk to another:

An educated woman regarded her talk as her personal tool. Because of this, she talked whenever she felt the need. Talk in her world was power and freedom and the best means to understanding and intimacy.

It was strange – her use of the words 'power,' 'freedom,' 'understanding,' and 'intimacy' did not quite translate into the language of the primal people.

Being an individual connected by words, she often felt the need to talk.

She was on one side of the canyon; one side of the bridge.

Her mind was language mind, the mind rooted in *objects*, real and abstract.

Her mind was the problem solving mind and her world was a bag of problems, not an infinity of gifts.

Agreement in *opinion* was her great felt need – it was her deepest bond.

Silence was unfamiliar to her, as the world of talk is to an autistic.

Silence was frightening, fragmented and far from reality. Silence made her anxious.

In the void anything could happen.

The idea of responding to the silence made no sense to her – her word mind was confused and fearful before the great expanse.

She did not know the difference between kind silence and malicious silence, or between grasping and receptive silence.

Bravely she stepped onto the bridge in silence; she stepped from one piece of time to another – as though time was just a sequence of uncomfortable quiet moments.

Each step forward listened.

In the middle of the bridge her mind began to transform. Talk was now a tool for her tribe. In the middle of the bridge she spoke only when it was good for her people.

She respected the needs of the tribe over her personal needs, and respected her words, for they had value for her people and her world.

She respected especially her elders, for she lived in a world without change, where elders always knew more. She prayed only for her tribe, not for herself.

She respected the earth, and spat over the edge of the bridge on the other tribe – on the enemy below…the enemy of a thousand years.

Almost across the bridge, thoughts came to her as gifts from a deeper realm – like dreams. There was no desire for self – no desire to solve problems.

Thoughts were silent, sacred words – not tools.

She used words aloud as gifts only when gifts could not be given as gestures. They belonged to her no more.

Across the bridge, across the canyon, the dignity of the real and whole found her. Humility and pride found her.

She was the silent gift.

Here is another story:

In 'The Little Mermaid' by Hans Christian Andersen, the little mermaid yearned to transform into a human being and live among them. But there was a terrible price to pay for leaving the great ocean and becoming human – she had to lose her tongue.

Only in silence could she live among humans.

Only in silence could she hope to love.

Still she was out of place.

Soon she lost her life, and became a spirit.

She was granted the promise of entering the Kingdom of God in 300 years; less if children were good, more if they were bad.

A third tale: an episode related by Lawrence Osborne, referring to a high functioning autistic child:

We were told that he couldn't get into the Lab School for gifted children because he was 'too quiet.' Quiet? Since when is a kid singled out for being quiet?[2]

Fifty-One: '...'

Turn back the clock and you will find primal peoples.

Turn back the clock till time is no longer time and space is no longer space.

You will find human beings; you will find the same species – yet a different form of life.

You will find them wild in ways you do not understand, and domesticated in ways that you have forgotten. They are like autistics – or Wittgenstein's imaginary lions – lions that can speak, but their form of life is another world – they cannot be understood.[1]

Too many seasons have passed.

Too many snows have fallen.

You are no longer the same.

Ask them about time and they will reply, 'We flow on the river of the moon.'

Ask them about science and their holy man will pray to a stone by the fire.

Ask them about medicine and a healer will journey to a hill top and open his soul for your sake.

Ask them about art and they will speak of life.

Ask them if their rain dance will *cause* rain and they'll wince, as they manifest its creation, and the rain consents to show itself – to present itself, like the feeling of joy.

Ask them about morality and they will stand silently, like a bear.

Ask them what their petroglyphs *represent*, and they'll walk away.

It is tempting to give their world a name, like 'primal world' or 'participatory world.'

But if the name meant anything clear to us it would be wrong.

To respect their world as it is we will not name it.

We will call their world '....'

This is not what moderns do – they name everything.

Their form of life is the naming culture.

They are like cowboys who break horses – they domesticate for a living.

It must be frustrating not to name. Moderns exclaim: We *must* give their world a name.

We *must* represent it – no matter how poor or misleading the representation. No matter how poor or misleading the very use of representation.

We feel that we must *grasp* their world.

…as though in life hands could have no other role.

When we are not allowed to name, we are like sparrows with blindfolds.

We sit in our nests, frustrated, fearful, unable to fly.

Slowly the '…' world passed away.

Object world – the represented world – gathered force as we domesticated and named.

Reality became the external world – the represented world – separate from us.

The separate required justification: experiments to justify scientific theories, logic to justify math, ethical principles to justify our laws…theology to justify our worded religions and our images of God.

'Well – what's wrong with experiments justifying science?'

Nothing – nothing at all. And this is not said in a sarcastic tone. The world of objects *needs* justification.

Modern mythology says that all things can be named, for the world *is* things, and language can do anything.

To primal peoples the nameless fill the world.

To the mystics of ancient history the great deity was nameless.

Simone Weil wrote: *We know by means of our intelligence that what the intelligence does not comprehend is more real than what it does comprehend.*[2]

Emily Dickinson never named her poems.

Fifty-Two: Raw Faith

Raw faith is not belief. Concepts are not involved.

It is an openness – a feeling of peaceful certitude – an unburdening – a form of life. Mystics speak of it as flowing through them in moments of grace.

Wittgenstein's longing for raw faith was expressed in a heart rending letter to his close friend, Engelmann:

...I shall be on the wrong track and I shall never find a way out of the chaos of my emotions and thoughts so long as I have not achieved the supreme and crucial insight that the discrepancy is not the fault of life as it is, but of myself as I am...

...The person who has achieved this insight and holds onto it, and who will at least try again and again throughout his life to live up to it, is religious.

...He 'has the faith', from which it does not follow by any means that he must use mythological concepts – self-created or handed down – to buttress and interpret his insight into the fundamental relationship between himself and human existence in general.[1]

Religious beliefs – concept houses for communities and hearts – provided no escape from his inner chaos and insecurity. Nor did the patterns of science and logic.

Structured solutions – generic solutions – the modern world – offered nothing.

Only shouldering responsibility...only confessing his faults.

In a very low moment Wittgenstein confessed:

...We are in a sort of hell where we can do nothing but dream, roofed in, as it were, and cut off from heaven. But if I am to be REALLY saved, – what I need is certainty – not wisdom, dreams or speculation – and this certainty is faith. And faith is faith in what is needed by my heart, my soul, not my speculative intelligence.[2]

Wittgenstein needed raw faith; the faith of his heart, not his mind.

Many autistics try to find connections to life and reality in the certainty of their 'speculative intelligence.'

They seek the soul in the concept-mind. They are pattern hunters.

Hans Christian Andersen knew about patterns.

An extended quote from Andersen's 'The Snow Queen' follows – if there are any truly Aspergian fables, 'The Snow Queen' figures among the best:

Little Kay was quite blue, nay, almost black with cold; but he did not perceive it; for she had kissed away his shivering feelings, and his heart was like a lump of ice.

…He was dragging about some sharp, flat pieces of ice, and placing them in all manner of ways, for he wanted to make something out of them…

…This was the ice-game of reason. In his eyes the figures were very remarkable, and of the highest importance – owing to the little glass sliver that still stuck in his eye.

…He composed complete figures that formed a written word, but he never could manage to form the word he wanted, which was 'Eternity.'

…And the Snow-Queen had said: 'If you can find out this figure, you shall be your own master, and I'll give you the whole world, besides a new pair of skates.'

…but he could not accomplish it.[3]

In the end only the love of a dear friend could save little Kay… and it did.

In his descriptions of Native American life, Gabriel Horn noted that civilized man was insulated from reality; no longer able to sense its depths.[4]

Autistics are insulated by their wiring. Victims are insulated by their injuries. The proud who are not also humble are insulated by their inability to confess. The civilized are insulated by their civilization.

In a way, raw faith is the opposite of insulation.

Decades ago, Carl Delacato studied hundreds of severe cases of childhood autism.

Some of the children repetitively bit their hands.

He hypothesized that they were trying to *open a channel* between their hands and their brains – that they were unconsciously trying to treat themselves.

He applied the therapy of rubbing and brushing their hands. This halted the hand biting.

He applied this idea successfully in other cases, and noted that once the obsession was gently supplanted, the children were able to attend to their lessons and to learn.[5]

It Delacato is right, perhaps Wittgenstein's later work – writing down tens of thousands of remarks – consisted largely of an unconscious treatment – the attempt to open a number of neural channels...

...or in less clinical terms to scratch the detail of life – the life in every remark that is not seen *first* as a description of a fact...

...and to show the flaws and limitations of his own reasoning, knowledge and character – that is, to make an extended confession.

Fifty-Three: Raw Religion

Raw religion is very old – the opposite of explanation, a life of raw faith, a covenant with the nameless. It is one path – it is by no means the only path.

Raw religion is experienced. It is a gift. It is received, not grasped.

It is not yours to own. It is better than you – higher than you.

It is deeper than concepts. It is a part of gift world.

It is hard to imagine a completely raw religion. It is easier to hold on to the deep life of one's storied religion and its structures, rituals and close community…

…or to blend one's ancient stories with the raw.

Raised in a community of stories, the stories become one's living world.

Yet there are other living worlds.

Imagine someone asking, 'Are you a Christian?' and responding, 'That is not for me to say.'

That brief moment of response is a different world.

High functioning autistics develop their conceptual, social mentalities very late. When they are young, they may experience life directly…

…they may experience raw religious feelings well into their teens, and later. They may pine for the pure, sacred world of their youth and resent being removed and dumped into the flat concept world.

Donna Williams wrote that she was born alienated from the world. That is the autistic way.

But she also noted that being forced to respond to the domesticated world alienated her *from herself* – from her true nature.

Most people would call this 'true nature' her feral nature, but Donna and many other autistics are adamant about the damage done when one is required to develop by being force fit.

...so many attempts are made by well-meaning people to drag children's consciousness into the so-called complexities of 'the world' without first asking to what extent that world is worthy of them.[1]

One college student, an avowed Christian named Crocus, diagnosed with some of the symptoms of autism, wrote that he had experienced God in a *physically palpable, incarnational way...*[2]

...A God who can live with the wonder and horror of being human...

...this incarnational, relational faith that is deeply embedded in who I am has always been at odds with institutions that seek to control and order this God of mine...

...Institutions that have sought to play God—a lonely, stereotypically 'autistic' deity with more concern for modifying behavior or following a seemingly arbitrary rule than in seeking a Power outside of themselves to change their heart and mine.

...(God) had been misunderstood, even rejected, by His own people when He was human.[3]

And all of this may sound blasphemous to those who *see* God *as* a power threatened...

...a vulnerable authority...a vulnerable structure.

In the film *City Lights* Charlie Chaplin's Little Tramp fell asleep in the arms of a statue of peace and prosperity, and when the covering was removed, the citizens were outraged.

He saw in the statue the *invitation* of welcoming arms. They saw the image of something so important, that the image must be protected.

He responded to a gesture, they worshipped a symbol.

Each had a certain way of seeing, and each was blind to the life and spirit sensed by the other.

...excellent comedy, or tragedy, depending on how you see it.

Temple Grandin wrote that because her thoughts were logical, not emotional, she could entertain theories but not faith.[4]

However, she certainly experienced raw religious feelings, and in situations one might not expect – as when tearing out a shackle hoist system…

…time stopped, reality fell away, and she was *one with the universe*.[5]

The fact that most people do not, in general, recognize a life of deeply affective personal experiences as a religion says volumes about the predominant culture, where religion is domesticated, not raw…

…where God is *distant* – he sets up rules to bind the tribe that has grown too large to be a family…

…like the autistic brain that has grown too fast in childhood, so deep instincts are missing, and rules must substitute for life.

Raw religion carries with it transcendent feelings, and sometimes notions of the mystical.

Einstein cherished his feelings of mystical union, but was harshly critical of mystical beliefs and fads (séances, disembodied spirits, etc.)[6,7]

Donna Williams wrote: *For me, God is that internal self where we cannot go with consciousness and mind…*[8]

There are thousands of glimpses of raw religion in the remarks of ancient texts, like the Bible and the Upanishads.

Zen Buddhism is one form of raw religion. The student requests wise advice from his master. The master slaps the student, 'You settle for second hand wisdom!'

The Tao Te Ching presents another form of raw religion:

The Tao which can be expressed in words is not the eternal Tao…

Ceaseless in action, it cannot be named…

…the law of Tao is its own spontaneity…as soon as Tao creates order, it becomes nameable.[9]

Sufism, in many ways, is raw. The Sufi poet, Rumi, wrote:

Form is born of That which is without form…[10]

The Gnostic Gospel of Philip contains bits and pieces of yet another kind of raw religion:

Names given to worldly things are very deceptive...

...Faith receives, love gives...[11]

...but the Gospel of Thomas is richly raw. Jesus does not respond to his followers questions about what to eat and how to pray or whether to fast, but speaks instead of entering the Kingdom.

When they ask him to *Show us the place where You are...*, he speaks not of a physical place, but of the light within.[12]

He continues that the sons of men are blind in their hearts and do not have sight.

They ask when the new world will come, and he responds, *What you look forward to has already come, but you do not recognize it.*[13]

...as though his disciples saw only a literal world where every kingdom was a place, and every act was governed by rules...

...and they lived in this strange, literal world and cherished it... invited by reality as if to a wedding, but ignoring it.

He speaks as if they were autistic and they loved what autism, in its blindness and confusion, grasps for so very desperately – rules of conduct and social order.

Jesus said his disciples were like children who settled in a field that was not theirs.

...

Is this the end of the story? Only for some. Reality is larger than a single path, deeper than a single view. Life is deeper than theory – therefore it is manifold.

For some raw religion is only a way station...a way to open the heart – to free it from the demands of the self and the imagery limited by concepts.

...so that faith in *someone* or *something* might then be unfettered, naïve, and in the best way, fully immature...

...loving, selfless, boundless and pure...childlike, innocent...

...some would say, the substance of God.

Fifty-Four: Four Worlds

Imagine a succession of four worlds.

They begin in silence and move towards sound.

They are, in sequence, the four worlds of one growing, maturing autistic mind. They are also, in part, the strange story of modern society.

Think of these four worlds as metaphors of mind and soul…and culture. They are not scientific worlds, not supported or verified by evidence.

They have been put to paper by instinct. They feel right.

The first world is a world of gray stones and pebbles, and the sun never sets. Awareness is constant.

The sun is fixed in the sky, never moving, never changing.

The sky is always blue – never a cloud.

The stones lie on the beach by an ocean, and the ocean is perfectly calm. There are no waves, not even a ripple. The water is perfectly smooth; a mirror of the sky.

The stones are dimly aware, but the awareness of each stone merges with the awareness of the other stones…the sun…the sky…the ocean; there is nothing to distinguish them.

It is a world of unity – but not a unity of parts, for only we, outsiders, see parts.

The second world is like the first, yet now differences are allowed.

…like the color of a flower or the movement of a pine bough in the wind.

In the second world there are simple *reactions*…

…like the surface of a pond reacting to a leaf that falls on its surface – producing ripples that spread outwards and gradually fade away.

There is no communication, no response, no back and forth.

The second world is reaction world – one way streets, everywhere.

Communication is shunned. This *preserves* solidarity with the world – it insures the absence of self awareness.

Response is shunned, as in the childhood autistic world of Donna Williams, where her mind could relax only if she was not forced to be made aware of herself...

...only if she was not forced to be made self-aware by responding to a gift...

The best way I could have been given things would have been for them to be placed near me with no expectation of thanks and no waiting for a response...

...To expect a thank-you or a response was to alienate me from the item that prompted the response.[1]

In the second world it is polite to receive what outsiders call a gift and *not* respond.

It is more than polite not to respond – it is sacred.

Even the simplest response would carve the gift-human in two.

The third world is the world of response.

There is self-awareness.

The third world is like the Hopi world or the Wintu world. The mind is a tribe; each part on an equal footing. There are thoughts, feelings, emotions and a sense of being an individual, but none dominates.

It is a kinship world, based on the giving and receiving of gifts.[2]

Possibilities of *connection*: When meeting a stranger in the deep woods one can fight them, kill them, surrender and become their captive, run away, trade with them, ignore them, or greet them and exchange gifts. It is the same in meeting the strangers within one's own maturing mind.

Gifts are the language of life; gifts of food, water, warmth, friendship, love, insight, creativity...mercy.

Gifts connect the mind that is a tribe.

Thoughts are given to feelings, to enrich and bond with them, like the thought of crossing a frigid stream providing the feeling before the feeling, and *this* feeling returning a new thought.

Emotions are given to identity to enrich and bond with it, like the memory of a kiss enhancing one's sense of being special, and in return, the stronger identity responding with new emotions.

Sensations of color are given to the sense of reality to enrich and bond with it, like the color of a sunrise opening the door to a more deeply felt reality.

Songs, poetry, parables and stories are gifts. They are close to life.

The Wintu third world, like some childhood autistic worlds, is a third person world – there is 'you' and 'she' but seldom 'I.'

The *world* is the center, not one's self.

The phrase, 'I'm sun burnt on the right side of my face' could never be uttered by a Wintu man. He would say, 'My north face is sun burnt,' and turning around, 'My south face is sun burnt.'[3]

The writer Kent Nerburn accompanied Dan, a Lakota elder. One day he wondered how Dan, whose vision was poor, was able to spot a buffalo on a distant ridge.

Dan explained that he had not seen the buffalo – the buffalo had shown himself.[4]

At intervals there is war between different tribes – disconnected from others, that is, connected only by power.

Yet war is more noble than barbaric, for the battles are never wholly between men. Men are part tribe and part story, part earth and part sky.

The fourth world is a world of individuals.

Social identity – one's place – is very slow to develop.

Talk is the language of the fourth world. Gifts are no longer its subtle glue.

The fourth world is filled with creative genius – art of astonishing beauty – music to amaze the soul – the works of individuals, sparkling in the night.

…and trust in the powers and life of the verbal mind – sequences of thought…

…colorful, cutting lines…ideas everywhere – evocative, beautiful, connective – within a space, but not the full space.

In the fourth world war is more barbaric than noble.

The idea of finding one's place in life by a great struggle culminating in a deep connection has disappeared. The autistic instinct for transformation has receded.

The fourth world is brimming with professionals – music, dance, science, religion, literature, education, government, repair, sports…

There are many specialists – many careers – the world is more pointillist painting than tribal patchwork.

Still, the amateur stands in the shadows alive with joy, presenting the kinship of a flat note and the humor of a forgotten word. He is forgiven for a dropped ball, and in his fallibility there is the innocent sincerity and richness of human relation.

The fourth world is a world of rights.

Simone Weil worried about this. She worried that the notion of rights has a commercial flavor – something measured – you get some, he gets some, she gets some.

'Rights talk' is used in legal claims, in contention – in contracts. A right is a quantity – an abstract object. It must be defended by force.

In the fourth world individuals have rights. They believe that placing rights at the foundation of culture is very good.

But Weil felt that making rights the foundation of a culture was a 'grave error.'[5]

What's wrong with rights as foundation? (And here it is easy to feel offended.)

Weil imagined someone being injured and crying out. The cry is innocent and sacred. It could be put into words – 'Why am I being hurt?'

But to cry out, 'I have my rights,' is to evoke contention and legalism and inhibit impulses to forgiveness and charity. It is to start a fight.

In the terms of this book, rights talk mechanizes the world, forcing it from life to object, making the foundation of culture and the reality in its train a contest of power.

Weil imagined a farmer defending his right to sell eggs at a price he chooses – a material, legal situation where the term 'rights' is appropriate.

She then compared this with a girl being forced to work in a brothel, where a protest in terms of rights would be an incredible cheapening of the soul – a reduction to a legal petition.

But the fourth world often does just this. It is stuck at the level of individuals with rights – in education, in culture, in vocabulary. It is stuck with the monarchy of the self and contests of power, and thinks it is done.

Rights emphasize personal satisfaction rather than the impersonal good – what is best.

Some years ago, a disturbing science fiction story was written that accentuated this.

In this tragic future, terrible abuses were committed on women who worked at a circus.

They consented to the abuses because they were anesthetized and well paid. But because they consented, no rights were violated, and in the logic of this fictional world, it followed that nothing was wrong.

The women did not react. They did not respond. They were inert. Even the simplest response would have carved the object-humans in two.

The women could not imagine that they possessed an intrinsic value higher than the legal value they saw in themselves.

…and their system of rights and laws, like an apathetic servant, could imagine no higher calling than to grudgingly address his master's complaints.

To Weil, thinking in terms of rights is spiritually mediocre; the sign of a confused language and the 'dimmed understanding' of a modern era.

Yes, there are great rights – great freedoms – won at great cost, held and defended. In this world they are still gravely needed. And in a world consisting *only* of individuals, powers and laws, rights are the foundation of that world.

The movement in this chapter is the way that some autistics develop and are subsequently raised – from *motionless unity…* to *reaction without response*…to the *near social world* of friends and relatives…to the *far social world* of strangers and laws – the great problem solving world of facts, talk and individuals with rights.

Weil glimpsed the possibility of an entirely different progression – a path towards participatory solitude, the sacred and the transcendent.

It may be that society must first tread on the most dangerous paths to finally arrive in Weil's idyllic world.

Imagine a man who sees himself as nothing more than a collection of rights.

He is the isolated center of the world. His respect extends to no one; especially not himself.

Disconnected, he speaks without listening. His brother complains of this, but the man is so free in his disconnection that he retorts 'Don't criticize me! You have no right!'

He is the autistic God, stumbling through the back alleys of Mount Olympus.

He utters defensive phrases like, 'The pay is good,' 'They're adults…'

…and 'No rights were violated.'

Fifty-Five: The Pilgrim

A business man from Chicago was on a trip to Atlanta, Georgia. On the last night of the trip, the night before returning home, he decided to go downtown to shop.

Perhaps he would find a nice souvenir – something to remind him of the gracious South.

He discovered a small bookstore and went inside.

Pausing to examine the books on one table, he was surprised when a woman asked, 'Are you a man of faith?'

'What?' he replied, as though catapulted into an alien world.

She pointed at the books on the table, all of which had Christian titles.

He didn't know what to say. Out of instinct, he peered into her eyes and studied them and then muttered, 'I don't know.'

The question was too rich and too deep. He thought her question must mean, 'Are you a Christian?'

It bothered the businessman that 'faith' had one meaning to her and another to him. Was it only about belonging to a community?

He returned to his hotel room and pondered her question.

The woman's world of faith was her church.

…and in his drifting mind her church seemed like the ghost of some Indian tribe, no longer living together in body, no longer sharing the same food and fire, but meeting in spirit for an hour each Sunday to reminisce – to share a little food and sing the old songs of gratitude and devotion to higher powers, and feel the warmth of community and spiritual fire.

He had seen the inviting warmth and community in her eyes. But he had also seen the tribe – the anxiety of meeting outsiders.

If he had seen in her eyes only love, he would have answered her question, 'Yes.'

The businessman felt that he had touched the truth, but he did not understand.

Like all truths without understanding, it did not stay.

The next day he returned to Chicago and to his office. He started at the beginning.

He asked himself, 'What is faith?'

He wondered if faith was trust that everything has a purpose. That seemed comforting and warm, but was that all – warmth?

He recalled a friend who had an autistic boy. The friend comforted his disabled son. He said to his son, 'Don't worry, some day it will all make sense.'

The businessman then imagined a science fiction story about a planet populated only by autistics, and their motto was, 'Don't worry, some day it will all make sense.'

The businessman then found a book that said Native Americans don't worry about such things: for them everything is sacred – the earth, the sky, animals, human beings – everything – and every human is both good and bad, and everything makes sense – it's obvious, nature shows this – in a living sense, not a mechanical sense.

But the businessman did not live in nature. His noisy, modern mind was too strong; his silent, natural mind, too weak. He wanted answers and mechanical comfort – a coherent theory – not life at the price of superstition – ancestors dotting the sky.

Besides, he couldn't live in silence like the Indians. For them the world of silence was the great community of nature. For him it was the lonely, empty world.

For the businessman, silence was either boring or terrifying – like being in the infantry – like war – silence was war.

The businessman's friends said that faith was belief, but that idea seemed to miss the mark. Words disguised so much.

Their beliefs were not really theories, not ideas to be investigated by experiment, but agreements within a group...

...and the agreements were not so much opinions but the shared realities of common actions and behaviors.

...like the social reality of a school of fish that turns and moves together, as one.

To accept without thought the gestures and movements of others – it was like joining the army to avoid the stress and competition of the rat race – or like answering 'yes' to some young evangelist who would come to the door – joining the society of the orderly and the well groomed.

It was never, 'Have faith,' but 'Have faith – join us.'

Then the image of a single fish came to mind. The fish was reaching up and touching the surface of a great and transcendent ocean…

…and somehow to the businessman this was faith – touching something that bounded the great ocean of life.

Yet the image was not enough.

He sat in his high window office in Chicago, high in a skyscraper, and gazed out at the city.

Musing over his skyscraper life he thought, 'How can I see so much and so little?'

In his search for an answer he decided to leave Chicago and journey across the world.

The businessman packed his bags and set out on a pilgrimage. He traveled to many lands.

One day he came to a remote and terribly poor village.

The inhabitants of this village had suffered from war, disease, tyranny and brutality. Many had died, all had suffered.

He remained in the village, hoping that their suffering would somehow bring him closer to life. He felt guilty for the idea.

He sat alone at night in a small hut, pondering his quest.

To find life he wondered how hard life had to be…

…so that every pain would be a connection, and every respite would be a gift.

He imagined an autistic child biting her small arm. He imagined a drug addict on the streets of Chicago. He imagined a teenage girl, dressed in black, walking down a dirt road, aimless and ungrounded, headed towards the dark city.

On his last evening in the village he met two women who were hungry and ill, dirty, rank, and covered with marks and scars. They scarcely slept. They never smiled.

He offered them some food and clean water, and together they shared his supplies.

He asked for their stories, but they refused. He asked again, but again they refused.

But something was forcing him on. 'Tell me!' he begged, 'Tell me! I need to breathe!'

Over the long dinner and well into the night they recalled their stories.

The businessman listened and absorbed their tragic lives. By the end of the evening he realized that these two women were special. They were sacred, for they had suffered more than anyone – more than anyone on the face of the Earth.

The businessman was overwhelmed. He saw them sitting quietly in their rags, by the fire.

He then asked, 'Are you women of faith?'

One woman was vehement, 'No – never!' The other replied, 'Yes, of course.'

In silence the words came to the businessman, 'I have no right to assert my beliefs – no right to argue – no matter what the answer – no matter what my beliefs! Not before these women!'

The businessman was transformed. His need for a philosophy was extinguished in the flames of the fire.

He gained a heart and surrendered his pilgrimage.

He wandered through the deserts of the world for a time, free of concerns.

And whenever someone asked him, 'Are you a man of faith?' he replied, 'I have no right. I have no right.'

The businessman returned to the United States.

He returned to his office, gazed out through his window, down at the city.

Then a wave of loneliness swept through him and he thought, 'I have to have a belief – I must have a belief – some belief – I must! I'm alone without it.'

And, in a way, so he was.

Fifty-Six: Gift World

Giving lies near the heart of reality and life. 'Sacrifice' and 'sacred' – the words are kin.

Following the autistic path, we observe the act of giving from many angles and assemble the lot into a single *children's story* and a single world – Gift World.

Gifts are complicated because they are so rarely given or accepted simply *as* gifts, as bonds that enlarge identity and the heart and move everyone towards life.

Instead they are transformed – used as means for other ends – used even to dissolve bonds.

A little girl, carrying five beautiful pearls in her hand came to a small village. She gave one pearl to each family. But there were six families in the village, so, sadly, one family received nothing.

The Winner family bragged about their gift. They placed their pearl on a satin pillow and carried it before them, tooting horns and clashing cymbals as they strutted about the tiny village, displaying their great possession.

'Clearly,' they announced, 'we are special!'

From their high position of wealth and prestige they felt that the world was their plaything – a great toy beneath their feet.

They transformed their gift into a possession more valuable to them than the gift itself – status and the entitlement to power.

One very old man in the Winner family did not brag. He saw the end of his days nearing. To him, status meant nothing. He thanked the little girl and returned to his quiet life.

The Squander family briefly thanked the little girl, but then held the pearl up to the light and gazed through it with great intensity, far into the distance, with the eyes of hawks.

They sold their pearl for a great sum of money and then spent it all as fast as they could, and when their money was gone they were shocked.

They had transformed the gift into a possession more valuable to them than the gift itself – pleasure.

Desperate, they began to buy lottery tickets, where no bond is established and no life is bestowed, but there is hope of a sort.

The Apathy family let the dog play with the pearl. She chewed on it until it cracked and broke. They didn't notice.

Nothing changed – nothing for the better, nothing for the worse, except this – they never thanked the little girl.

Perhaps they chose their apathy, for the vulnerability of receipt and new life was too much to endure. Perhaps they did so without knowing this.

The Loser family received no pearl. They felt cheated. And it was not enough to suffer an injustice.

They transformed the absence of a gift into the *mentality* of victims.

Now, like autistic children, but with connections severed by injury, they had the right to complain, fail and lash out, and to close their ears to everyone.

A very good woman in the Loser family resented the injustice – she traveled from village to village, working for equality, giving gifts to the poor, not as an innocent gesture, but as a noble means to justice and a heartfelt exercise of compassion.

Her gifts were transformed into bread, the warmth of a roof over one's head, health, strength, hope for a better future, gratitude, resentment, weakness and self-pity.

All the flaws, she felt, could be eliminated…with enough knowledge, enough compassion and fortitude…with enough effort.

Gifts of time, gifts of structure, gifts of tools, gifts of insight – they formed an endless parade of hope in her imagination and heart.

The Castle family opened their castle door a crack and snatched the pearl. They did not show their faces to the little girl but whispered through the crack, 'Got it.'

They hid their great pearl behind the castle walls. They bolted their doors and posted guards. They buried their gift in a metal box in a dark and secret corner of the castle.

The Castle brother who had received the pearl crowned himself head of the family, and the rest obeyed his orders, for in their anarchy and conflict they craved a strong leader.

Rules were instituted: no one may leave the castle. Outsiders were thieves. To speak ill of the gift was blasphemy and punishable by death.

The Castle family became Castle guards.

Their gift was holy in the way that all prisons are holy.

The Crime family was at first suspicious. They smiled and accepted the gift and politely responded, 'Thank you,' but in the strangest way – their words sounded like cardboard.

They put their pearl aside, thinking it must be a ruse. They thought the little girl wanted something in return.

They lay awake at night, wondering when she would return, worrying what she or someone else would want or demand. But she did not return.

After a time they thought well of the gift and wanted more. They prayed to heaven, they offered sacrifices; they even gave money to their priest, but to no avail.

The father and mother went out and preached to their neighbors that it was good to be generous, but their neighbors only turned their eyes askew and grinned.

The Crime family transformed their gift into the desire for more gifts.

Yet they also had a small daughter who gazed at the pearl one night and thought, 'We can't be deserving – we're the Crime family. Whoever gave us this gift must have made a mistake.'

So the next day she took the pearl and walked down the road to the village of innocents and gave it away.

Her parents were horrified. The Castle family was astonished. The Winner and Loser families shook their heads until they almost came off.

Especially concerned was the compassionate woman, who lived not in the innocence of gift world, but in a considerate world, where love is plentiful but always a logical tool.

To the eyes of these people a gift to the village of innocents was worthless – unable to transform itself into status, pleasure, power, justice, bread, or the expectation of more gifts.

'Worthless,' they cried, 'worthless.' To the eyes of these families the gift was indeed worthless, hobbled and poor – a disabled gesture.

But in the village of innocents the gesture of giving was pure, and in this way it was able to grow.

The ancient gesture of giving – innocent, vulnerable and selfless – was magnified, as was life, in all its rich and terrible poverty.

Fifty-Seven: 'That Looks Close'

One afternoon many years ago, I listened to a lecture by a philosophy professor, who said (more or less):

It's not at all clear what we really, ultimately mean by 'courage,' but we feel that the answer is there – if only we could find the right definition. ...

...we try and try...

...Of course, no one's ever found a completely satisfactory definition, but people keep adding insights...

...In a way, this is where Socrates started; this is where Western philosophy began...

...He (and his interlocutors) failed to find a satisfactory definition of courage, but at least the search for better definitions had begun.

Soon after, I attended a lecture on aphasia (problems with language and meaning due to brain damage). The lecturer described one special case of aphasia:

A women who had suffered a stroke was given the word, 'Hallo_een,' and was asked to fill in the blank...

...She struggled and struggled but couldn't guess. Her doctor said,

'How about the letter "a"?'

'No – that's not it.'

'How about the letter "b"?'

'No – that's not it.'

This went on until finally the doctor asked her about the letter 'w.'

She exclaimed, 'That's it!'

I returned to the philosophy building and announced to my advisor, 'I think philosophy is all about brain damage.'

He winced.

I began to wonder if people couldn't find all sorts of things, but kept searching. They might spend their whole lives searching.

And even when they were *shown* the answer, they might not exclaim, 'That's it!'

They might respond, 'Hmm, that looks close.'

Fifty-Eight: Professional World

Autistic children do not 'pick-up' social behavior. They must be taught. They learn it as one might learn the law – in a classroom, one law at a time.

To do so they must be little professionals.

They must organize everything in their domain, plan well into the future, pay particular attention to cause and effect, and make dispassionate decisions.

They must be well oiled machines, for *their* world is dangerous and time consuming.

Modern cultures – communities – nations – are similar.

Like autistic minds, they must have artificial structures to survive – refined, intricate but stable systems of machines, laws and rules.

To prosper they require professionals, all of whom are selflessly concerned with the long term...*planners*, who carry a dispassionate and deep understanding of a host of interrelated causes and effects – attending to detail, but caring for the whole.

Professional cultures falter when they are not good autistic minds; not professional, not dispassionate, not planning ahead, not adapting to new situations, and not aware of every angle and minute cause and effect.

The Wright brothers are role models for professional cultures and little professionals.

They loved flight – the exhilaration – freedom from the chains of the earth.

For this freedom they were willing to take risks.

They knew that they would have to test their ideas in piloted gliders – dangerous and time consuming trials.

They brilliantly chose Kitty Hawk, where the winds are strong and constant.

They planned to glide *slowly* downhill *into* the rising wind...

…so that every landing would be gentle…and every crash would be easy…

…and they could settle *nearby*, and not waste time and energy dragging their machine a great distance up a hill after every flight.

Only they thought of methodical testing. Only they realized that the tremendous power of mechanized flight requires tremendous care…and control so effortless and natural that man and aircraft form a living unity.

Everyone else rushed at some preconceived design…some urgent inspiration…where the Wright bothers let their experiments gradually decide the best design. Everyone else thought that flight was a matter of power. Everyone else thought that an aircraft was *just* a machine.

Fifty-Nine: Mask World

Autism is a mask, and living with autism is living in mask world.

A mask breaks eye contact.

It hides a face from recognition.

It breaks the connections of belonging and status. How do you greet a mask?

Surrounded by masks, the social world crumbles.

The wearer of the mask is the mask, a caricature – a one dimensional being – a frozen face – a rule...

Hidden, the wearer is free and dangerous – free to reach other realms, free to transform...

...an angel – a beast – a human – a dream.

Sixty: Remarks

Why is this book written as a collection of remarks?

It must be frustrating for the reader to see the world in fragments. Especially to read a remark and wonder whether it connects to the remarks that immediately precede and follow it – we are so accustomed to the sequential style.

In sequence, we can glide over and forget, as if each remark were a wave on an ocean over which we were smoothly sailing.

That style has its place.

By contrast, the style of this book encourages the reader to pause and respect each thought on its own merits – not to always see a thought as part of a tight sequence.

In this way each thought – each instant of life – may also be seen as an end in itself, not just as a means to an end, not just as a tool.

It is possible to pause and forget the accumulation of information, pause and ponder the remark…like slowly turning over a stone in one's hands.

A remark can stand alone, or it can connect to others. We are not telling it what to do. A remark is free – not in a box or a bubble.

Each remark might *connect* in a rich way, and not just to other remarks.

Imagine Wittgenstein in his study, alone, desperately hunting for life. He suddenly exclaims, 'The color of green eyes cannot be painted on a wall.'

This connects.

'*Connects*? Don't you mean disconnects? The color of green eyes is different – unique. That's what the remark implies.'

No. Significance that deeply felt is life – it is not alone. You are abstracting a concept, not experiencing it. You are reading for information, not for life.

The color of green eyes – experienced, entered into – is life itself.

Have you read *every* remark in this book only for information?

Look for multiplicity in remarks – for information *and* life.

'So we have a relationship of sorts – with green eyes?'

Consider – one man says there are two *things*: tall prairie grass and the blowing wind.

Another says there is a *relationship* between the wind and the grass.

A third says the wind *lives* in the grass.

A fourth is silent; he stands on the hill. But you see him as an object, alone.

In reading only remarks, it will seem to some that the question is put: 'Will you abandon your arguments and conclusions?' (as though they were ornaments or possessions).

'Where is the argument so that I can dispute it?'

Do you see the world then – always – as a collection of conclusions?

'Where are the rules so that I may follow them?'

Perhaps you are accustomed to reading books that try to simplify for some purpose – tool books. We are not here to simplify.

The author once told a long story about his life to a young woman. She listened carefully and then said, 'I don't think I can summarize that in a few words. I can't simplify it and I don't think I should.'

It's fun to note all the occurrences of words like 'grasp,' 'celebrate,' 'idolatry,' and a hundred others in this book, and try to tie them into gossamer stories.

Perhaps that is what you imagined.

Well, these connections are rich, too.

And there are subtler kinds.

Imagine seeing a remark as two things at the same time – like seeing an antique child's sled, with rusted runners, gray wood and faded paint, and imagining the young child who played on it long ago.

Imagine seeing the great age and the innocent youth, together.

When you read the remarks of an ancient figure of life, do you see the spark of youth in his words, and his antiquated culture – all at once – like a child on a rusty gray sled?

In multiplicity there is life.

Imagine meeting a pretty young woman, and seeing her as four and twenty-four and ninety-four, all at the same time.

You see this in her face, just as you see emotions. Does this change the significance of her remarks? Of her appearance?

Perhaps now she is more than an abstraction, for abstractions have no multiplicity.

It must be frustrating to read an isolated remark, for the intention is sometimes unclear.

…a burden to a culture whose conclusions are automatic and easy.

In this book the significance must be supplied by the reader.

It forces one to be responsible for the remark.

It forces one to grow up in a way that this culture resists.

It's like being forced off the road. Where do you drive? The road made it so easy.

Remarks lack conclusions. They are like fables without a moral attached.

They live in a world where, out of respect, one *must* pause.

In a book of fiction one is absorbed in the story – the pages disappear, the ink disappears – the story becomes the world. That is story absorption – absorption in the close continuity of sentences that are not remarks. It is absorption in a form of life.

In a book of non-fiction, one is absorbed in a theory – the pages disappear, the ink disappears, and the theory becomes the world.

In a book of remarks, the remarks cluster around themes like life or gifts or striving to see, and one is absorbed in these themes. The pages disappear, the ink disappears, and the themes become the world.

Imagine a rare and beautiful disorder called 'anti-autism' – or perhaps 'super-autism.'

People with this 'disorder' see reality as life.

…not as alive – it has nothing to do with animism.

They see a face in all things, so to speak – yet not a face. They keep speaking of life when others see nothing but objects and people. They live in a world spoken of by ancient figures of life.

How do they behave? Do they act differently?

Perhaps they would touch the world with gentler hands.

Perhaps they would be forced to speak in strange similes: 'His gift was as the living water,' and so on.

Some would point to the differences between their world and ours.

Their world is the world of covenants, lived in multiplicity and unity.

A covenant is wordless, a contract is written.

A covenant is lived, a contract is signed.

A covenant is felt, a contract is seen.

A covenant is an end in itself, a contract is a means to an end.

A covenant is based on trust, a contract on distrust.

A covenant listens. A contract has no ears.

A covenant lives on vulnerability, a contract on invulnerability.

A covenant requires courage and faith, a contract requires fear.

A covenant allows as much freedom to the other as they need; a contract restricts the other's freedom for one's own needs.

How much freedom does reality need?

Friendship and love are covenants.

Parables are covenants, as are many ancient poems and stories.

...they are examples of life and calls to life, like the mother who calls to her autistic child.

...like a hand extended. Not like an unknown object whose motion must be dissected.

They are movements of life, far more than information.

They are gestures in words.

Like remarks.

Sixty-One: Tony

We end this book with a story – a short piece about a boy named Tony, and another path from object to life (not a thinly veiled tale about the author).

When Tony was young he was usually very kind, but sometimes he was remarkably thoughtless and rude. On these occasions he used people; mostly his friends or family, but sometimes strangers.

When he was three and his mother took him to the grocery store, he stepped on a woman's foot to reach what he wanted. He may have heard her cry, but if he did he ignored it.

He ignored her cry because he wanted something badly, and when he wanted something *that* much, the rest of the world disappeared.

When he was four he sat in a small red wagon and *ordered* his best friend to pull him around in a circle. His friend replied, 'I'm not your servant.'

Tony's parents were patient with him because they understood his nature.

When he was six his parents took him to the movies. Impatient from waiting in line, he commanded the woman in front to move. His mother gently scolded him, 'That's not what you really want to say, is it?'

He didn't understand…of course that was what he wanted to say. He said it, didn't he?

Tony spent his youth making mistakes like these, and when his parents weren't there to correct him, he managed to offend a lot of people.

When he was fourteen and in school, Tony's assignment was to write an essay. He completed the essay and was pleased with his effort.

But his teacher returned his work with the remark, 'You can do better.'

Tony complained, 'I tried as hard as I could – I can't do any better!'

'No,' she replied, 'I don't want you to work harder – I want you to look closer. Look inside yourself. That's not what you really want to say, is it?'

Tony grimaced. He explained that he had high-functioning autism, and that it was hard for autistics to put their thoughts and feelings into words.

She shook her head and replied, 'That's not what I meant.'

A few years later Tony got a summer job in a paper factory, working a fork lift. He enjoyed moving things around. He liked putting things in order.

Finishing his duties one morning he sat down to lunch with some of his co-workers.

A man at the table named Frank was telling a story about a baseball game. As Frank finished his story he smiled and said, 'And then that guy just sailed one over the fence – I swear to God!'

Everyone at the table appreciated the story, but Tony listened a little too closely. He asked Frank, 'What do you mean when you swear by God? Does it mean that people will believe you more? Is God like the gold standard? What about his other uses?'

Not a word – Frank clammed up – they all clammed up. Silence at the table. You couldn't have done better with a sign over the door commanding the same.

Everyone's mind momentarily went blank, save for Tony's.

To his mind came the image of a great blue sky and a shining hardware store poised on a white cloud, and the store had a smiling face.

But the silence at the table informed Tony that he had blundered once again.

He missed the friendly mood of the lunch room and the easy character of Frank's story.

He missed the casual, offhand nature of Frank's concluding remark about God. The atmosphere – the human context – had simply floated by.

To Tony remarks about ultimate things were deadly serious. They were about reality. They were literal. They were about the big picture. What could be more important?

To Tony it was wrong to swear by God or swear by heaven, for it transformed these ultimates into mere things – mere tools, making religion nothing more than an instruction book for using tools in the sky.

Was this all there was to civilization? Tool use? Endless domestication?

Maybe Frank had to name the nameless to make it real. Maybe he *had* to.

Tony repeated to himself, 'Not everything is a tool, not everything is a possession.'

He finished work that day and went home.

He was angry with Frank and himself, and puzzled and angry with the world.

Finally he fell asleep.

The next day, a woman who had eaten with Tony and Frank approached Tony and whispered, 'I heard your question about God yesterday. I didn't want to speak in front of everyone, but now that we're alone I'll tell you what I believe.'

Tony instinctively drew back. The image of a heart drawing lines bore into his mind, but he tried to be clever and replied, 'That's not what you really want to say, is it?'

The woman was baffled, 'I don't understand.'

'You can do better than that,' offered Tony.

He was confusing her – interrupting her. She ignored his strange remarks and began.

She disclosed her deepest feelings, illuminating the darkest corners of her life.

She confessed the terrible, painful errors of her youth…her many regrets…

…and then poured forth images of repentance, acceptance, forgiveness, love and mercy…

She revealed her true heart.

Tony listened, and as he listened he began to see. He saw her now not as a woman needing direction, not as an object in need of repair. He saw, standing before him, the plain, sacred, human soul – the genuine soul, the soul of flaws and tears.

He grew eyes to see.

...and then she swore by heaven that everything she said was true, and she swore by God that her church was the only true church, and that her religion was the only true religion, for through them alone had she been healed. And she prayed before him and displayed her piety...

...and she encased all her wounds and all of her healings in a great and sacred story, and she put this story in a great and sacred box and closed the lid to this box and called it 'the truth.'

When she finished, Tony stood silently for a moment.

Then in gratitude he uttered, 'I feel unworthy of your confidence.'

In his mind he saw an image of himself standing at the end of the long, long line of humanity.

She wiped her eyes and asked him what he meant when he said that she could do better.

Tony replied, 'Never mind. Forget what I said. I was anxious. I just wanted something so bad – the rest of the world disappeared...I don't know anything. I'm sorry.'

The woman nodded and then apologized for imposing on Tony. He gently grasped her hand and she smiled.

He returned her smile with the words, 'At your service.'

About the Author

David Duncan lives in upstate New York.

He has two older sisters, both married, who live in New England.

His father, recently deceased, was a creative, humorous and energetic writer who worked many years in advertising, delighted in books of facts and collected over a thousand books on American history. A devoted family man and political activist, when he retired he wrote and published several history books – most of them picture books.

According to his mother, when David was very young, he was the most placid child she had ever seen.

He never said, 'I'm bored,' or 'What do I do?' He was content playing with his toys.

His kindergarten teacher reported that he had difficulty socializing, but this passed.

As a youth he was quite normal and usually happy – he enjoyed playing with kites and balsa wood airplanes and improving their performance.

He liked to play with his friends and sit in the branches of a maple tree in his yard and day dream.

He did not understand the tendency of his classmates in grade school to want to socialize with more than one or two people or to follow the dictates of a group or some leader. That was an alien world.

He was thrown out of the cub scouts for imitating the den father – David did not care for the arbitrary exercise of authority by adults, whatsoever.

He loved watching the *Twilight Zone* with his sister, and to this day admires the stories that were written or co-written by Rod Serling.

Only after writing this book did the author realize why Rod Serling's stories are so extraordinarily appealing…

…like the story of the astronauts who return to Earth but feel that they don't quite belong…

…and the New York businessman unable to stand the stress of the modern world, who hungers for an idyllic past…

…the used car salesman who is forced to tell the truth by a car – a haunted mechanism…

…the murderous cowboy who is transported in time but finds modern life is far too confused – far too noisy…

…the perpetually annoyed and annoying businessman who uses his power of concentration to make everyone else disappear, but eventually his conscience returns…

…an alien (appearing to be human) who arrives in a small Mexican village, bringing a great gift for humanity. By accident, he kills someone. The villagers lack faith and he is killed. They lose the great gift…

…a man who hallucinates being lost in an empty town. In reality he is an astronaut trapped in an isolation booth, being trained for future missions in a far larger, far emptier space…

…the aging movie star who has departed reality, living the fiction of a life in the ritualized imagery of her antiquated films…

…the woman who feels trapped in a house only to discover that she is a robot, unable to fully love…

…the woman pursued by a hitchhiker. Terrified by the prospect of death, she discovers that she has been dead all along…

…the pretty young woman lost among shoppers in a department store, who finally recalls that she is a mannequin. For a moment she imagined that she was real.

…the blissfully happy but odd young man who is magically presented with a stable life and occupation, but relinquishes these gifts to return to the joy of his innate eccentricities…

…the peddler in an old western town who pretends to resurrect the dead, but whose service is refused because the townspeople prefer the dead as they are…

…the dying man who requires his greedy inheritors to wear grotesque masks. They inherit every penny of his wealth, but their faces become the masks.

...the convict confined to a lonely desert world. He happily marries a robotic woman.

...the group of utopians who long ago searched for a perfect world, but their spaceship crashed on a harsh and alien planet. An iron-fisted leader helps them to survive. When another ship from Earth finally arrives, allowing them to escape, he desperately tries to hold onto them, appealing to their immaturity and dependence – calling them his children. He fails and retreats to the isolation and power of his barren cave...

...the talkative young man who accepts a wager to be silent for a year – locked in a glass room...

...the man whose magic watch stops time. This is a joy and a wonder, but then the watch breaks, freezing the eternal moment, and all companionship is lost...

...the field officer in battle, whose terrible blood thirst transforms into mercy only after he is forced to see through the eyes of his enemy...

...the five characters stranded in a strange cylindrical chamber, who finally discover that they are dolls in a Christmas donation barrel – inanimate, caricatured objects – gifts in a lonely, hollow, symmetric world...

...the corporate boss who replaces all of his employees with machines, but because of his obsession, the board of directors replace him with a robot.

...a terrifying episode in which a ventriloquist is controlled by his smiling wooden dummy...

...the man who stands against the tyranny of a fascist state, and shows by his courage that the tyrant is only a bully and the bully is only a coward...

...the drunk who loves most to give and magically transforms into Santa Claus...

...and the astronauts who think that they are stranded and alone on an alien planet, but in reality they are at home, on Earth.

Serling displayed no clinical traits of Asperger's or autism.

At the end of grade school, asking himself what he planned to do with his life, the author of this book responded, 'It won't be like anything anyone else does; I may as well be living on another planet.'

The idea of being born in the wrong century or placed on the wrong planet haunted him from then on.

In the 7th and 8th grades he was astonished by the strange behavior of his peers. He greatly preferred collecting model airplanes to school.

To this day he feels that biplanes have a certain charm to them; hand crafted, slow, fragile craft, struggling to fly.

He was a poor student early in high school, flunking Spanish and nearly flunking math. He was assigned a math tutor.

His father said, 'You seem to approach every problem as though it's completely new.'

High School seemed to revolve around groups, status and competition – clubs, teams, bands, contests, grades…

He ignored it. The world outside was a great clamor. The world inside was magic.

The author's favorite subjects were Art and English. He found that making little abstract sculptures like those of Henry Moore was easy – amorphous human forms, waiting to be defined.

His performance in school was 'spiky' and he received mediocre grades. His sister complained that he never studied. Once in a while something would catch his interest, like the idea of designing a better sun-dial, and he would devote all his time and energy to that project.

He learned that many of his classmates found a place in the world and formed an identity by joining with others, in shop or French club, or band or the baseball team…

But the author's interests were personal, and his identity was a matter of following an internal compass.

To the author, societies, clubs and teams, no matter how ostensibly enjoyable or interesting, always carried the tinge of the cult – the lessening of the soul.

When his friends asked him what he wanted to be, he joked – 'I just want to understand. My talent is not understanding.'

His mother liked church; his father didn't care to be lectured to. The author liked the feel of church but intensely disliked the idea of being accepted into a community on condition of agreeing with them.

His senior year in high school the author built a telescope, staying out late each clear night to view the beautiful sky.

He postponed going to college for a year, explaining to his parents that his brain needed time to mature.

He worked as a stock boy in a department store, packed boxes in a warehouse, picked up garbage and gave planetarium shows to the public on weekends.

He discovered great joy in music and taught himself how to play acoustic guitar by ear in a few months (it was impossible to *read* guitar music).

In college he majored in astronomy until learning that modern astronomers don't much look at the sky; they stare at computer monitors.

He switched majors and received a bachelor's in physics from Boston University in 1976.

As a senior he was warned that it was unhealthy to concentrate for so long (eight hours). One *should* on occasion get up and take a break.

His good friend Theo Bloom, with whom he had shared a dormitory suite for a year, laughed until he almost keeled over when Dave remarked, 'My parents said your last name sounds Jewish – are you Jewish?'

He had no sense for and no interest in such distinctions.

His friends complained that sometimes he walked by in a kind of haze – more than once they yelled unsuccessfully to get his attention as he passed by, oblivious.

Theo gave the author a book about philosophy which included a chapter on an eccentric fellow – someone named Wittgenstein.

The author's girlfriend gave him the poems of Tennyson.

The author memorized just one of Tennyson's poems – the only poem he ever put to memory:

Flower in the crannied wall,
I pluck you from the crannies;
Hold you here, root and all, in my hand,
Little flower – but if I could understand
What you are, root and all, and all in all,
I should know what God and man is.

The author came close to marrying his girlfriend. She complained that when something stressful happened he often stared off into the distance, as though she wasn't there. 'You're usually carefree Dave, but sometimes you are so serious, and I lose you!'

In the summer after his junior year in college, the author wrote a small, unpublished book on Fourier Series and Integrals in the form of an illustrated dialogue, not because he understood the subject, but because he had to explain it to himself with diagrams and dialogue.

The idea in this kind of mathematics is to build the whole out of an infinity of smaller pieces, and not forget the pieces.

In his senior year he decided to mimic Richard Feynman's style in all his physics homework assignments. (Feynman was refreshingly candid and tried to motivate every step of his work.)

The author's professor, Wolfgang Franzen, wrote a recommendation praising the way he approached every problem – 'David, I like the way you think,' and he was, perhaps on these false pretenses, accepted into the graduate physics program at Dartmouth.

The classes were too stressful and abstract, and after handing in 50, then 60, then 70 pages of equations for each week's homework in physics, he dropped out.

His old advisor, John Stachel, offered him a part time job sorting Einstein's papers down in Princeton.

He visited, and was thrilled to speak with Helen Dukas, Einstein's secretary, but Stachel noted the minimal salary and advised the author: 'Be practical – don't take the job.'

The author made a great mistake – he followed this advice. He taught for one year at a private school in rural New York State.

One of the women there called him 'Chippy,' after the movie, *Goodbye Mr. Chips*.

Returning to Dartmouth, he was very lucky to find a professor in the physics department, Dr. John Kidder, as kind and intelligent a man as ever lived (Kidder recently passed away).

Dr. Kidder had built a device to flicker lights of different hues at different rates and intensities, and he left it to the young graduate student to figure out why humans see strange things when they stare at flickering lights.

We see hue shifts – changes in color – because of different kinds of sensory inhibitions in the retina.

The author was given for his office the entire optics lab – lenses, mirrors, prisms, spinning wheels, lights, filters, colors by the bucketful, and nearby, a great library of old books amidst the great forests of New England, and best of all, time to ponder and solve the mysteries of perception.

Flickering a light in just the right way will allow (some) color blind people to actually distinguish different colors – to lose their blindness.

The author explained a few phenomena of flickering color perception and proposed a new optical flow invariant (a signal from the eye to the brain indicating how fast one is moving past nearby objects) for which he received a Master's in physics.

He did not attend graduation – too much fuss…and the pretense of a reward for learning when he felt that still, he understood nothing.

A few months later he found a job in Minnesota.

He worked on computer graphics and image processing for Honeywell avionics, and for a time, under their auspices, on the Mars Lander program for NASA.

The main concern was how to get a computer to recognize objects.

The difficulty was figuring out how to put primitive image fragments and features together so as to recognize different objects, regardless of orientation, distance or partial occlusion – a search for invariants.

It was a pleasant way to earn a living.

While close to friends and family, he displayed in his apartment no photos of people – faces were too distracting.

In his spare time the author thought about another interest: explanation. He made charts that formalized the structures of explanation, showing every conceivable way of thinking about or visualizing each topic that came to mind.

Most professors easily jump about in their explanations of a single phenomenon –'Here is a picture…now a diagram…now an equation…now another equation in a different space…' but to the author each form of explanation was a completely different world…a new reality – a whole – not just another way of seeing.

The author also researched what the world looked like in all wavelengths. He wanted to visualize the full spectral world, not peek through some small visible window.

We sparkle in coherent radar, we glow in infrared, we are black in ultra-violet, and grainy in gamma rays.

The author invented a tomography based method for obtaining images at sub-pixel resolution, in effect, seeing more detail by viewing from all angles.

For a year or two he designed t-shirt logos for all the engineers in image processing. The first design was an indistinct acronym – a pattern half buried in visual noise.

His boss once prohibited him from going on a business trip because a co-worker warned the boss, 'Dave won't be able to tell the customer how wonderful our product is and keep a straight face.'

The author usually ate lunch with co-workers who were from China, Iran, Lebanon and Peru, because he felt more at home with them. With his friend Hatem Nasr he edited a one page weekly satire on life and politics at Honeywell.

They agreed that he didn't belong in Minnesota – they suggested many countries where he might better fit in – Peru, Brazil, Vietnam, Scotland, Israel, Turkey, England, Lebanon…

The author enjoyed making up stories about a clever dog named Guido for the children of his friend Bill Larson. Guido was asked whether Rome was really built in a day. He found the answer in an ancient text, but it was a hot day – he drooled on the passage, and so to this day, no one knows the truth of the matter.

The author had a wonderful time talking with his friend Karl Fant about revolutionizing computer science.

'Karl and Dave' (as the waitresses called them) went to the same restaurant for lunch each week for years, chatting about everything.

Karl wagged his finger, 'Nobody understands computers correctly – the foundations of computer science are completely misguided.' Dave wagged back, 'Nobody understands anything correctly.' They were peas in a pod.

…except that Karl was exasperated when he asked Dave for the title or author of a book, and Dave replied, 'You mean the green one with the large white letters or the purple one that smells bad?'

Dave thought in colors. He remembered his books by their color, shape, size, texture and smell, not by titles or authors…and streets not by their names but by pictures in his head.

In the 80's the author decided to study philosophy of science at the University of Minnesota part time, eventually obtaining a doctorate in philosophy.

At first he considered writing a dissertation about Mach's Principle – the idea that nature is relational – that things that seem to be absolute (like mass) are not, for their nature depends essentially on context and interaction. The math was too hard, and he had nothing important to say.

The author's dissertation was finally about Wittgenstein and how scientific explanation could not be reduced to logic (as many philosophers then believed).

It was a good choice of topic because Wittgenstein was deep and, as far as the author was concerned, no one explained anything completely; that is, few scientists seemed to care about the boundaries where scientific explanations failed.

They liked to *use* tools, not to question them.

The author loved looking into the depths for answers, but he had no taste for the academy. To his ears, philosophical words like 'realist,' 'metaphysical,' and 'objectivism,' were painful. They felt unreal.

The author loved reality. Theory worship and the social ladder of University life seemed pointed in exactly the wrong way.

Besides, the idea of more competition, more proving of oneself, and more stress was too much.

For two years the author worked part time on technology transfer for the blind and disabled, and helped with infant perception studies on strabismus (lazy eye).

In the 90's he worked part time as a consultant, designing clockless (self-timed) computer logic for Karl's small company, Theseus Logic.

All of the author's technical work was done on 2' x 3' sheets of paper – he loved the big picture, literally. To write on a large rock face – that would have been heaven.

He holds the patent on the 'Null-Convention Full Adder' – a clockless computer device which works by automatically alternating between states of operation and states where it clears itself of all data, to momentarily rest. (Karl initiated this idea.)

Compared to the full adders in current computers, they save a lot of energy.

This is far from a complete or representative summary of the author's life, but that some elements are absent is right and good. It is a superficial, purposely incomplete 'whiff of autism' – a partial, diagnostic biography – not an accurate one.

The author still feels that he understands almost nothing, but now the less he understands the better.

He is and always has been a creature of instinct.

For 30 years the author collected books by or about Einstein, Wittgenstein, David Bohm, Simone Weil, Gabriel Marcel, Native Americans and Sufis, because he liked the way they thought.

For the past two decades, before learning about autism or Asperger's, he (privately) wrote fables and short stories about unusual topics…compelling ideas that bubbled up…

...like the story of the little girl whose language is silence...but her silence frightens others...

...children of the distant future, playing in the dark with flashlights, illuminating scary toy beasts of the past – the tyrannosaurus, the allosaurus and *humans*...

...an angel who is sent to purgatory to suffer because he does not appreciate the feel of wooden steps...

...a rabbit who, because he is nameless, is more powerful than a fox...

...a fox who thinks he is cleverer than the other animals for he sees in the rocks every crevice and knows the motion of every star. But then he sees the ocean.

...a young man who works at a rectangular computer on a rectangular desk in a cubicle in a square building, drives a boxy car, lives in a cellular apartment, watches TV on a box, discovers he's an android, and falls in love with a woman who collects cubist paintings...

...a mirror maker who prefers looking in mirrors to looking at people directly. He adds mirror after mirror and forms a cascade of reflections, multiplying the distortions of the images until someone he knows appears as a monstrosity. The mirror maker shatters his mirrors and regains reality...

...a bird who makes too many rules for itself...

...a fish who asks too many questions, who wants to be filled with answers but decides it is better to be filled by nature...

...frog twins who debate whether dreams are real...

...an Indian elder who speaks of the magic of being young and old at the same time...

...two college students who share their lives by wearing glasses that transmit what the other is seeing...

...a woman who invents a way for computers to morph images of television personalities into animal caricatures – the hero becomes a lion, the coward becomes a chicken...but she gets into trouble...

...a Buster Keaton-like character who makes incredibly elaborate plans to win the hand of his girl...

...a father and son who exchange their covenant for a contract...

...a sumptuous elfin dinner, where sprites, trolls and humans are invited to the table, but the humans can't eat and think simultaneously...

...an Appalachian woodsman who concentrates with such extraordinary power that he wins a marksmanship contest indirectly, by disturbing a bird with a pea-shooter...

...a Soviet scientist who invents a way to make emotions visible – but they are alive...

...a Latino gardener who is frozen and stored away because he feels that he doesn't belong in this time, but ironically the distant future is populated with an advanced species that ministers to him as veterinarians would to a dog...

...an ex-con who keeps being given gifts until he finally understands the act of giving...

...an acorn that is worried because his shell is cracking – but the acorn is only becoming a tree.

Notes

One: Introduction

1.1. Rumi, Maulana Jalalu-'d-din Muhammad. *The Masnavi I Ma'navi*. (1898). E.H. Whinfield (trans.). book VI, story IX. <www.sacred-texts.com>. These lines were a marvelous shock. I had fancied myself clever for making an analogy with color-blindness later in this chapter, but subsequently discovered that Rumi had preceded me by over 700 years. His insight now serves as an epigraph for the chapter and the book.

1.2. Fitzgerald, M. (2005). *The Genesis of Artistic Creativity: Asperger's syndrome and the arts*. London: Jessica Kingsley Publishers.

1.3. Weil, S. (1997). *Gravity and Grace*. NY: Routledge, p.11.

1.4. French, A.P., (Ed.). (1979). *Einstein: A centenary volume*. Cambridge, MA: Harvard University Press, p.153. Original source: Seelig, C. (1956). *Albert Einstein: A documentary biography*. M. Savill (trans.). London: Staples Press.

1.5. Wittgenstein, L. (1980). *Culture and Value*. G.H. von Wright (Ed.). P. Winch (trans.). Chicago: University of Chicago Press, p.18e.

Three: The City Under Repair

3.1. Osborne, L. (2002). *American Normal*. NY: Copernicus Books, pp.x, 5.

3.2. Fitzgerald, M. (2005). *The Genesis of Artistic Creativity: Asperger's syndrome and the arts*. London: Jessica Kingsley Publishers.

3.3. Stillman, W. (2006). *Autism and the God Connection*. Naperville, IL: Sourcebooks.

3.4. Hewetson, A. (2002). *The Stolen Child*. Westport, CT: Bergin & Garvey. This is an excellent, modern survey of autism.

3.5. Paradiz, V. (2002). *Elijah's Cup: A family's journey into the community and culture of high-functioning autism and Asperger's syndrome*. NY: Free Press, pp.143, 147.

Four: Raw World

4.1. Snyder, A.W. & Mitchell, D.J., Is integer arithmetic fundamental to mental processing?: The mind's secret arithmetic, *Proc Roy Soc Edinb B Biol*, 266, (1999): 587-592.

4.2. Snyder, A.W., Bossomaier, T. & Mitchell, D.J., Concept formation: 'Object' attributes dynamically inhibited from conscious awareness, *J Integr Neurosci*, 3(1), (2004): 31-46.

4.3 Sloman, S. (2005). *Causal Models: How people think about the world and its alternatives.* Oxford: Oxford University Press. This book is an excellent introduction to the ways in which people represent and simplify the world.

4.4. Ibid. ref.2. Original source is Pascalis, O., de Haan, M. & Nelson, C.A. Is face processing species-specific during the first year of life?, *Science*, 296, (2002): 1321-1323.

4.5. Ibid. ref.2. Original sources are (1) Cheour, M., Ceponiene, R., Lehtokoski, A., Luuk, A. Allik, J., Alho, K. & Naatanen, R., Development of language-specific phoneme representations in the infant brain, *Nat Neurosci*, 1, (1998): 351-353, and (2) Kuhl, P.K., Williams, K.A., Lacerda, F., Stevens, K.N. & Lindblom, B., Linguistic experience alters phonetic perception in infants by 6 months of age. *Science*, 255, (1992): 606-608.

4.6. Ibid. ref.1. Original source is: Selfe, L. (1977). *Nadia: A case of extraordinary drawing ability in children.* London: Academic Press.

4.7 Ibid. ref.2. Original sources are: (1) Edwards, B. (1993). *Drawing on the right side of the brain.* London: HarperCollins. (2) Snyder, A.W. & Barlow, H.B., 'Revealing the Artist's Touch' in *Nature*, 331, (1986): 117-118, and (3) Snyder, A.W. & Thomas, M., Autistic artists give clues to cognition, *Perception*, 26, (1997): 93-96.

Five: Absorption World

5.1. Paradiz, V. (2002). *Elijah's Cup: A family's journey into the community and culture of high-functioning autism and Asperger's syndrome.* NY: The Free Press.

5.2. Julien, W. (1999). *Carrousels and Storms: Mysticism from an autistic mind.* Maestro Media, p.53.

5.3. Williams, D. (1998). *Autism and Sensing: The unlost instinct.* London & Philadelphia: Jessica Kingsley Publishers.

5.4. Williams, D. (1992). *Nobody Nowhere.* NY: Times Books, p.127.
5.5. Frith, U. (2003). *Autism: Explaining the enigma,* 2nd edn. Malden, MA: Blackwell Publishing, p.146. Original reference: Humphrey, N., Cave art, autism, and the evolution of the human mind, *Camb Archaeol J*, 8(2), (1998): 165-191.
5.6. Robinson, J.M. (director). (1977). 'The Gospel of Philip' in *The Nag Hammadi Library: In English.* Trans. by Members of the Coptic Gnostic Library Project of the Institute for Antiquity and Christianity. San Francisco: Harper & Row, p.137.

Six: The Eternal Moment

6.1. Wittgenstein, L. (1983). *Tractatus Logico-Philosophicus.* London: Routledge & Kegan Paul, #6.4311.

Seven: The Eternally New World

7.1. Prince-Hughes, D. (Ed) (2002). *Aquamarine Blue 5: Personal Stories of College Students with Autism.* Athens, OH: Swallow Press, Ohio University Press, p.62.
7.2. Wittgenstein, L. (1975). *Zettel.* G.E.M. Anscombe & G.H. von Wright (Eds.). G.E.M. Anscombe (trans.), Berkeley, CA: University of California Press, #33.
7.3. Miller, A. (1981). *Albert Einstein's Special Theory of Relativity.* Reading, MA: Addison-Wesley, p.173.

Eight: Bubble World

8.1. Williams, D. (1998). *Autism and Sensing: The unlost instinct.* London and Philadelphia: Jessica Kingsley Publishers.

Nine: Detachment

9.1. Bloom, P. (2004). *Descartes' Baby.* NY: Basic Books, p.37. The original reference is the excellent collection of case studies, and case # 9 in particular in Kanner, L., Autistic disturbances of affective contact, *Nervous Child*, 2, (1943): 236. <http://www.neurodiversity.com/library_kanner_1943.pdf>.
9.2. French, A.P. (Ed.). (1979). Pais, A., in *Einstein: A centenary volume.* Cambridge, MA: Harvard University Press, p.35.
9.3. Frith, U. (2003). *Autism: Explaining the enigma,* 2nd edn. Malden, MA: Blackwell Publishing, pp.24-25.

9.4. Fitzgerald, M. (2005). *The Genesis of Artistic Creativity: Asperger's syndrome and the arts*. London: Jessica Kingsley Publishers, p.84.

9.5. Marcel, G. (1965). *Being and Having*. NY: Harper Torchbooks, Harper & Row, pp.20-21.

9.6. Ibid., Marcel, G. Marcel may have had some Aspergian traits. See his autobiography in Marcel, G. (1965). *The Philosophy of Existentialism*. NY: The Citadel Press, p.21.

9.7. Lessing, D. (1987). *Prisons We Choose to Live Inside*. NY: Harper & Row.

9.8. Weil, S. (1956). *The Notebooks of Simone Weil*. A. Wills (trans.). NY: G. P. Putnam's Sons, vol.2, p.334.

9.9. Weil, S. (1997). *Gravity and Grace*. NY: Routledge, p.13.

9.10. Pfeiffer, F. (1956). *Meister Eckhart*. London: John M. Watkins, pp.341-345.

Ten: Object World

10.1. Prince-Hughes, D. (Ed). (2002). *Aquamarine Blue 5: Personal stories of college students with autism*. Athens, OH: Swallow Press, Ohio University Press, p.108.

10.2. Williams, D. (1992). *Nobody Nowhere*. NY: Times Books, pp.107-108.

10.3 Ibid. Williams, *Nobody Nowhere*, p.5.

10.4. Bloom, P. (2004). *Descartes' Baby*. NY: Basic Books, p.17. Original Reference: Heider, F & Simmel, M. An experimental study of apparent behavior, *Am J Psych*, 57(2), (1944): 243-259.

10.5. Wittgenstein, L. (1975). *Zettel*. G.E.M. Anscombe & G.H. von Wright. (Eds.). G.E.M. Anscombe (trans.). Berkeley, CA: University of California Press, #238.

10.6. Ibid., #711.

10.7. Einstein, A. (1994). *Ideas and Opinions*. NY: Modern Library, p.41.

10.8. Fitzgerald, M. (2005). *The Genesis of Artistic Creativity: Asperger's syndrome and the arts*. London: Jessica Kingsley Publishers.

10.9. Hane, R.E. (2003). 'On a Clear Day' in *Sharing our Wisdom: A collection of presentations by people within the autism spectrum*. G. Gillingham & S. McClennen (Eds.). North Plymouth, MA: The National Autism Committee, p.22.

10.10 Chiu, P.H. & Kayali, M.A. et. al., Self responses along cingulate cortex reveal quantitative neural phenotype for high-functioning autism, *Neuron*, 57, (2008): 463-473.

10.11. Williams, D. (1998). *Autism and Sensing: The unlost instinct.* London & Philadelphia: Jessica Kingsley Publishers, p.16.

10.12. Bohm, D. (1996). *On Dialogue.* L. Nichol (Ed.). London: Routledge, p.88.

10.13. St. Augustine. (401). *Confessions.* (1907). H. Chadwick (trans.). New York: Dutton, book V. <www.sacred-texts.com>.

Eleven: Picture World

11.1. Grandin, T. (1996). *Thinking in Pictures.* NY: Vintage Books.

11.2. Ibid., 33,34.

11.3. Nerburn, K. (1994). *Neither Wolf Nor Dog.* Novato, CA: NewWorld Library, pp.242-243.

11.4 Palmer, M. (1991). *The Elements of Taoism.* Dorset: Element Books, p.35.

11.5. Pauli, W. (1994). *Writings on Physics and Philosophy.* C.P. Enz & K. von Meyenn (Eds.). Berlin: Springer-Verlag, p.221.

Twelve: Exposure World

12.1. Williams, D. (1992). *Nobody Nowhere.* NY: Times Books, p.216.

12.2. Williams, D. (2003). *Exposure Anxiety – The Invisible Cage.* Jessica Kingsley Publishers, London and Philadelphia.

12.3. Ibid., Williams. *Exposure Anxiety – The Invisible Cage.* Mostly pgs. 13, 14.

Thirteen: Detail World

13.1. Frith, U. (2003). *Autism: Explaining the enigma,* 2nd edn. Malden, MA: Blackwell Publishing, p.152.

13.2. Wittgenstein, L. (1979). *Notebooks 1914-1916,* 2nd edn. G. H. von Wright & G.E.M. Anscombe (Eds.). G.E.M. Anscombe (trans.). Chicago: University of Chicago Press, p.5e.

13.3. Wittgenstein, L. (1980). *Culture and Value.* G. H. Von Wright (Ed.). P. Winch (trans.). Chicago: University of Chicago Press, p.34e. Original reference: Longfellow, H.W. (1850). 'The Builders' in *Seaside and the Fireside.* Boston: Ticknor, Reed and Field.

13.4. Julien, W. (1999). *Carrousels and Storms: Mysticism from an autistic mind.* Maestro Media, p.14.
13.5. Robinson, J.M. (director). (1977). 'The Gospel of Truth' in *The Nag Hammadi Library: In English.* Trans. by Members of the Coptic Gnostic Library Project of the Institute for Antiquity and Christianity. San Francisco: Harper & Row, p.41.

Fourteen: Wittgenstein the Philosopher

14.1. Wittgenstein, L. (1983). *Tractatus Logico-Philosophicus.* London: Routledge & Kegan Paul.
14.2. Engelmann, P. (1967). *Letters from Wittgenstein, with a memoir.* NY: Horizon Press, p.97.
14.3. Ibid., p.98.
14.4. Wittgenstein, L. (1958). *Philosophical Investigations,* 3rd edn. G.E.M. Anscombe (trans.). NY: Macmillan Publishing, Basil Blackwell & Mott, p.156e.

Fifteen: Simone Weil

15.1. Weil, S. (1951). *Waiting for God.* E. Craufurd (trans.). NY: G.P. Putnam's Sons, Harper Perennial Classics Edition, 2001, p. 23.
15.2. Fitzgerald, M. (2005). *The Genesis of Artistic Creativity: Asperger's syndrome and the arts.* London: Jessica Kingsley Publishers.
15.3. Weil, S. (1956). *The Notebooks of Simone Weil.* A. Wills (trans.). NY: G. P. Putnam's Sons, vol.2, p.365.
15.4. Ibid. *Notebooks,* p.527.
15.5. Ibid., *Waiting for God,* p.29.
15.6. Weil, S. (1997). *Gravity and Grace.* NY: Routledge, pp.viii-ix.

Sixteen: Wittgenstein the Autistic

16.1. Wittgenstein, L. (1980). *Culture and Value.* G.H. von Wright (Ed.). P. Winch (trans.). Chicago: University of Chicago Press, p.11e.
16.2. Wittgenstein, H. (1984). 'My Brother Ludwig' in *Recollections of Wittgenstein.* R. Rhees (Ed.). Oxford: Oxford University Press, pp.1, 2, 11.
16.3. Ibid. p.2.

16.4. Fitzgerald, M. Did Ludwig Wittgenstein have Asperger's syndrome? *Eur Child Adolesc Psychiatr*, 9, (2000): 61-65. See this paper for a comprehensive discussion of Wittgenstein's autistic traits.

16.5. Wittgenstein, L. (1979). *Notebooks 1914-1916*, 2nd edn. G.H. von Wright & G.E.M. Anscombe (Eds.). G.E.M. Anscombe (trans.). Chicago: University of Chicago Press, p.50e.

16.6. Ibid., pp.47e-48e.

16.7. Bouwsma, O.K. (1986). *Wittgenstein Conversations 1949-1951*. J.L. Craft & R.E. Hustwit (Eds.). Indianapolis: Hackett, p.74.

16.8. Wittgenstein, L. (1980). *Culture and Value*. G.H. von Wright (Ed.). P. Winch (trans.). Chicago: University of Chicago Press, p.11e.

16.9. Ibid., p.11e.

16.10. Wittgenstein, L. (1975). *Philosophical Remarks*. Chicago: University of Chicago Press, p.67.

16.11. Wittgenstein, L. (1980). *Culture and Value*. G.H. von Wright (Ed.). P. Winch (trans.). Chicago: University of Chicago Press, p.39e.

16.12. Genova, J. (1995). *Wittgenstein: A way of seeing*. NY: Routledge, p.xiv.

16.13. Ibid., p.xv.

16.14. McGinn, M. (1997). *Wittgenstein and the Philosophical Investigations*. London: Routledge, p.10.

16.15. Drury, M.O'C. (1996). 'Conversations with Wittgenstein,' in *The Danger of Words and Writings on Wittgenstein*. Bristol: Thoemmes Press, p.109.

16.16. Wittgenstein, L. (1979). *Notebooks 1914-1916*, 2nd edn. G.H. von Wright & G.E.M. Anscombe (Eds.). G.E.M. Anscombe (trans.). Chicago: University of Chicago Press, p.13e.

16.17. Grandin, T. (2006). *Thinking in Pictures: My Life with Autism*, 2nd edn. NY: Vintage Books, p. 74.

16.18. Wittgenstein, L. (1988). *Remarks on the Philosophy of Psychology*, vol. 1. G.E.M. Anscombe & G.H. von Wright (Eds.). G.E.M. Anscombe (trans.). Chicago: University of Chicago Press, #896.

16.19. Wittgenstein, L. (1975). *Zettel*. G.E.M. Anscombe & G.H. von Wright (Eds.). G.E.M. Anscombe (trans.). Berkeley, CA: University of California Press, #10.

16.20. Ibid., #254.
16.21. Grandin, T. (1996). *Thinking in Pictures*. NY: Vintage Books, pp.73, 20.
16.22. Monk, R. (1990). *Ludwig Wittgenstein: The duty of genius*. NY: Penguin Books, p.29. Originally from an unpublished letter from Wittgenstein to his sister, Hermine. Manuscript # 17.5.08 from Wren Library, Trinity College, Cambridge.
16.23. Prince-Hughes, D. (Ed). (2002). *Aquamarine Blue 5: Personal stories of college students with autism*. Athens, OH: Swallow Press, Ohio University Press, p.xvii.
16.24. Williams, D. (1992). *Nobody Nowhere*. NY: Times Books, p.4.
16.25. Ibid., Monk, pp.33-34.
16.26. Wittgenstein, L. (1979). *Wittgenstein's Lectures, Cambridge, 1932-1935*. A. Ambrose (Ed.). Chicago: University of Chicago Press, p.99. See also pp.98, 110.
16.27. Shields, P.R. (1997). *Logic and Sin in the Writings of Ludwig Wittgenstein*. Chicago: University of Chicago Press, p.109.
16.28. Bouwsma, O.K. (1986). *Wittgenstein Conversations 1949-1951*. J.L. Craft & R.E. Hustwit (Eds.). Indianapolis: Hackett, p.62.
16.29. Ibid., Monk, p.182-183. Original Reference: Letter from Bertrand Russell to Lady Ottoline Morrell. Harry Ransom Humanities Center, University of Texas at Austin. Manuscript # 20.12.19 from Wren Library, Trinity College, Cambridge.
16.30. Ibid., Monk, p.244. Original Reference: Carnap, R. (1963). *The Philosophy of Rudolph Carnap*. P. Schilpp (Ed.). The Library of Living Philosophers, v. XI. LaSalle, IL: Open Court Publishing, pp.25-26.

Seventeen: Association World

17.1. Prince-Hughes, D. (Ed.). (2002). *Aquamarine Blue 5: Personal stories of college students with autism*. Athens, OH: Swallow Press, Ohio University Press, p.xii.
17.2. Williams, D. (1992). *Nobody Nowhere*. NY: Times Books, pp.116-117.
17.3. Andersen, H.C. (1847). *A Picture-Book without Pictures*. From the German Translation of *De La Motte Fouqué* by Meta Taylor. London: David Bogue. See the chapter heading, 16th

Evening. Other translations may place this very short story in other, nearby chapters.
17.4. Grandin, T. & Johnson, C. (2005). *Animals in Translation*. NY: Scribner.
17.5. Grandin, T. (1996). *Thinking in Pictures*. NY: Vintage Books, p.32.
17.6. Ibid., p.25.

Eighteen: David Bohm

18.1. Peat, F.D. (1997). *Infinite Potential: The life and times of David Bohm*. Reading, MA: Addison–Wesley, p.18.
18.2. Ibid., p.18.
18.3. Ibid., p.13.
18.4. Ibid., p.13.
18.5. Ibid., p.13.
18.6. Ibid., p.117.
18.7. Ibid., p.119.
18.8. Ibid., p.237.
18.9. Rovelli, C. (2008). *Relational Quantum Mechanics*. <http://arxiv.org/PS_cache/quant-ph/pdf/9609/9609002v2.pdf>.
18.10. Christensen, J.D. & Crane, L., Causal sites as quantum geometry, *J Math Phys*, 42, (2005): 122502.
18.11. Domenech, G., Holik, F. & Krause, D. (2008). *Quasi-spaces and the Foundation of Quantum Mechanics*. <http://philsci-archive.pitt.edu/archive/00003957/01/QM_in_Q_Spaces.pdf>.
18.12. Ibid., Peat, p.273.
18.13. Ibid., Peat, pp.3-4.

Nineteen: From Eternity's Point of View

19.1. Einstein, A. (1994). *Ideas and Opinions*. NY: The Modern Library, p.41.
19.2. Holton, G. (1981). 'Thematic Presuppositions and the Direction of Scientific Advance' in *Scientific Explanation*. A.F. Heath (Ed.). Oxford: Oxford University Press, p.19.
19.3. Hermanns, W. (1983). *Einstein and the Poet: In Search of the Cosmic Man*. Brookline Village, MA: Branden Press, p.27.
19.4. Ibid., Holton, p.20.
19.5. Ibid., Hermanns, p.12.

19.6. Ibid., Einstein, p.319.
19.7. Wittgenstein, L. (1979). *Notebooks 1914-1916*, 2nd edn. G.H. von Wright & G.E.M. Anscombe (Eds.). G.E.M. Anscombe (trans.). Chicago: University of Chicago Press, p.83e.
19.8. Einstein, A. (1979). *Albert Einstein, The Human Side: New glimpses from his archives*. H. Dukas & B. Hoffmann (Eds.). Princeton: Princeton University Press, p.52.

Twenty: Reddish-Green

20.1. Wittgenstein, L. (1977). *Remarks on Colour*. G.E.M. Anscombe (Ed.). L.L. McAlister & M. Schättle (trans.). Berkeley: University of California Press, p.3e.
20.2. Ibid., p.3e.
20.3. Shah, I. (1971). *The Sufis*. Garden City, NY: Anchor Books, Doubleday, pp.158, 164.
20.4. Weil, S. (1956). *The Notebooks of Simone Weil*. A. Wills (trans.). NY: G.P. Putnam's Sons, vol.1, p.87.
20.5. Weil, S. (1997). *Gravity and Grace*. NY: Routledge, p.xviii.
20.6. Pfeiffer, F. (1956). *Meister Eckhart*. London: John M. Watkins, p.17.

Twenty-One: The Well Adapted Concept World

21.1. Bohm, D. (1995). *Thought as a System*. London: Routledge, p.101.

Twenty-Two: If You Complete It, You Falsify It

22.1. Wittgenstein, L. (1988). *Remarks on the Philosophy of Psychology*, vol. 1. G.E.M. Anscombe & G.H. von Wright (Eds.). G.E.M. Anscombe (trans.). Chicago: University of Chicago Press, #257.

Twenty-Three: The World Seen from Every Angle

23.1. Wittgenstein, L. (1980). *Culture and Value*. G.H. von Wright (Ed.). P. Winch (trans.). Chicago: University of Chicago Press, p.7.
23.2. Ibid., pg.28.
23.3. Weil, S. (1956). *The Notebooks of Simone Weil*. A. Wills (trans.). NY: G.P. Putnam's Sons, vol.2, p.334.
23.4. Nerburn, K. (1994). *Neither Wolf Nor Dog*. Novato, CA:

NewWorld Library, pp.143-144.
23.5. Wittgenstein, L. (1958). *Philosophical Investigations*, 3rd edn. G.E.M. Anscombe (trans.) NY: Macmillan Publishing, Basil Blackwell & Mott, #66.
23.6. Jacobs, D.T. (1998). *Primal Awareness*. Rochester, VT: Inner Traditions.
23.7. Shah, I. (1971). *The Sufis*. Garden City, NY: Anchor Books, Doubleday, p.283.
23.8. Leong, K.S. (1995). *The Zen Teachings of Jesus*. NY: Crossroad Publishing, p.140.
23.9. Ekai, called Mu-Mon. (1934). 'Buddha Twirls a Flower' in *The Gateless Gate*. N. Senzaki & P. Reps (trans.). <www.sacred-texts.com>.

Twenty-Four: Parallel Angles

24.1. Weil, S. (1956). *The Notebooks of Simone Weil*. A. Wills (trans.). NY: G.P. Putnam's Sons, vol.2, p.334.

Twenty-Seven: What is Joy?

27.1. Wittgenstein, L. (1958). *Philosophical Investigations*, 3rd edn. G.E.M. Anscombe (trans.). NY: Macmillan Publishing, Basil Blackwell & Mott, #435, also see #126.
27.2. McGinn, M. (1997). *Wittgenstein and the Philosophical Investigations*. London: Routledge, p.44.

Twenty-Eight: What's for Dessert?

28.1. Hacker, P.M.S. (1996). *Wittgenstein's Place in Twentieth-Century Analytic Philosophy*. Oxford: Blackwell Publishers, p.109.
28.2. Edwards, J.C. (1983). *Ethics without Philosophy: Wittgenstein and the moral life*. FL: University Press of Florida, p.197.
28.3. Wittgenstein, L. (1958). *Philosophical Investigations*, 3rd edn. G.E.M. Anscombe (trans.). NY: Macmillan Publishing, Basil Blackwell & Mott, p.102e.
28.4. Ekai, called Mu-Mon. (1934). 'Joshu's Dog' in *The Gateless Gate*. N. Senzaki & P. Reps (trans.). <www.sacred-texts.com>.

Thirty: Logic Fills the World

30.1. Wittgenstein, L. (1983). *Tractatus Logico-Philosophicus.* London: Routledge & Kegan Paul, #5.552.
30.2. Ibid., #5.61.
30.3. Ibid., #1.13.
30.4. Wittgenstein, L. (1979). *Notebooks 1914-1916,* 2nd edn. G.H. von Wright & G.E.M. Anscombe (Eds.). G.E.M. Anscombe (trans.). Chicago: University of Chicago Press, p.2e.
30.5. Wittgenstein, L. (1958). *Philosophical Investigations,* 3rd edn. G.E.M. Anscombe (trans.). NY: Macmillan Publishing, Basil Blackwell & Mott, Ltd., #97.
30.6. Szatmari, P. (2004). *A Mind Apart.* NY: The Guilford Press, pp.52-53.
30.7. Ibid., pp.54-57.
30.8. Ibid., *Philosophical Investigations,* #101.
30.9. Genova, J. (1995). *Wittgenstein: A Way of Seeing.* NY: Routledge, pp.58-60.
30.10. Monk, R. (1990). *Ludwig Wittgenstein: The duty of genius.* NY: Penguin Books, p.19.
30.11. Williams, D. (1992). *Nobody Nowhere.* NY: Times Books, pp.101-103.
30.12. L'Heritier, M.-J. (1696). 'Ricdin-Ricdon' in *Spells of Enchantment.* (1991). J. Zipes (Ed.). NY: Penguin Books.

Thirty-One: Raw Math

31.1. Wittgenstein, L. (1975). *Zettel.* G.E.M. Anscombe and G.H. von Wright (Eds.). G.E.M. Anscombe (trans.). Berkeley, CA: University of California Press, #295.

Thirty-Two: Bubble-Gum in the Storm

32.1. Pauli, W. (1994). Bohr in *Writings on Physics and Philosophy.* C.P. Enz & K. von Meyenn (Eds.). Berlin: Springer-Verlag, p.41.
32.2. Heisenberg, W. (1958). *Physics and Philosophy: The revolution in modern science.* NY: Harper Torchbooks, Harper & Row, p.106.
32.3. Schrödinger, E. (1977). *What is Life?* with *Mind and Matter.* Cambridge: Cambridge University Press, pp.126–150.
32.4. Vallentin, A. (1954). *The Drama of Albert Einstein.* Garden

City, NY: Doubleday. p.155.
32.5. Schilpp, P.A. (Ed.). (1991). *Albert Einstein: Philosopher-scientist.* LaSalle, IL: Open Court, p.13.
32.6. Pauli, W. (1994). *Writings on Physics and Philosophy.* C.P. Enz & K. von Meyenn (Eds.). Berlin: Springer-Verlag, p.221. See also Heisenberg, W. (1974). *Across the Frontiers.* NY: Harper & Row, p.32.
32.7. Putnam, H. (1987). *The Many Faces of Realism.* LaSalle, IL: Open Court, p.8.

Thirty-Three: Lumps of Dough

33.1. Hall, K. (2001). *Asperger Syndrome, the Universe and Everything.* London: Jessica Kingsley Publishers, p.66.
33.2. Meyerding, J. (1998). *On Finding Myself Differently Brained.* <http://mjane.zolaweb.com>.

Thirty-Four: Sighted Ethics

34.1. Stringer, L. (1998). *Grand Central Winter: Stories from the street.* NY: Washington Square Press. National Public Radio interview.
34.2. Grandin, T. (1996). *Thinking in Pictures.* NY: Vintage Books, p.83.
34.3. Monk, R. (1990). *Ludwig Wittgenstein: The duty of genius.* NY: Penguin Books, p.44. Original Reference: Letter from Bertrand Russell to Lady Ottoline Morrell. Harry Ransom Humanities Center, University of Texas at Austin. Manuscript # 17.3.12 from Wren Library, Trinity College, Cambridge.
34.4. Ibid., p. 52. Original Reference: Letter from Bertrand Russell to Lady Ottoline Morrell. Harry Ransom Humanities Center, University of Texas at Austin. Manuscript # 1.6.12 from Wren Library, Trinity College, Cambridge.
34.5. Ibid, p. 52.
34.6. Williams, D. (1992). *Nobody Nowhere.* NY: Times Books.

Thirty-Five: Mystical Views

35.1. Kornfield, J. & Feldman, C. (Eds.). (1996). *Soul Food.* San Francisco: Harper, p.227.

Thirty-Six: Sufism

36.1. Angha, N. (1991). *Principles of Sufism*. Fremont, CA: Asian Humanities Press. p.99.
36.2. Shah, I. (1971). *The Sufis*. Garden City, NY: Anchor Books, Doubleday, p.54.
36.3. Ibid., Shah, p.xiv.
36.4. Ibid., Shah, pp.1-11.
36.5. Witteveen, H.J. (1997). *Universal Sufism*. Shaftesbury, Dorset: Element Books. This book is devoted to the teachings of Inayat Khan.

Thirty-Seven: One Night in the Sistine Chapel

37.1. Julien, W. (1999). *Carrousels and Storms: Mysticism from an Autistic Mind*. Maestro Media, p.59.
37.2. Heisenberg, W. (1971). Dirac in *Physics and Beyond: Encounters and conversations*. NY: Harper & Row, p.86.

Thirty-Eight: The Wheels Have Come Off

38.1. Lakoff, G. & Johnson, M. (1999). *Philosophy in the Flesh: The embodied mind and its challenge to Western thought*. NY: Basics Books. Examples from pp.236-240.

Thirty-Nine: From Faulkner to Harry Potter

39.1. Maslow, A.H. (1976). *The Farther Reaches of Human Nature*. NY: Penguin Books. p.242.
39.2. Faulkner, W. (1964). 'The Bear' in *Bear, Man and God*. Utley, F.L., Bloom, L.Z. & Kinney, A.F. (Eds.) NY: Random House.
39.3. Horn, G. (White Deer of Autumn). (1996). *Contemplations of a Primal Mind*. Novato CA: New World Library, p.29.
39.4. Rowling, J.K. (1997). *Harry Potter and the Sorcerer's Stone*. NY: Scholastic, p.300.

Forty: Abstraction

40.1. Hayakawa, S.I. (1990). *Language in Thought and Action*. San Diego: Harcourt Brace & Co.
40.2 Versluis, A. (1992). *Sacred Earth: The spiritual landscape of Native America*. Rochester, VT: Inner Traditions International, p.45.

Forty-One: Free from Pictures

41.1. F. Pfeiffer (Ed.). (1956). 'Tractate VII, Signs of the True Ground' in *Meister Eckhart*. C. de B. Evans (trans.). London: John M. Watkins, p.334.

41.2. Wittgenstein, L. (1958). *Philosophical Investigations*, 3rd edn. G.E.M. Anscombe (trans.), NY: Macmillan Publishing, Basil Blackwell & Mott, p.102e.

41.3 Müller, M. (trans.). (1879). *The Upanishads*, Part I. (Sacred Books of the East). Talavakara or Kena-Upanishad, Khanda II. <www.sacred-texts.com>.

41.4. Ekai, also called Mu-Mon. (1934). 'Everyday Life is The Path' in *The Gateless Gate*. N. Senzaki & P. Reps trans.). <www.sacred-texts.com>.

41.5. Weil, S. (1997). *Gravity and Grace*. NY: Routledge, p.107.

Forty-Two: Idolatry

42.1. Isanon, A. (2001). *Spirituality and the Autism Spectrum*. London: Jessica Kingsley Publishers, p.108.

42.2. Barfield, O. (1988). *Saving the Appearances: A study in idolatry*, 2nd edn. CT: Wesleyan University Press, pp.111, 161.

42.3. Rumi, Maulana Jalalu-'d-din Muhammad. (13th century). *The Masnavi I Ma'navi*. (1898). E.H. Whinfield (trans.), book IV, story IV. <www.sacred-texts.com>.

Forty-Three: The Land of Black Grass

43.1. Nerburn, K. (1994). *Neither Wolf Nor Dog*. Novato, CA: New World Library, pp.108-109.

43.2. Hamilton, E. (1957). *The Echo of Greece*. NY: W.W. Norton.

Forty-Four: Mountains and Desert

44.1. David-Neel, A. (1970). *Initiations in Tibet*. London: Rider, p.16.

44.2. Weil, S. (1970). *First and Last Notebooks*. R. Rees (trans.). NY: Oxford University Press, p.335.

44.3. Robinson, J.M. (director). (1977). 'The Gospel of Truth' in *The Nag Hammadi Library: In English*. Trans. by Members of the Coptic Gnostic Library Project of the Institute for Antiquity and Christianity. San Francisco: Harper & Row, p.39.

Forty-Five: Celebration

45.1. Paradiz, V. (2002). *Elijah's Cup: A family's journey into the community and culture of high-functioning autism and Asperger's syndrome.* NY: The Free Press, p.58.
45.2. Bouwsma, O.K. (1986). *Wittgenstein Conversations 1949-1951.* J.L. Craft & R.E. Hustwit (Eds.). Indianapolis: Hackett, p.62.
45.3. Personal conversation.
45.4. Highwater, J. (1981). *The Primal Mind.* NY: Meridian Books, p.65.
45.5. Ibid., pp. 61-62.
45.6. Williams, D. (1992). *Nobody Nowhere.* NY: Times Books, pp.3-4.
45.7. Murdoch, I. (1971). *The Sovereignty of Good.* London & NY: Routledge, p.64.
45.8. Leong, K.S. (1995). *The Zen Teachings of Jesus.* NY: Crossroad Publishing, p.40.

Forty-Six: Wittgenstein as Human

46.1. Wittgenstein, H. (1984). 'My Brother Ludwig' in *Recollections of Wittgenstein.* R. Rhees (Ed.). Oxford: Oxford University Press, p.3.
46.2. Pascal, F. (1984). 'Wittgenstein: A personal Memoir' in *Recollections of Wittgenstein.* R. Rhees (Ed.). Oxford: Oxford University Press, p.18.
46.3. Bouwsma, O.K. (1986). *Wittgenstein Conversations 1949-1951.* J.L. Craft & R.E. Hustwit (Eds.). Indianapolis: Hackett, p.68.
46.4. Drury, M.O'C. (1996). 'Conversations with Wittgenstein' in *The Danger of Words and Writings on Wittgenstein.* Bristol: Thoemmes Press, p.110.
46.5. Ibid., Drury, p.105.
46.6. Ibid., Wittgenstein, H. *Recollections of Wittgenstein.* p.11.
46.7. Wittgenstein, L. (1980). *Culture and Value.* G.H. Von Wright (Ed.). P. Winch (trans.). Chicago: University of Chicago Press, pp.6e-7e.
46.8. Monk, R. (1990). *Ludwig Wittgenstein: The duty of genius.* NY: Penguin Books, p.489.

46.9. Ibid., Monk, p.491.
46.10. Ibid., Bouwsma, p.75.

Forty-Seven: Gabriel Marcel

47.1. Marcel, G. (1965). *The Philosophy of Existentialism*. NY: The Citadel Press, p.104, see also pp.113-114.
47.2. Ibid., p.115.
47.3. Marcel, G. (1963). *The Existential Background of Human Dignity*. Cambridge, MA: Harvard University Press, p.21.
47.4. Marcel, G. (1973). *Tragic Wisdom and Beyond*. Evanston, IL: Northwestern University Press, pp.253-254.
47.5. Ibid., *Tragic Wisdom and Beyond*, pp.xxiii, xxxiii.
47.6. Marcel, G. (1967). *Problematic Man*. NY: Herder & Herder.
47.7. Marcel, G. (1982). *Creative Fidelity*. NY: Crossroad Publishing, p.51.
47.8. Ibid., *The Existential Background of Human Dignity*, p.20.
47.9. Ibid., *The Existential Background of Human Dignity*, pp.20-21.
47.10. Conversations between Paul Ricoeur and Gabriel Marcel, in Marcel, G. (1973). *Tragic Wisdom and Beyond*. Evanston, IL: Northwestern University Press.
47.11. Ibid., *The Philosophy of Existentialism*, p.10.
47.12. Ibid., *The Philosophy of Existentialism*, p.12.
47.13. Ibid., *The Philosophy of Existentialism*, p.13.
47.14. Ibid., *Tragic Wisdom and Beyond*, p.213.
47.15. Ibid., *Tragic Wisdom and Beyond*, p.221.
47.16. Ibid., *Tragic Wisdom and Beyond*, p.29.
47.17. Ibid., *Tragic Wisdom and Beyond*, pp.251-252.

Forty-Eight: Creatures of Abstraction and Creatures of Life

48.1. Watson, R. (2002). *Cogito, Ergo Sum: The life of René Descartes*. Boston: David R. Godine.

Forty-Nine: Silence

49.1. Isanon, A. (2001). *Spirituality and the Autism Spectrum*. London: Jessica Kingsley Publishers, pp.93-94.
49.2. Weil, S. (1997). *Gravity and Grace*. NY: Routledge, p.106.

49.3. Deloria Jr., V. (1994). *God Is Red: A native view of religion.* Golden, CO: Fulcrum Publishing, pp.67, 155.
49.4. Cain, S. (1963). *Gabriel Marcel.* NY: Hillary House Publishers, p.41.
49.5. Ibid., p.73.

Fifty: Talk

50.1. Nerburn, K. (1994). *Neither Wolf Nor Dog.* Novato, CA: NewWorld Library, p.58.
50.2. Osborne, L. (2002). *American Normal.* NY: Copernicus Books, p.58.

Fifty-One: "..."

51.1. Wittgenstein, L. (1958). *Philosophical Investigations.* 3rd edn. G.E.M. Anscombe (trans.). NY: Macmillan Publishing, Basil Blackwell & Mott, p.223.
51.2. Weil, S. (1997). *Gravity and Grace.* NY: Routledge, p.116.

Fifty-Two: Raw Faith

52.1. Engelmann, P. (1967). 'Wittgenstein' in *Letters from Wittgenstein, with a Memoir.* NY: Horizon Press, p.77.
52.2. Wittgenstein, L. (1980). *Culture and Value.* G.H. von Wright (Ed.). P. Winch (trans.). Chicago: University of Chicago Press, p.33e.
52.3. Andersen, H.C. (1852). 'The Snow Queen' in *Tales and Fairy Stories.* Mme de Chatelain (trans.). London: G. Routledge & Co., pp.72-73.
52.4. Horn, G. (White Deer of Autumn). (1996). *Contemplations of a Primal Mind.* Novato, CA: New World Library, pp.35-36.
52.5. Delacato, C.H. (Ed.). (1974). *The Ultimate Stranger: The autistic child.* Novato, CA: Academic Therapy Publications, p.83.

Fifty-Three: Raw Religion

53.1. Williams, D. (1992). *Nobody Nowhere.* NY: Times Books, p.207.
53.2. Prince-Hughes, D., (Ed.). (2002). *Aquamarine Blue 5: Personal stories of college students with autism.* Athens, OH: Swallow Press, Ohio University Press, pp.52-55.

53.3. Ibid. pp.52-55.
53.4. Grandin, T. (1996). *Thinking in Pictures.* NY: Vintage Books, pp.189-191.
53.5. Ibid., pp.204-205.
53.6. Einstein, A. (1979). *Albert Einstein: The human side.* H. Dukas, & B. Hoffman (Eds.). Princeton: Princeton University Press, pp.23, 33.
53.7. Ibid., p.39.
53.8. Williams, D. (2003). *Exposure anxiety – The Invisible Cage.* London & Philadelphia: Jessica Kingsley Publishers, p.318.
53.9. Lao-Tzu. (Ancient). (1905). *The Sayings of Lao-Tzu.* L. Giles (trans.). pp.19-21. <www.sacred-texts.com>.
53.10. Rumi, Maulana Jalalu-'d-din Muhammad. (13th century). *The Masnavi I Ma'navi.* (1898). E.H. Whinfield (trans.). book I, story V. <www.sacred-texts.com>.
53.11. Robinson, J.M. (director). (1977). 'The Gospel of Philip' in *The Nag Hammadi Library: In English.* Trans. by Members of the Coptic Gnostic Library Project of the Institute for Antiquity and Christianity. San Francisco: Harper & Row. pp.132, 137.
53.12. Ibid. (The Gospel of Thomas) p.121.
53.13. Ibid. (The Gospel of Thomas) p.123.

Fifty-Four: Four Worlds

54.1. Williams, D. (1992). *Nobody Nowhere.* NY: Times Books, p.216.
54.2. Whiteley, P.M. (Nov. 2004). 'Ties That Bind' in *Natural History*, pp.28-29.
54.3. Lee, D. (1959). *Freedom and Culture.* NJ: Prentice-Hall, pp.138-139.
54.4. Nerburn, K. (1994). *Neither Wolf Nor Dog.* Novato, CA: NewWorld Library, p.131.
54.5. Weil, S. (1986). *Simone Weil: An anthology.* S. Miles (Ed.). NY: Grove Press, pp.50-55. Also see Plant, S. (1997). *Simone Weil.* Liguori, MO: Triumph, pp.70-79.

Bibliography

Aczel, A.D. (2005). *Descartes' Secret Notebook*. New York: Broadway Books.

Allen, D. & Springsted, E.O. (1994). *Spirit, Nature, and Community: Issues in the thought of Simone Weil.* NY: State University of New York Press.

Andersen, H.C. (1847). *A Picture-Book without Pictures.* From the German translation of *De la Motte Fouqué* by M. Taylor. London: David Bogue.

Andersen, H.C. (1852). 'The Snow Queen' in *Tales and Fairy Stories.* Mme. de Chatelain (trans.). London: G. Routledge.

Angha, N. (1991). *Principles of Sufism.* Fremont, CA: Asian Humanities Press.

Barfield, O. (1988). *Saving the Appearances: A study in idolatry,* 2nd edn. CT: Wesleyan University Press.

Baron-Cohen, S., Baldwin, D.A. & Crowson, M., Do children with autism use the speaker's direction of gaze strategy to crack the code of language? *Child Dev,* 68, (1997): 48-57.

Bloom, P. (2004). *Descartes' Baby.* NY: Basic Books.

Bohm, D. (2000). *On Creativity.* London: Routledge.

Bohm, D. (1996). *On Dialogue.* L. Nichol (Ed.). London: Routledge.

Bohm, D. (1995).*Thought as a System.* London: Routledge.

Bohm, D. (1985). *Unfolding Meaning.* London: Routledge.

Bouwsma, O.K. (1986). *Wittgenstein Conversations 1949-1951.* J.L. Craft & R.E. Hustwit (Eds.). Indianapolis: Hackett.

Brenner, W.H. (1999). *Wittgenstein's Philosophical Investigations.* Albany, NY: State University of New York Press.

Brill, S.B. (1995). *Wittgenstein and Critical Theory.* Athens, OH: Ohio University Press.

Cain, S. (1963). *Gabriel Marcel.* NY: Hillary House Publishers.

Carnap, R. (1963). *The Philosophy of Rudolph Carnap.* P. Schilpp (Ed.). The Library of Living Philosophers, vol. XI, LaSalle, IL: Open Court Publishing.

Cavell, S. (1979). *The Claim of Reason.* Oxford: Oxford University Press.

Chang, H. (2004). *Inventing Temperature.* Oxford: Oxford University Press.

Cheour, M., Ceponiene, R., Lehtokoski, A., Luuk, A., Allik, J., Alho, K. & Naatanen, R., Development of language-specific phoneme representations in the infant brain, *Nat Neurosci,* 1, (1998): 351-353.

Chiu, P.H. & Kayali, M.A. et. al., Self responses along cingulate cortex reveal quantitative neural phenotype for high-functioning autism, *Neuron,* 57, (2008): 463-473.

Christensen, J.D. & Crane, L., Causal sites as quantum geometry, *J Math Phys,* 42, (2005): 122502.

David-Neel, A. (1970). *Initiations in Tibet.* London: Rider & Co.

Delacato, C.H. (Ed.). (1974). *The Ultimate Stranger: The autistic child.* Novato, CA: Academic Therapy Publications.

Deloria Jr., V. (1994). *God Is Red: A Native view of religion.* Golden, CO: Fulcrum Publishing.

Diamond, C. (1995). *The Realistic Spirit: Wittgenstein, philosophy, and the mind.* Cambridge, MA: MIT Press.

Drury, M.O'C. (1996). *The Danger of Words and Writings on Wittgenstein.* Bristol: Thoemmes Press.

Edwards, B. (1993). *Drawing on the Right Side of the Brain.* London: HarperCollins.

Edwards, J.C. (1983). *Ethics without Philosophy: Wittgenstein and the moral life.* FL: University Press of Florida.

Einstein, A. (1979). *Albert Einstein, The Human Side: New glimpses from his archives.* H. Dukas & B. Hoffman (Eds.). Princeton: Princeton University Press.

Einstein, A. (1954). *Ideas and Opinions.* NY: Bonanza Books.

Ekai, also called Mu-Mon. (1934). *The Gateless Gate*. N. Senzaki & P. Reps (trans.). <www.sacred-texts.com>.

Engelmann, P. (1967). *Letters from Wittgenstein, with a Memoir*. NY: Horizon Press.

Fant, K.M. (2005). *Logically Determined Design*. Hoboken, NJ: Wiley-Interscience.

Faulkner, W. (1964). 'The Bear' in *Bear, Man and God*. F.L. Utley, L.Z. Bloom & A.F. Kinney (Eds.). NY: Random House.

Feynman, R.P., Leighton R.B. & Sands, M. (1963). *The Feynman Lectures on Physics*. Reading, MA: Addison-Wesley.

Finch, H.L. (2001). *The Vision of Wittgenstein*. NY: Vega.

Fine, A. (1996). *The Shaky Game: Einstein realism and the quantum theory*, 2nd edn. Chicago: University of Chicago Press.

Fitzgerald, M., Did Ludwig Wittgenstein have Asperger's syndrome? *Eur Child Adolesc Psychiatr*, 9, (2000): 61-65.

Fitzgerald, M. (2005). *The Genesis of Artistic Creativity: Asperger's syndrome and the arts*. London: Jessica Kingsley Publishers.

Fogelin, R.J. (1995). *Wittgenstein*, 2nd edn. London: Routledge.

French, A.P. (Ed.). (1979). *Einstein: A centenary volume*. Cambridge, MA: Harvard University Press.

French, A.P. & Kennedy, P.J. (1985). *Niels Bohr: A centenary volume*. Cambridge, MA: Harvard University Press.

Frith, U. (2003). *Autism: Explaining the enigma*, 2nd edn. Malden, MA: Blackwell Publishing.

Genova, J. (1995). *Wittgenstein: A way of seeing*. NY: Routledge.

Grandin, T. (1996). *Thinking in Pictures*. NY: Vintage Books.

Grandin, T. (2006). *Thinking in Pictures: My Life with Autism*, 2nd edn. NY: Vintage Books.

Grandin, T. & Johnson, C. (2005). *Animals in Translation*. NY: Scribner.

Grayling, A.C. (2001). *Wittgenstein: A very short introduction*. Oxford & NY: Oxford University Press.

Hacker, P.M.S. (1996). *Wittgenstein's Place in Twentieth-Century Analytic Philosophy*. Oxford: Blackwell Publishers.

Hall, K. (2001). *Asperger Syndrome, the Universe and Everything*. London: Jessica Kingsley Publishers.

Hamer, D. (2004). *The GOD Gene*. NY: Doubleday.

Hamilton, E. (1957). *The Echo of Greece*. NY: W.W. Norton.

Hane, R.E. (2003). 'On a Clear Day' in *Sharing our Wisdom: A collection of presentations by people within the autism spectrum*. G. Gillingham & S. McClennen (Eds.). North Plymouth, MA: The National Autism Committee.

Hanson, N.R. (2002). 'Seeing and Seeing As' in *Philosophy of Science: Contemporary readings*. Y. Balashov & A. Rosenberg (Eds.). London & NY: Routledge.

Happe, F. (2001). 'Why Success is More Interesting than Failure: Understanding Assets and Deficits in Autism' in *Autism: The search for coherence*. J. Richer & S. Coates (Eds.). London: Jessica Kingsley Publishers.

Hawking, S. (1990). *A Brief History of Time*. NY: Bantam Books.

Hay, D. & Nye, R. (2006). *The Spirit of the Child*. London: Jessica Kingsley Publishers.

Hayakawa, S.I. (1990). *Language in Thought and Action*. San Diego: Harcourt Brace.

Heider, F. & Simmel, M., An experimental study of apparent behavior, *Am J Psych*, 57(2), (1944): 243-259.

Heisenberg, W. (1958). *Physics and Philosophy: The revolution in modern science*. NY: Harper Torchbooks, Harper & Row.

Heisenberg, W. (1971). *Physics and Beyond: Encounters and conversations*. NY: Harper & Row.

Heisenberg, W. (1974). *Across the Frontiers*. NY: Harper & Row.

Hermanns, W. (1983). *Einstein and the Poet: In search of the cosmic man*. Brookline Village, MA: Branden Press.

Hewetson, A. (2002). *The Stolen Child*. Westport, CT: Bergin & Garvey.

Highwater, J. (1981). *The Primal Mind*. NY: Meridian Books.

Hintikka, J. (2000). *On Wittgenstein*. Belmont, CA: Wadsworth Publishing.

Holton, G. (1981). 'Thematic Presuppositions and the Direction of Scientific Advance' in *Scientific Explanation*. A.F. Heath (Ed.). Oxford: Oxford University Press.

Horn, G. (White Deer of Autumn). (1996). *Contemplations of a Primal Mind*. Novato, CA: New World Library.

Humphrey, N., Cave art, autism, and the evolution of the human mind, *Camb Archaeol J*, 8(2), (1998): 165-191.

Isanon, A. (2001). *Spirituality and the Autism Spectrum*. London: Jessica Kingsley Publishers.

Ishiguro, H. (2001). 'The So-called Picture Theory' in *Wittgenstein: A critical reader*. H.-J. Glock (Ed.). Malden, MA: Blackwell Publishers.

James, I. (2006). *Asperger's Syndrome and High Achievement*. London: Jessica Kingsley Publishers.

Janik, A. & Toulmin, S. (1973). *Wittgenstein's Vienna*. NY: Touchstone, Simon & Schuster.

Julien, W. (1999). *Carrousels and Storms: Mysticism from an autistic mind*. Maestro Media.

Kanner, L., Autistic disturbances of affective contact, *Nervous Child*, 2, (1943): 217-250.

Kornfield, J. & Feldman, C. (Eds.). (1996). *Soul Food*. San Francisco: Harper.

Kuhl, P.K., Williams, K.A., Lacerda, F., Stevens, K.N. & Lindblom, B., Linguistic experience alters phonetic perception in infants by 6 months of age, *Science*, 255, (1992): 606-608.

Lakoff, G. & Johnson, M. (1999). *Philosophy in the Flesh: The embodied mind and its challenge to Western thought*. NY: Basics Books.

Lao-Tzu. (1905). *The Sayings of Lao-Tzu*. L. Giles (trans.). <www.sacred-texts.com>.

Lee, D. (1959). *Freedom and Culture*. NJ: Prentice Hall.

Leong, K.S. (1995). *The Zen Teachings of Jesus*. NY: Crossroad Publishing.

Lessing, D. (1987). *Prisons We Choose to Live Inside*. NY: Harper & Row.

L'Heritier, M.-J. (1696). 'Ricdin-Ricdon' in *Spells of Enchantment*. (1991). J. Zipes (Ed.). NY: Penguin Books.

Longfellow, H.W. (1850). 'The Builders' in *Seaside and the Fireside*. Boston: Ticknor, Reed & Field.

Malcolm, N. (1984). 'Introduction' in *Recollections of Wittgenstein*. R. Rhees (Ed.). Oxford: Oxford University Press.

Malcolm, N. (1995). *Wittgensteinian Themes: Essays 1978–1989*. Ithaca, NY: Cornell University Press.

Marcel, G. (1965). *Being and Having*. NY: Harper Torchbooks, Harper & Row.

Marcel, G. (1982). *Creative Fidelity*. NY: Crossroad Publishing.

Marcel, G. (1963). *The Existential Background of Human Dignity*. Cambridge, MA: Harvard University Press.

Marcel, G. (1965). *Philosophical Fragments 1909–1914*. IN: University of Notre Dame Press.

Marcel, G. (1965). *The Philosophy of Existentialism*. NY: The Citadel Press.

Marcel, G. (1967). *Problematic Man*. NY: Herder & Herder.

Marcel, G. (1973). *Tragic Wisdom and Beyond*. Evanston, IL: Northwestern University Press.

Maslow, A.H. (1976). *The Farther Reaches of Human Nature*. NY: Penguin Books.

Menn, S. (1998). *Descartes and Augustine*. Cambridge: Cambridge University Press.

Merton, T. (1967). *Mystics and Zen Masters*. NY: Noonday Press.

Merton, T. (1986). *Thoughts in Solitude*. NY: Farrar, Straus & Giroux.

Meyerding, J. (1998). *On Finding Myself Differently Brained*. <http://mjane.zolaweb.com>.

McGinn, C. (1999). *The Mysterious Flame.* NY: Basic Books.

McGinn, M. (1997). *Wittgenstein and the Philosophical Investigations.* London: Routledge.

Miller, A. (1981). *Albert Einstein's Special Theory of Relativity.* Reading, MA: Addison-Wesley.

Mitchell, S. (Ed.). (1991). *The Enlightened Mind.* NY: HarperCollins.

Monk, R. (1990). *Ludwig Wittgenstein: The duty of genius.* NY: Penguin Books.

Murdoch, I. (1971). *The Sovereignty of Good.* London & NY: Routledge.

Neihardt, J.G. (1932). *Black Elk Speaks.* Lincoln & London: University of Nebraska Press.

Nerburn, K. (1994). *Neither Wolf Nor Dog.* Novato, CA: New World Library.

Orwell, G. (1950). 'Politics and the English Language' in *Shooting an Elephant and Other Essays.* NY: Harcourt, Brace & World.

Osborne, L. (2002). *American Normal.* NY: Copernicus Books.

Pagels, E. (1979). *The Gnostic Gospels.* NY: Random House.

Pagels, E. (2003). *Beyond Belief: The secret gospel of Thomas.* NY: Vintage Books.

Palmer, M. (1991). *The Elements of Taoism.* Dorset: Element Books.

Paradiz, V. 2002. *Elijah's Cup: A family's journey into the community and culture of high-functioning autism and Asperger's syndrome.* NY: Free Press.

Pascal, F. (1984). 'Wittgenstein: A personal memoir' in *Recollections of Wittgenstein.* R. Rhees (Ed.). Oxford: Oxford University Press.

Pascalis, O., de Haan, M. & Nelson, C.A., Is face processing species-specific during the first year of life? *Science,* 296, (2002): 1321-1323.

Pauli, W. (1994). *Writings on Physics and Philosophy.* C.P. Enz & K. von Meyenn (Eds.). Berlin: Springer-Verlag.

Pears, D. (1987). *The False Prison.* Oxford: Clarendon Press.

Peat, F.D. (1997). *Infinite Potential: The life and times of David Bohm.* Reading, MA: Addison–Wesley.

Pétrement, S. (1976). *Simone Weil: A life.* R. Rosenthal (trans.). NY: Pantheon Books.

Pfeiffer, F. (Ed.). (1956). *Meister Eckhart.* C. de B. Evans (trans.). London: John M. Watkins.

Plant, S. (1997). *Simone Weil.* Liguori, MO: Triumph.

Price, A.F. & Wong M.-L. (trans.). (1969). *The Diamond Sutra and the Sutra of Hui Neng.* Boulder, CO: Shambala.

Prince-Hughes, D. (Ed.). (2002). *Aquamarine Blue 5: Personal stories of college students with autism.* Athens, OH: Swallow Press, Ohio University Press.

Putnam, H. (1987). *The Many Faces of Realism.* LaSalle, IL: Open Court.

Robinson, J.M. (director). (1977). *The Nag Hammadi Library: In English.* Trans. by Members of the Coptic Gnostic Library Project of the Institute for Antiquity and Christianity. San Francisco: Harper & Row.

Rowling, J.K. (1997). *Harry Potter and the Sorcerer's Stone.* NY: Scholastic.

Rumi, Maulana Jalalu-'d-din Muhammad. (13th century). *The Masnavi I Ma'navi.* (1898). E.H. Whinfield (trans.). <www.sacred-texts.com>.

St. Augustine. (401). *Confessions.* (1907). H. Chadwick (trans.). NY: Dutton. <www.sacred-texts.com>.

Saturday Evening Post (The). Jan./Feb. 2005. Indianapolis: Benjamin Franklin Literary and Medical Society.

Schilpp, P.A. (Ed.). (1991). *Albert Einstein: Philosopher-scientist.* LaSalle, IL: Open Court.

Schrödinger, E. (1977). *What is Life?* with *Mind and Matter.* Cambridge: Cambridge University Press.

Sedgwick, M.J. (2003). *Sufism: The essentials.* Cairo: American University in Cairo Press.

Selfe, L. (1977). *Nadia: A case of extraordinary drawing ability in children*. London: Academic Press.

Shah, I. (1978). *Learning How to Learn*. NY: Penguin Books.

Shah, I. (1971). *The Sufis*. Garden City, NY: Anchor Books, Doubleday.

Shah, I. (1994). *The Commanding Self*. London: Octagon Press.

Shields, P.R. (1997). *Logic and Sin in the Writings of Ludwig Wittgenstein*. Chicago: University of Chicago Press.

Sloman, S. (2005). *Causal Models: How people think about the world and its alternatives*. Oxford: Oxford University Press.

Sontag, F. (1995). *Wittgenstein and the Mystical*. Atlanta, GA: Scholars Press.

Snyder, A.W. & Mitchell, D.J., Is integer arithmetic fundamental to mental processing?: The mind's secret arithmetic, *Proc Roy Soc Edinb B Biol*, 266, (1999): 587-92.

Snyder, A.W., Bossomaier, T. & Mitchell, D.J., Concept formation: 'Object' attributes dynamically inhibited from conscious awareness, *J Integr Neurosci*, 3(1), (2004): 31-46.

Snyder, A.W. & Barlow, H.B., 'Revealing the Artist's Touch' in *Nature*, 331, (1986): 117-18.

Snyder, A.W. & Thomas, M., Autistic artists give clues to cognition, *Perception*, 26, (1997): 93-96.

Stillman, W. (2006). *Autism and the God Connection*. Naperville, IL: Sourcebooks.

Stringer, L. (1998). *Grand Central Winter: Stories from the street*. NY: Washington Square Press.

Swenson Jr., L.S. (1979). *Genesis of Relativity: Einstein in context*. NY: Burt Franklin.

Szatmari, P. (2004). *A Mind Apart*. NY: Guilford Press.

Szegedy-Maszak, 'Mysteries of the Mind: Your unconscious is making your everyday decisions' in *US News & World Report*, (Feb. 28, 2005).

Trilling, L. (1972). *Sincerity and Authenticity*. Cambridge, MA: Harvard University Press.

Vallentin, A. (1954). *The Drama of Albert Einstein*. Garden City, NY: Doubleday.

van Peursen, C.A. (1970). *Ludwig Wittgenstein: An introduction to his philosophy*. NY: Dutton.

Versluis, A. (1992). *Sacred Earth: The spiritual landscape of Native America*. Rochester, VT: Inner Traditions International.

Wall, S. (1993). *Wisdom's Daughters: Conversations with women elders of Native America*. NY: Harper Perennial.

Watson, R. (2002). *Cogito, Ergo Sum: The life of René Descartes*. Boston: David R. Godine.

Weil, S. (1997). *Gravity and Grace*. NY: Routledge.

Weil, S. (1956). *The Notebooks of Simone Weil*. A. Wills (trans.). NY: G.P. Putnam's Sons.

Weil, S. (1970). *First and Last Notebooks*. R. Rees (trans.). NY: Oxford University Press.

Weil, S. (1951). *Waiting for God*. E. Craufurd (trans.). G.P. Putnam's Sons: Harper Perennial Classics Edition, 2001.

Weil, S. (1986). *Simone Weil: An anthology*. S. Miles (Ed.). NY: Grove Press.

Whiteley, P.M. 'Ties that Bind' in *Natural History*. (Nov. 2004).

Williams, D. (1998). *Autism and Sensing: The unlost instinct*. London & Philadelphia: Jessica Kingsley Publishers.

Williams, D. (2003). *Exposure anxiety – The invisible cage*. London & Philadelphia: Jessica Kingsley Publishers.

Williams, D. (1992). *Nobody Nowhere*. NY: Times Books.

Witteveen, H.J. (1997). *Universal Sufism*. Shaftesbury, Dorset: Element Books.

Wittgenstein, H. (1984). 'My Brother Ludwig' in *Recollections of Wittgenstein*. R. Rhees (Ed.). Oxford: Oxford University Press.

Wittgenstein, L. (1965). *The Blue and Brown Books*. NY: Harper Colophon Books, Harper & Row.

Wittgenstein, L. (1980). *Culture and Value*. G.H. Von Wright (Ed.). P. Winch (trans.). Chicago: University of Chicago Press.

Wittgenstein, L. (1979). *Notebooks, 1914-1916*, 2nd edn. G.H. von Wright & G.E.M. Anscombe (Eds.). G.E.M. Anscombe (trans.). Chicago: University of Chicago Press.

Wittgenstein, L. (1958). *Philosophical Investigations*, 3rd edn. G.E.M. Anscombe (trans.). NY: Macmillan Publishing, Basil Blackwell & Mott.

Wittgenstein, L. (1975). *Philosophical Remarks*. Chicago: University of Chicago Press.

Wittgenstein, L. (1977). *Remarks on Colour*. G.E.M. Anscombe (Ed.). L.L. McAlister & M. Schättle (trans.). Berkeley: University of California Press.

Wittgenstein, L. (1988). *Remarks on the Philosophy of Psychology*, vol. 1. G.E.M. Anscombe & G.H. von Wright (Eds.). G.E.M. Anscombe (trans.). Chicago: University of Chicago Press.

Wittgenstein, L. (1983). *Tractatus Logico-Philosophicus*. London: Routledge & Kegan Paul.

Wittgenstein, L. (1980). *Wittgenstein's Lectures, Cambridge, 1930-1932*. D. Lee (Ed.). Chicago: University of Chicago Press.

Wittgenstein, L. (1979). *Wittgenstein's Lectures, Cambridge, 1932-1935*. A. Ambrose (Ed.). Chicago: University of Chicago Press.

Wittgenstein, L. (1975). *Zettel*. G.E.M. Anscombe & G.H. von Wright (Eds.). G.E.M. Anscombe (trans.). Berkeley, CA: University of California Press.

Acknowledgements

I am grateful to Pari Publishing for accepting my work for publication, and in particular to Maureen Doolan and F. David Peat of the Pari Center for New Learning, for their heartfelt and unstinting support. I also thank friends and family for their continuing moral support, and a host of less tangible though equally important gifts like cover ideas, photographs, shelter and food.

Grateful Acknowledgement is made to the following for their kind permission to reprint previously published material:

Branden Press: Excerpts from *Einstein and the Poet: In Search of the Cosmic Man* by Hermanns, William, copyright © 1983 by Branden Press, Inc., Brookline Village, Mass. Courtesy, Branden Books, Boston.

Christopher Little Literary Agency (Lucy Rogers): for an excerpt from *Harry Potter and the Sorcerer's Stone* by Rowling, J. K., Scholastic, Inc., NY. Courtesy, *Harry Potter and the Sorcerer's Stone* © JK Rowling 1997.

Continuum Books: Excerpt from *The Danger of Words and Writings on Wittgenstein* by Drury, M. O'C. 1996. Thoemmes Press, Bristol. By permission of Continuum Books, *Danger of Words and Writings on Wittgenstein* © Thoemmes Press, 1996.

Duncan-Baird Publishers: Excerpts from *Meister Eckhart* by Eckhart, ed. by Pfeiffer, Franz. 1956 (1924). John M. Watkins, London. Out of copyright.

Fulcrum Publishing: Excerpts from *God Is Red: A Native View of Religion* by Deloria Jr., Vine. 1994, Golden, Colorado. Copyright © 1994 by Vine Deloria, Jr. Unable to reach Fulcrum after repeated attempts.

Hackett Pub. Co: *Wittgenstein: Conversations 1949-1951* by O. K. Bouwsma and edited by J. L. Craft and Ronald E. Hustwit. Copyright © 1986 by J. L. Craft and Ronald E. Hustwit. All rights reserved.

Harper & Collins: excerpts from three books:

> *Physics and Beyond: Encounters and Conversations* by Heisenberg, Werner. 1971. Harper and Row, Publishers, NY. Copyright © 1971 by Harper &Row Publishers, Inc. All rights reserved.

> *Physics and Philosophy: The Revolution in Modern Science* by Heisenberg, Werner. 1958, Harper Torchbooks, The Science Library, Harper and Row Publishers, NY. Copyright © 1958 by Werner Heisenberg. All rights reserved.

> *The Nag Hammadi Library*: *In English.* Robinson, James M.(director) 1977, tr. by Members of the Coptic Gnostic Library Project of the Institute for Antiquity and Christianity. Harper and Row, Publishers, San Francisco. Copyright © 1977 by E. J. Brill, Leiden, The Netherlands. All rights reserved.

Horn, Gabriel (White Deer of Autumn): Excerpt from *Contemplations of a Primal Mind.* New World Library, Novato, CA.,1996. Copyright ©1996 by Gabriel Horn, by kind permission of Gabriel Horn.

Jessica Kingsley Publishers: Excerpts from three books:

> *Exposure Anxiety – The Invisible Cage by* Williams, Donna. 2003 Jessica Kingsley Publishers, London and Philadelphia. ISBN 1-84310-051-7.Copyright © Donna Williams 2003. All rights reserved.

> *The Genesis of Artistic Creativity (Asperger's Syndrome and the Arts)* Fitzgerald, Michael. 2005. Jessica Kingsley Publishers, London. ISBN -13: 978-1-84310-334-9. Copyright © Michael Fitzgerald 2005. All rights reserved.

> *Nobody Nowhere* by Williams, Donna. 1992.Times Books, NY. ISBN 0-8129-2042-2. Copyright © 1992 by Donna Williams. All rights reserved.

Kensington Books: Excerpts (86 words) from *The Philosophy of Existentialism by* Marcel, Gabriel. 1965.The Citadel Press, NY. Copyright © 1956 by the Philosophical Library. We are grateful for Kensington's allowance of fair use.

Maestro Media: Excerpts from *Carrousels and Storms: Mysticism from an Autistic Mind* by Julien, William.1999. Maestro Media. Copyright © 1999 by William Julien.

Meyerding, Jane: *On Finding Myself Differently Brained*. Copyright © 1998. http://mjane.zolaweb.com.

New World Library: Excerpts from the book *Neither Wolf nor Dog*, copyright © 1994, 2002 by Kent Nerburn. Reprinted by permission of New World Library, Novato, CA. www.newworldlibrary.com.

Northwestern University Press: Excerpts from *Tragic Wisdom and Beyond* by Gabriel Marcel, 1973, tr. by Stephen Jolin and Peter McCormick, Evanston. Copyright © 1973 by Northwestern University Press. Our gratitude for US permission. (See Plon for UK and Commonwealth.)

Ohio University Press: Excerpts from *Aquamarine Blue 5: Personal Stories of College Students with Autism,* ed. by Dawn Prince-Hughes. Published by Ohio University Press/Swallow Press, Athens, Ohio (www.ohioswallow.com). Copyright © 2002 by Dawn Prince Hughes.

Open Court Publishing: Excerpts reprinted by permission of Open Court Publishing Company, a division of Carus Publishing Company, Peru, Il, from *The Many faces of Realism* by Hilary Putnam, © 1987 by Open Court Publishing Company.

Paradiz, Valerie (Through Melissa Sarver): Excerpts from *Elijah's Cup: A Family's Journey into the Community and Culture of High-Functioning Autism and Asperger's Syndrome.* 2002. The Free Press, NY. Copyright © 2002 by Valerie Paradiz. All rights reserved. Our gratitude for rights to reprint in the British Commonwealth. (For US, see Simon & Schuster.)

Peat, F. David: excerpts from *Infinite Potential: The Life and Times of David Bohm.* 1997. Helix Books, Addison-Wesley, Reading, Mass. Copyright © 1997 by F. David Peat. Our gratitude for British Commonwealth permission. (For US, see Perseus.)

Penguin Group: Excerpts from two books:

> 'Notes on Cognition,' from *The Farther Reaches Of Human Nature* by Abraham H. Maslow, copyright © 1971 by Bertha G. Maslow. Used by permission of Viking Penguin, a division of Penguin Group (USA) Inc.

> From *Waiting For God* by Simone Weil, translated by Emma Craufurd, copyright 1951, renewed © 1979 by G. P. Putnam's Sons. Used by permission of G. P. Putnam's Sons, a division of Penguin Group (USA) Inc.

Perseus Books: Excerpts from two books:

> *Philosophy in the Flesh (The Embodied Mind and its Challenge to Western Thought)*. 1999, by Lakoff, George and Johnson, Mark. Basics Books, NY. Copyright © 1999 by George Lakoff and Mark Johnson.

> *Infinite Potential: The Life and Times of David Bohm* by Peat, F. David, 1997. Helix Books, Addison-Wesley, Reading, Mass. Copyright © 1997 by F. David Peat. Our gratitude for US permission. (For BC, see Peat.)

Plon: Excerpts from: *Pour Une Sagesse Tragique Et Son Au-Dela* by Gabriel Marcel © PLON, 1968. Our gratitude for UK and Commonwealth permission. (For US, see Northwestern.)

Random House Group, Ltd: Excerpts from *Ludwig Wittgenstein: The Duty of Genius* by Ray Monk, published by Jonathan Cape. Reprinted by permission of The Random House Group Ltd. Copyright © Ray Monk, 1990. Our gratitude for UK, Commonwealth and Canadian rights. (For US, see Simon & Schuster.)

Simon & Schuster: excerpts from two books:

> *Elijah's Cup: A Family's Journey into the Community and Culture of High-Functioning Autism and Asperger's Syndrome*. Valerie Paradiz. Copyright 2002 by Valerie Paradiz. Reprinted by permission of the Free Press, a Division of Simon & Schuster, Inc. All rights reserved. Our gratitude for US permission. (For BC, see Paradiz.)

> *Ludwig Wittgenstein: The Duty of Genius* by Raymond Monk. Copyright © 1990 by Raymond Monk. Reprinted with permission of The Free Press, a Division of Simon &Schuster, Inc. All rights reserved. Our gratitude for US permission. (For UK, BC and Canadian rights, see Random House.)

Springer: An excerpt from *American Normal* by Lawrence Osborne, Copernicus Books, NY, 2002, ch. 2, 'Little Professors,' pg. 58. Copyright © 2002 by Lawrence Osborne. With kind permission of Springer Science and Business Media.

Taylor and Francis: Excerpts from three books:

> *Tractatus Logico-Philosophicus* by Wittgenstein, Ludwig. 1983. First published by Routledge & Kegan Paul Ltd., London, 1922. Excerpts from pages 27,185, 31, 149, 145, by kind permission of Taylor & Francis.

> *Gravity and Grace* by Simone Weil,1997. Routledge, NY. Tr. from the French by Emma Crauford. Excerpts from pgs. 116, 107, 11, 13, xviii, viii, ix.

> *The Notebooks of Simone Weil* by Simone Weil. (Tr. by Arthur Wills). G. P. Putnam's Sons. NY. 1956. Excerpts from pgs. 334, 527, 87.

University of California: Excerpts from two books (fair use):

> *Zettel, by* Ludwig Wittgenstein. 1975. Ed. by G.E.M. Anscombe and G.H. von Wright. Tr. by G.E.M. Anscombe, University of California Press, Berkeley, Ca. Copyright © 1967 by Basil Blackwell.

> *Remarks on Colour* by Ludwig Wittgenstein. 1977. Ed. by G.E.M. Anscombe. Tr. by Linda L. McAlister and Margarete Schättle, University of California Press, Berkeley. Copyright © G.E.M. Anscombe 1977.

University of Chicago Press and Blackwell: Excerpts from three books (fair use):

> *Culture and Value* by Ludwig Wittgenstein. 1980. Ed. by G. H. Von Wright in collaboration with Heikki Nyman. Tr. by Peter

Winch. The University of Chicago Press, Chicago. English translation copyright © 1980 by Basil Blackwell.

> *Notebooks 1914-1916* by Ludwig Wittgenstein, 1979. 2nd Edition. Ed. by G. H. von Wright and G.E.M. Anscombe. Tr. by G.E.M. Anscombe. The University of Chicago Press, Chicago. Copyright © 1961, 1979 by Basil Blackwell.

> *Remarks on the Philosophy of Psychology, v. 1.* by Ludwig Wittgenstein. 1988. Ed. by G.E.M. Anscombe and G.H. von Wright. Tr. by G.E.M. Anscombe. University of Chicago Press, Chicago. Copyright © 1980 by Basil Blackwell.

University Presses of Florida: An excerpt from *Ethics without Philosophy: Wittgenstein and the Moral Life* by Edwards, James C. 1983. U. of South Florida.

Wiley: Extracts from three books (fair use):

> *Philosophical Investigations* by Ludwig Wittgenstein. 1958. 3rd edition. Tr. by G.E.M. Anscombe, Macmillan Publishing Co., NY., Basil Blackwell & Mott, Ltd. Copyright © Basil Blackwell & Mott, Ltd., 1958.

> *Autism: Explaining the Enigma* by Uta Frith. 2003. (2nd Ed.) Blackwell Publishing, Malden, Mass. Copyright © 1989, 2003 by Uta Frith.

> *Letters from Wittgenstein, with a memoir* by Paul Engelmann, 1967, Horizon Press, NY. Copyright © Basil Blackwell, Oxford, 1967.

Pari Publishing is an independent publishing company, based in a medieval Italian village. Our books appeal to a broad readership and focus on innovative ideas and approaches from new and established authors who are experts in their fields. We publish books in the areas of science, society, psychology, and the arts.

Our books are available at all good bookstores or online at
www.paripublishing.com

If you would like to add your name to our email list to receive information about our forthcoming titles and our online newsletter please contact us at **newsletter@paripublishing.com**

Visit us at **www.paripublishing.com**

Pari Publishing Sas
Via Tozzi, 7
58045 Pari (GR)
Italy

Email: info@paripublishing.com